*Ecologies of Empire
in South Asia, 1400–1900*

Culture, Place, and Nature

Studies in Anthropology and Environment

K. SIVARAMAKRISHNAN | SERIES EDITOR

Centered in anthropology, the Culture, Place, and Nature series encompasses new interdisciplinary social science research on environmental issues, focusing on the intersection of culture, ecology, and politics in global, national, and local contexts. Contributors to the series view environmental knowledge and issues from the multiple and often conflicting perspectives of various cultural systems.

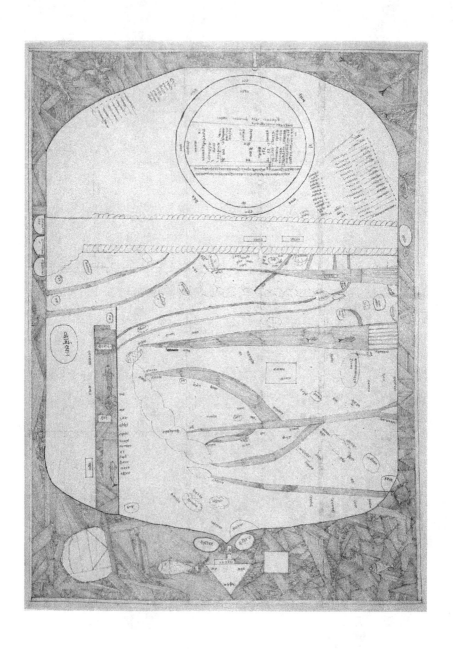

SUMIT GUHA

Ecologies *of* Empire *in* South Asia, 1400–1900

University of Washington Press | Seattle

Copyright © 2023 by the University of Washington Press

Design by Mindy Basinger Hill

Composed in Adobe Caslon Pro

Maps by Crixter Designs.

All rights reserved. No part of this publication may be reproduced or transmitted in any form or by any means, electronic or mechanical, including photocopy, recording, or any information storage or retrieval system, without permission in writing from the publisher.

UNIVERSITY OF WASHINGTON PRESS

uwapress.uw.edu

LIBRARY OF CONGRESS CONTROL NUMBER: 2023002467
ISBN 9780295751481 (hardcover)
ISBN 9780295751498 (paperback)
ISBN 9780295751504 (ebook)

∞ This paper meets the requirements of ANSI/NISO Z39.48-1992 (Permanence of Paper).

FRONTISPIECE: This Maratha map from the late eighteenth century illustrates the confluence of new geographical knowledge and Indic cosmology. It shows the location of the Puranic heaven, stylized Indian mountains and rivers but also the land of the Arabs and the small islands whence the Europeans were believed to have come. Finally, the tax assessments of the sixteen provinces of the north are written on it in the *modi* script. Map image from a manuscript in the British Library, catalogued at Mar.G28.1. © The British Library Board.

Contents

List of Maps — ix

Foreword *by K. Sivaramakrishnan* — xi

Acknowledgments — xv

A Note on Spelling Conventions and Abbreviations — xvii

Introduction — 1

ONE Inequality, Complexity, and Ecology — 18

TWO South Asia in the Imperial Gaze — 44

THREE Imperial Gaze, Lordly Grasp — 79

FOUR The Village and Its Inhabitants — 110

FIVE Lands of Resistance, Terrains of Refuge — 139

SIX Colonialism, Disarmament, and the Closing of the Forest Frontier — 167

Conclusion — 188

Notes — 191

Bibliography — 213

Index — 235

Maps

1. Asian Agroclimates   45
2. South Asia Rainfall Patterns   46
3. Southern Asia geopolitical c. 1800   66
4. British India c. 1900   170

Foreword

IN THIS STUDY, WHICH SPANS THE BETTER PART OF FIVE CENTURIES, Sumit Guha provides a fine-grained account of how landscapes and their dynamic ecology played a role in the formation and decline of empires in South Asia. These empires were able to concentrate and wield power and influence in varying degrees and over variable expanses at different historical moments. Part of the consequence of their overlapping ambitions and sway over some of the same terrain meant that they warred with each other. This led, as Guha writes, to the creation and manipulation of landscapes of war with eco-systemic consequences in specific regions where conflict occurred over extended periods.

Through the clash of empires, this book also takes up the rarely treated topic of war and ecology in South Asia. Another notable accomplishment is the sophisticated blending of modern and premodern periods to tell a story of landscape change, cultural and political conflict, and transformation of human–environment relations in South Asia. A third admirable feature is the attention to both what Guha terms practical geography and symbolic cosmology in the way the landscape was altered, understood, and represented and in the way it expressed itself in varied environmental processes in the making and breaking of empires in South Asia.

World environmental history, especially as it engages with global discussions around the emergence of the epoch of the Anthropocene, has focused on human transformation of the earth system but almost entirely in material and physical terms, letting economic and energy history and allied topics lead the way.[1] However, Guha delves deeply into conflicting cultural perspectives on land, animals, forests, agriculture, coastal zones, and ecosystems to show the continuing importance of paying attention to values, ethics, ideologies, and social construction. Some of this he discusses as the evaluative gaze and mental maps, within a political ecology framework in writing the history of ecology and empire, and he illustrates this point beautifully from the vantage of South Asia. In that sense the book is also making a major contribution to the environmental humanities and the writing of long duration accounts of the relations between nature and empire.

The book proceeds from the larger expanse to the more regional dimensions of Western India, in the last five hundred years or so, where the Maratha polity was established in conflict with the Mughal Empire and later the British Empire, which ultimately ended Maratha hegemony in Western India by the beginning of the nineteenth century. In doing so, Guha is attuned to ecological complexity and social inequality as they come to interact and shape each other in the formation and fortune of empires. One aspect of these inequalities was the uneven development and influence of knowledge systems that were reaching beyond their places of origin to influence empire building. Plant classification and understanding animals and their value were inimitably local practices before they were broadcast as branches of modern science.

Other forms of knowledge—including systematics, cartography, astronomy, navigational technology, and geology—laid the foundations of modern European empires. Along with military technology, meteorology, epidemiology, and telecommunication technology, they facilitated the spread of these empires. Guha ranges across Asian and European history at the cusp of the modern period to bring these developments into his analytical focus. We learn, for instance, that Mughal and Maratha Empires developed little cartography, a form of local knowledge and its spatial representation that was so central to the British Empire.[2] The British evaluative gaze took many forms, as the empire worked to compile the knowledge and shape the ecology that would consolidate its rule.[3]

Such knowledge production resulted in a cosmology of land and human relations to landscapes that differed sharply from existing South Asian ones, even as it learned from them assiduously at least till the late nineteenth century. Then, as Guha notes, and as others have written as well, these cosmological systems were rendered unequal in the colonial gaze, and scientific racism took over as the dominant way to characterize colonized people and their livelihoods in their own land, in their forests, across coastal areas, and in the semi-arid zones on which Guha focuses.

As he notes, each empire strove to reach deeper into the village and worked to understand more granularly the classification and use of land for farming and other purposes and the hierarchy of rights in land that directed the access and utilization of the land for various purposes. Such imperial efforts had their effects on ecology and village organization, as others have also shown for different parts of South Asia.[4] They also encountered recalcitrance or, in other words, ecological and social changes that arose from activities not emerging from the impulses of imperial knowledge production and resource control. This could be the work done by elephants or less charismatic animals, demographic changes in human settlement patterns, and relations that linked sedentary farmers to itinerant peoples. Most important, as Guha notes, it had to do with the tenuous grip of straining imperial authorities over regional and local structures of power, authority, and land management. Intermediate power structures were more often of consequence in shaping the ecology of empire.

As the latter half of the book turns a more sustained gaze on the Western and Central Indian regions that came under Maratha sway and then were occupied by the British, Guha addresses the advance of specific crops, their episodic abandonment, the introduction of new commercial cultivars, and the recomposition of village life and human endeavor in land, forest, and coast as it responded to both climate and colonization. This is where the book descends into the intricacies of village life and land control and use practices, presenting the constant struggle for recognition by each other of the view from below and that from above. Ecological change from this scale of analysis is subtle and not predictably in one direction till late in the nineteenth century; a few seasons of abandonment or even less intensive cultivation could change edaphic conditions, alter plant communities or patterns of woodland succession, and thereby remake animal habitats.[5]

As it spends more time in the last part of the nineteenth century and the first part of the twentieth, this book reprises some more familiar topics relating to forest history. It does so from the Western Indian perspective, noting similarities to accounts already written for Central and Eastern India. Guha observes the enlarging and standardized forestry regime that the British colonial empire built across its holdings in South Asia but also considers similar efforts with irrigation and the latest transformation of village society, especially as its sedentary aspects were once again recalibrated to proximate mobile communities, the growth of migration over longer distances, and the dispossession of forest-based crafts and livelihoods that had serious adverse effects for Adivasis and their polities.

This book ably covers a very consequential half millennium in the history of South Asia. It does so by scaling and rescaling the analysis from global processes to local events and practices even while attending to the importance of varied regional mediations of these scales. Guha has, thus, provided a clear, concise, and creatively researched study of the relation between ecological change and the formation of empires as well as their limitations and ultimately their decline.

K. Sivaramakrishnan | YALE UNIVERSITY

NOTES

1. See, for instance, John R. McNeill and Peter Engelke, *The Great Acceleration: An Environmental History of the Anthropocene since 1945* (Cambridge, MA: Belknap Press, 2016); and Andreas Malm, *Fossil Capital: The Rise of Steam Power and the Roots of Global Warming* (London: Verso, 2016).

2. The authoritative work on British colonial mapping and surveying remains: Matthew H. Edney, *Mapping an Empire: The Geographical Construction of British India, 1765–1843* (Chicago: University of Chicago Press, 1997).

3. Two works illustrative of this point are Om Prakash Kejariwal, *The Asiatic Society of Bengal and the Discovery of India's Past, 1784–1838* (Delhi: Oxford University Press, 1988); and Bernard S. Cohn, *Colonialism and Its Forms of Knowledge: The British in India* (Princeton, NJ: Princeton University Press, 1996).

4. An excellent example is, of course, Neeladri Bhattacharya, *The Great Agrarian Conquest: The Colonial Reshaping of a Rural World* (Albany: State University of New York Press, 2019).

5. A point made more broadly in K. Sivaramakrishnan, "Forests and the Environmental History of Modern India," *Journal of Peasant Studies* 36, no. 2 (2009): 299–324.

Acknowledgments

I HAVE INCURRED MANY DEBTS DURING THE WRITING OF THIS BOOK. Indrani Chatterjee's work has deepened my understanding of maps and mapping as geographical representation. Thomas Trautmann read a very incomplete project and then a draft of this book with a keen and sympathetic eye. Raymond Hyser assisted in editing an early version of this work. K. Sivaramakrishnan has read several drafts and provided valuable inputs for each iteration. Brian Lander permitted me to read his unpublished PhD thesis and helped organize a stimulating cross-regional session at the American Society for Environmental History in 2018. Discussions with Kathleen Morrison over a decade ago enabled me to think differently about political ecology generally. Her discussion of the social effects of rice production informs my understanding of that subject. Trevor Birkenholtz introduced me to the politics of water geography and water knowledge in today's India. I am grateful to Ajay Skaria for sharing a copy of his unpublished doctoral dissertation and permitting me to quote from it. I am indebted to Jonathan Seefeldt for permission to read and cite his unpublished dissertation on the history of a royal water management project of the seventeenth century. Isaac Ullah shared his ideas about the archaeology of early farming in Inner Asia. Timothy Beach patiently explained how modern techniques of remote sensing are applied for the recovery of past landscapes. Nayanjot Lahiri deepened my understanding of empire and archaeology in India. Upinder Singh helped me trace references to her own early work on perceived landscapes. Pamela K. Crossley has read and patiently corrected sections on Inner Asia and Northeast China. Prachi Deshpande permitted me to read her important forthcoming book on Marathi records and record keepers. She also helped me interpret an interesting but obscure Marathi poem from Kolhapur. Marina Chellini of the British Library tracked down the rare Maratha map, used as a frontispiece, which had been bound in another volume and was not easily traceable. I am likewise indebted to Tirthankar Roy for responding quickly to several queries made at busy times. Annette Schmiedchen answered my queries on the numerical descriptors attached to territories in South India during Chalukya and Shilahara times. Dirk Sachse took the time to answer my emails regarding the recovery of past vegetation and climate history in his work on the Lonar Lake deposits in Central India. I am deeply indebted to Emily Bowles, who completed a thorough developmental edit in record time and helped me organize a sprawling manuscript into orderly chapters and caught many minor errors as well. Her apparently simple but truly incisive questions have helped me sharpen my own thinking and writing.

I am grateful to Nicole L. Boivin for permission to cite her in the epigraph to chapter 1, Johns Hopkins University Press for the epigraph to chapter 4, and the University of Chicago Press for the epigraph to chapter 6.

V. Tokuto Zhimoni drew the maps. Lorri Hagman provided valuable inputs, and Joeth Zucco patiently steered the project through to completion. Alja Kooistra's copyediting spotted many missing references and minor errors.

I am also grateful to two anonymous reviewers whose perceptive comments enabled me to understand my own project better than I had before. This book owes much to their inputs.

A Note on Spelling Conventions & Abbreviations

THE ROMAN ALPHABET IS POORLY SUITED FOR ASIAN NAMES AND words. But an overuse of diacritics distracts the reader and clutters the page. I have therefore sought a via media: a contemporary, roughly phonetic "vernacular Anglo" spelling is used wherever possible, even at the cost of inconsistency. I have translated all references to and quotations from non-English sources and cited the translators in the bibliography if I relied on their translations.

Authors with accepted English forms of their names are cited by those. Colonial executive officials were traditionally distinguished by capitalizing their titles, but this has fallen foul of the *Chicago Manual of Style*. I trust that the reader will understand that a district collector administered a district, that a commissioner supervised the governance of millions, and that a conservator of forests governed hundreds of square miles of land classed as such.

First name–last name is used for all authors when possible. Citations are shortened in the notes and provided in full in the bibliography. Frequently cited sources are abbreviated, and the complete reference may be found in the bibliography, alphabetically listed under the abbreviated form.

*Ecologies of Empire
in South Asia, 1400–1900*

Introduction

THE INFORMED PUBLIC TODAY IS AWARE OF AND ANXIOUS ABOUT the dramatic environmental changes occurring around us and across the globe. Human action has clearly precipitated the earth into a new geological epoch, one shaped by human action and therefore newly dubbed the Anthropocene. This recognition is recent—it burst onto global consciousness in the last decades of the twentieth century. The famous series of observations at the Mauna Loa Observatory on Hawaii began to record a rise in carbon dioxide levels from 1958 onward. Global series of temperature readings began to multiply in the decades after. The satellites orbiting the earth moved from being instruments of Cold War competition and surveillance to more mundane purposes such as communication and weather observation. Increasing outlays added to the mass of data available to scientists and the interested public. Unprecedented amounts of funding allow large teams to work on single aspects of the past or of ongoing transformations, whether by sampling of ice cores in remote regions or drilling in deep ocean sediments. Satellite technologies and surveillance systems now allow remote sensing and grid mapping more granular than anything that earlier epochs could conceive.[1] Thus, ironically, small fractions of the vast resources generated by the unsustainable exploitation of the world enable us to launch satellites and operate computer systems that gauge the havoc we have wrought, and still wreak, every day. The outputs of this knowledge production process have now permeated the public domain and are widely available via free apps such as Google Earth.

I, like other historians, was initially just another member of the educated public, receiving knowledge from on high as digested by those able to master results from large teams of scientists and to interpret digital data streams from many sources. What could the smaller geographical areas and shorter periods of traditional historical inquiry hope to add to analyses that spanned the globe and interpreted local phenomena in terms of planetary orbital cycles lasting 28,000 years or longer? While my own research has covered longer spans than those of most historians of my region, my 1999 book *Environment and Ethnicity* stretched over only eight hundred years.[2] Yet the cosmic past uncovered by the new instruments is much more accidental, more historical than earlier generations thought. The making of our earth, Bruno Latour has recently observed, now resembles "a long string of historical events, random, specific, and contingent events . . . the temporary, fragile result of a geohistory."[3]

I began to read more widely on the history of the recent climate, especially the Holocene period, the epoch following the last Ice Age, which began 11,000 years ago. As I read more closely, I gradually began to realize that many scientists were, in fact, developing historical narratives that flattened out and oversimplified historical trajectories. One of the most widely used estimations, HYDE 3.2 (the History Database of the Global Environment), featured an undifferentiated humanity that collectively cleared land and set fires across the earth. In this model, humans' effect upon the world was density-dependent, or determined by their number in any territory.[4] And human numbers were subject only to what Thomas Malthus termed "positive checks": poverty followed by hunger and disease. Therefore, human numbers are best represented by a logistic function, one where the rate of population growth begins to slow down as it approaches the limit of the environment's capacity to sustain it. The fact that the Holocene saw a great increase not only in human numbers but also of inequality was largely neglected in HYDE and therefore by its users. Yet the said inequality is every day more apparent as billions of humans live on a few dollars a day while a handful spend $50 million or more for a brief recreational rocket flight that pollutes all levels of the atmosphere. Additionally, HYDE and many other models assumed that modern land use categories reported to the Food and Agriculture Organization (FAO) are objective traits that can be unproblematically projected back in time to estimate the human effect upon the land. Yet a scrutiny of the data classes reveals modernist assumptions about how humans historically interacted with our planet and its biota.[5]

When this began to dawn on me, I was already exploring the interactions of people and land through time within a segment of South Asia and over a few hundred years. These interactions were strongly differentiated by class and community. I realized that differences between human societies and their cultures were absent from the HYDE model. Having previously researched population history, I knew that historical demography had made vast strides after World War II and developed sophisticated theories of population behavior.[6] Pioneers starting with John Hajnal in the 1950s had shown that human fertility was not an easily modeled biological phenomenon and that large countries have undergone major changes in demographic behavior in relatively short periods.[7] The striking decline in Asian fertility—often to below replacement—in the past fifty years has demonstrated this afresh. I therefore argue that no density-dependent model such as HYDE can capture these social and culturally determined variations.

I begin my critique with HYDE because it is frequently the default model for scientists seeking a historical summary of earth history. Natural scientists before Kees Klein Goldewijk and colleagues have also made efforts at reaching the educated public.[8] The ornithologist Jared Diamond's 1997 bestseller *Guns, Germs, and Steel* developed a geographically determinist theory of human history. In 2005, the oceanographer and earth scientist William F. Ruddiman published a highly readable study of the Holocene in which he assigns a controversially extended role to human action in adding to the global stock of greenhouse gases over the past five millennia.[9] Diamond and Ruddiman have, however, developed their historical models of regional and planetary change on the basis of limited historical investigation.

In *Plows, Plagues, and Petroleum*, Ruddiman launches a contrarian challenge to the idea that it was modern, fossil-fueled industrialization that explained the rise in atmospheric carbon dioxide and global warming. He claims to identify a long-term role for human activity in changing the climate through past millennia and, specifically, in warming the earth. He is thus contesting arguments that the Anthropocene began with the Industrial Revolution or yet later with the detonation of nuclear devices in 1945. Instead, he argues that there was a slowly cumulative human role in increasing the global stock of greenhouse gases before the Industrial Revolution. The slow net addition, he declares, grew to have significant effects through the millennia, effects that counteracted a geoplanetary trend to cooling that should have set in five thousand years ago. Here he moves on to historical territory—Babylonia, Harappa, Northeast China—that historians have long studied.[10]

Ruddiman also offers interpretations of shorter and more recent periods. He argues that the destruction of the Indigenous peoples of the Amazon basin led to a regrowth of forest that took so much carbon out of the atmosphere as to cool the planet during the well-known seventeenth-century cold phase that caused droughts in Asia and shortened growing seasons in the northerly latitudes. The events Ruddiman invokes are recent historical ones. When considering changes to greenhouse gas (GHG) output as a result of colonization, it is insufficient to only consider human populations. There were no bovines or ovines in the Americas before 1500. But if we consider 1600, we should ask how many sheep, cattle, and horses were adding their methane emissions to the atmosphere as a result of the colonization of the Americas. How much more woodland could be hacked and burned by peoples with iron tools than by those with stone ones? An estimation of these magnitudes and other countervailing effects in the Americas requires a close training in the evaluation of relevant archives and sources that only specialists possess. It also turns upon an understanding of the political processes that generated the records we must depend on. Those records were themselves created even as the biota and terrain of the Americas were drastically transformed by the actions of a few and the decisions of even fewer.

These tremendous inequalities shaped the fates of millions of lives of many kinds, but we cannot understand them without understanding the structural settings that animated them. So understanding our modern predicament undoubtedly has a historical dimension. History, in my view, deals with sequences of events that succeed one another in unique combinations through an irreversible time. Roads not taken cannot be retraced; one cannot wash one's feet in the same river twice. Efforts by natural scientists and non-scientists to find iron laws in history and predict the future from the past have so far failed. At the same time, ecologists are moving to a similar view of change through time, one that must incorporate the historical.

As I have earlier indicated, today's commonsense cosmological vision is only made possible by a large and expensive infrastructure. The cosmological gaze began reaching out to deep space in the later nineteenth century, first with larger telescopes and then with a range of sensors directed out from the earth's surface and deep beneath it. Carbon dioxide measurements that began at the Mauna Loa Observatory in Hawaii in the 1950s produced the first indications of CO_2 increase that explained the rise in temperatures globally. Meanwhile, aircraft made aerial photography possible from the

1930s. Initially, it was only used for military purposes, but after World War II, it was also gradually applied to landscape surveys. A visual extra-planetary perspective on the earth came with the launch of the first satellites. In 1972, NASA released a photograph of the earth from space that, as Sara Pritchard writes, "became an icon of American environmentalism."[11] Many features of remote sensing have been added since, including many satellites devoted to recording climate change, land use, soil moisture levels, ocean temperatures, or the individual location of hundreds of millions of individual global positioning system (GPS) units.[12] The latter, now perceived as almost a feature of the landscape itself, requires an array of thirty-one satellites with a GPS device connecting to a minimum of four of them at any one time.[13] Users of these ubiquitous devices unconsciously also self-install a singular view of the world embedded in the apparatus that guides them. But the GPS network that creates near-instantaneous maps is a pragmatic construct. It is sustained at great expense for an array of functions needed in the modern, high-consumption, globalized society. It is a commercial spin-off from the kind of globalization that was launched by the Cold War. It will decay if and when the flow of energy and expertise needed to sustain it shrink.

The social scientists Sverker Sörlin and Nina Wormbs have recently proposed the term *environing* as an integral term to label the new knowledge process. They use it to mean "the knowledge-based representation of the material world in which humans and their actions are embedded." Humans, Sörlin and Wormbs declare, make environments, both pragmatically and perceptually. Humans, they continue, differ vastly in their capacities for action upon the world and their access to knowledge about it. This is an important insight, but the phrase perhaps suggests that *humans* is a single entity.

Humans, however, neither affect nor comprehend in equal measure. This book demonstrates the enduring nature of environmental inequality through deep historical time. Similarly, *knowledge* is a problematic category. Technology in the broadest sense creates knowledge. A vast and expensive apparatus of observation, analysis, and record is what enables scientists to grasp the existence of an earth system and estimate its changing dynamics. Educated contemporaries are recipients of information via "the comprehensive environing technology" formed by "the nexus of computers, monitoring devices, climate models, and concerted research programs and collaborations. . . . In reality, there has always been 'climate'—multiple local and regional climates. The environing technology of computerized climate science brought into being a *global* climate that hitherto had not existed."[14]

Sörlin considers George P. Marsh's pioneering 1864 study of the changes in the earth resulting from human action the baseline for a concept of the "environment" as a *planetary* process. A well-educated American of the mid-nineteenth century, Marsh automatically looked back to the Hellenic and Roman Empires when tracing the environmental history of the world. Their former lands from Libya to Turkey were favored travel destinations for the Western elite. Marsh came to believe that their transformation had resulted from the action of a differentiated humanity, one in which some members had great power and others little. "Savages," as he called them, had little technical capacity and so left few enduring effects upon the earth. Even their destructive ravages were, he thought, periodically undone. It took great imperial societies such as the Romans to actually denude and desertify vast regions of the Mediterranean basin.[15] A century later, an important collective volume reviewed these issues again.[16] Inequalities of power and consumption have only increased since Marsh's time. Some elites and some countries have had vastly more impact—for good and for ill—than others. The United Nations recognized this differential effect in a phrase in the 1992 Rio Declaration on Environment and Development on the need to address the emergent climate catastrophe. It assigned "common but differentiated responsibilities" to signatory nations.[17]

THE NEED FOR HISTORICAL ANALYSIS RECOGNIZED

The deep interactions of humans, their production systems and cosmologies, and their political projects with the biosphere have thus all been historical—indeed, they are "world historical" processes. The process is dynamic and what economists call "path-dependent," meaning that events earlier in time open and close paths to alternative states of the world, paths that the system cannot retrace. In a broad sense, this amounts to saying the processes in question are irreversible and *historical*.[18] But in the great age of Western empires (ca. 1880–1945), world historians who did not shape their projects around the "manifest destiny" of a nation or race searched for evolutionary models or, indeed, for "the laws of motion" of human society. Meanwhile, mainstream economists from Alfred Marshall on moved instinctively to equilibrium models. They thus abandoned the historical and contingent side of the "political economy" found in Adam Smith. Computable General Equilibrium models have become more sophisticated and complex in the century plus since Marshall wrote but still strive by definition to find equilibria and understand the laws of motion of the economy. Various dynamic models in early ecology also preferentially sought to find equilibria when modeling the processes they studied.

However, beginning in the 1960s, the ecological sciences have moved toward recognition of contingency, of the existence of "unknown unknowns." Environmental scientists therefore turned back to a more "historical" approach. Sharon Kingsland, the leading historian of ecological thought, observes that the history of the discipline may be seen as "a conflict between historical and ahistorical thinking." The latter, she argues, was a temptation for mathematical modelers such as Robert MacArthur to focus on populations in equilibrium, ones that could ignore the impact of unique and therefore historical events.[19] Yet equilibrium models cannot cope with single unique events—such as the great meteor strike at the end of the Cretaceous that opened up the earth for mammals. Peter Taylor in a "state of the field" survey also points to the importance of history. He writes that epidemiologists, paleontologists, historians, and ecologists all face the challenge of historical explanation. That is, they have to assemble a composite of past conditions sufficient for the subsequent outcome to have followed and not some other, although they must at the same time not obscure the provisionality of such accounts in the face of competition from other plausibly sufficient accounts. Since the 1980s, "ecologists in general have become increasingly aware that situations may vary according to historical trajectories that have led to them; that particularities of place and connections among places matter; that time and place is a matter of scales that differ among co-occurring species; that variation among individuals can qualitatively alter the ecological process; that this variation is a result of ongoing differentiation occurring within populations—which are specifically located and inter-connected—and that interactions among the species under study can be artifacts of the indirect effects of other 'hidden' species."[20] The Ecological Society of America has been at the forefront of such integrative thinking. A team of distinguished members recently declared that the reach of humans into the environment had proved far deeper than was previously thought. Consequently, "ecological science is virtually impossible to conduct in isolation, as humans are a large part of the ecosystems we study."[21]

These changes in ecological thought began to percolate back into the other human sciences. Anthropologists who studied little communities moved more quickly than historians to the study of political ecology. Michael Dove and Nancy Peluso are leading examples. K. Sivaramakrishnan began his field observations of social forestry programs in West Bengal (later published as *Modern Forests*) in the 1990s as well. He especially critiqued the widespread view that precolonial South Asia had been in harmonious equilibrium until colonial power disrupted it.[22] As a result of the "cultural turn" in the human sciences, however, many scholars in the 1980s eschewed grand narratives. They instead considered only the structures of printed texts or provided thick descriptions of little episodes. Indeed, John McNeill, a past president of the American Historical Association, has recently lamented that just as the evidence of human impacts on the globe was entering educated public discourse, scholars of history and the humanities were turning their backs on it. The rise of CO_2 to levels unknown for millions of years, the incineration of forests, the extinction of many species—"all this was unworthy of their powers, interesting only for the discourses that it aroused." The economists, he notes, were equally rapt in an unreal world of abstract models deriving from unexamined generalizations about universal human behavior. But, he adds, this was beginning to change.[23]

Still, it was only in 1998 that the annual series *Reviews in Anthropology* commissioned Ian Scoones of the University of Sussex to write an essay on the emerging field of political ecology. Scoones presents the crossover between the natural and social sciences thus: "New ecological thinking suggests that there is no straightforward relationship between people and environment in processes of environmental change." This, he continues, requires analysis to be "sensitive to the interaction of structural features and human agency across a range of scales from the local to the global."[24] This book is structured to cover these overlapping scales in historical time.

For example, the decimation of indigenous South American populations after the Iberian conquests that Ruddiman invokes was, after all, the (partly) unintended result of the deployment of military and political power by successive kings of Spain and Portugal. The same kings began the slave trade from Africa to the Americas. That long-sustained trade then brought not only millions of enslaved humans but also deadly new diseases including yellow fever to tropical America. McNeill shows that unintended lethal consequences then shaped the political life of the tropical Americas for three centuries. Many scholars agree that the Anthropocene began with the testing of nuclear devices made by the Manhattan Project. These detonations left markers in the form of new radioactive particles across the entire globe. But that was only possible for a great power that could intensively mobilize scientific knowledge, engineering capacity, and vast resources for it. Tens of thousands worked on the project, but billions have been impacted by it. Similar inequalities structured human impact upon the global environment even as the existence of a "global commons" to which all were entitled became a common theme in international policy discourse.[25] That change became evident only after many decades of environmental studies that focused on single nations or, indeed, regions within them, such as studies of highway noise and pollution or of the siting of waste dumps in the United States and Canada.

THE INDIAN INTERVENTION IN INTERNATIONAL POLITICAL ECOLOGY

Conflicting views on history and responsibility emerged as early as 1972, soon after the entomologist Paul Ehrlich and others published alarming books announcing that the world environment would be irretrievably damaged by Third World population growth.[26] Jairam Ramesh has recently uncovered the background to an increasingly powerful Third World—and specifically Indian—response in his biography of the then Indian prime minister Indira Gandhi as an environmentalist. With input from Pitambar Pant and T. N. Srinivasan in India, she critiqued the dominant stance that global environmental problems were mainly caused by population growth in the underdeveloped nations. She pointed to the overconsumption of small, high-income populations as more damaging than the subsistence consumption of poorer countries. She therefore defended the latter's right to grow and suggested that the burden of past pollution should be borne by its beneficiaries, the then high-income nations. Ramesh (who was a participant in a famous later debate as minister of environment and forests in India in 1992) observes how the 1972 speech became famous as a precursor of positions more widely adopted after 1992, when activists and representatives of major governments gathered at the United Nations Conference on Environment and Development, or the Rio Summit.[27] The meeting saw a sharp clash over burden-sharing between developing countries, led by India, and the developed West.[28] It turned crucially on the question of historical responsibility for the emerging crisis, but in this polemic historical responsibility was generally apportioned by country. At the meeting, representatives of several governments rejected plans that required their countries to bear the remedial burden of minimizing environmental damage, since historical evidence showed they had made minimal contributions to it. The political dimensions of the conflicts were also evident.[29]

The Indian delegation took an especially strong stance at the Rio Summit. That position derived in great measure from earlier Indian debates around political ecology. In a pioneering effort at bypassing the governmental grip on environmental knowledge that the Republic of India had inherited from the colonial state, the Centre for Science and Environment (CSE) in Delhi compiled the first Citizens' Report on the Indian environment in 1982.[30] Meanwhile, the World Resources Institute published a report analyzing global emissions of greenhouse gases and recommending that all countries be required to reduce their emissions. The CSE had by then developed the analytic strength to push back with another report and an alternative allocation of responsibility. That response contributed to the government of India's changed stance at the Rio Summit.[31] History and inequality had moved onto the stage of global debates.

REVIEW OF HISTORICAL LITERATURE

The aftermath of the 1992 Rio Summit prompted discussions of responsibility for past planetary damage. One of the most notable of these is Peter Hayes and Kirk Smith's *The Global Greenhouse Regime: Who Pays?*[32] Economists, geographers, and sociologists have since contributed to contemporary critical discourse. More Western environmental historians became aware of the international and historical dimensions of their research. Archaeological publications have for decades commonly begun with a discussion of the environmental setting of the study site, as major changes in it might be invoked to explain the collapse of even early urban civilizations.[33]

Archaeologists in South Asia had long advanced ecological arguments, especially after the discovery in 1924 of an unsuspected early civilization in the lower valley of the Indus. But there long was an odd division of labor in South Asia between archaeology, which was limited to the era before writing, and history, which began when texts became widespread. As a result there was little communication between materially oriented archaeologists and textually oriented historians. In South Asia, this only began to change in the 1970s and 1980s. In 1982, Thomas Trautmann's essay "Elephants and the Mauryas" developed an important argument about the relation between kingly power and forest policy.[34] In the same year, the historian Irfan Habib made a brave attempt at mapping textual evidence of local environments into his great *Atlas*.[35] John Richards collaborated with Elizabeth Flint to carry out a deep quantitative study of land use change in South Asia that appeared in 1994.[36] A pioneering work, it suffered from an insufficient interrogation of colonial land use classifications. It therefore simplistically assimilated older tax-based data into contemporary categories of land use classification such as "forest." This book will interrogate the foundations of historical classifications to uncover the power relations that generated them.

Meanwhile, however, efforts at uniting environmental study with historical sociology had been initiated by Madhav Gadgil and his collaborators in India in the 1970s. In 1989, Ramachandra Guha published *The Unquiet Woods* on the long history of local environmental activism in the middle Himalaya. He followed this by collaborating with Gadgil to publish the first full-scale environmental history of the Indian subcontinent in 1992.[37] This contained the germ of the idea that localization and stability led to prudent and sustainable management, while mobility was associated with destructive use. That idea was further developed in *Ecology and Equity*, a book that opens by highlighting the global reach of Victorian elite consumption in the era when the sun never set on the British Empire. It goes on to point to the intensification of colonial patterns in the asymmetric consumption of various fractions of Indian society in the authors' own time. A small elite—the "omnivores," they write—shared in global consumer life at a level resembling that of the West. Meanwhile, four-fifths of the population depended on the local environment to meet most of their material needs. Gadgil and Guha term these locavores "ecosystem people," direct consumers of nature and direct sufferers from its degradation. Struggles over natural resources were therefore political struggles.[38]

GOALS OF THIS MONOGRAPH

Sörlin and Wormbs end an important 2018 article with a call for a history that enables humanity "to see more clearly the relationship of technologies and environment."[39] Within that agenda, what I aim to specifically foreground is how effective technologies of measurement and record are bound up with inequalities of power and the working of resistance in environmental history. This book demonstrates how the historical apparatus of twentieth-century ecological thinking emerged from the concrete power structures of empires. It thereby uncovers the visions of the world capacitated by these historical projects. It does this by focusing concretely on two empires that succeeded each other in South Asia from the fifteenth to the mid-nineteenth century. Selecting this period avoids the tendency to tacitly consign the entire pre-British period to the hazy world of "traditional India" and instead allows a delineation of major continuities in the two projects of empire as well as the radical changes resulting from the arrival of techniques derived from the Industrial Revolution.

Several disciplines and many little-used sources inform this study of human environments in historical time in the frame of political ecology. The politics of nature begins with "the question of environmental knowledge, of how it is produced, contested, legitimated, and hybridized."[40] When I began writing this book six years ago, I, like many historians, conceived "the environment" as a distinct segment of a four-dimensional reality, solely framed in a neutral time and space. It was an entity whose characteristics could be objectively known and consistently evaluated. It had always been there. All human agents were therefore assumed to act upon the same objectively extant landscape.[41] The historically authentic would then be my reconstruction of a segment of that historical past. I now realize that to be untenable and instead argue that the perception, valuation, and manipulation of human environments all have their own histories. Since the evaluative gaze was typically followed by the manipulative grasp, I consider terrain and biota as perceived and acted upon by different layers of agents living at different scales—ranging from the feeble many to the powerful few.

This book therefore travels through different scales of perception, each of which was overlapped by, and also excluded by, others. Each scale—from the small neighborhood landscape of the peasant family, to the edge of the seagirt world that bounded traditional Indic kingship, to the software-generated planetary images of the space age—is framed by the hierarchy of power and resources that generated it. In every case, humans have acted upon their perceived world and learned of it through action. Their grasp of the world accompanied their gaze upon it, and their imagination—from cosmological to pragmatic—patterned their action.

Chapter 1 considers general patterns that characterize "humanity" and how human inequality shaped each habitus and its corresponding level of knowledge. State systems labored to measure, count, and surveil even as resistance to subjugation sought to limit the overlord's gaze and obstruct his reach. In turn, subaltern efforts at evasion, concealment, and resistance obscured the transparency that empires sought. In the process, such struggles enhanced some natural features of the landscape. The modified terrain, typically woodland, was not merely opaque to the gaze of the powerful; it was also resistant to their movement. Conflicts thus generated the ever-shifting boundaries of excluded and contested zones, or *zomia* and *mehwas*. Refuges can double as strongholds, and predation and protection shade into each other. Within the frontier, in the lands of the submissive, I go below the kingly gaze to learn how intermediate elites perceived the land and used their knowledge to control subordinates and exclude overlords.

This analysis goes beyond the simply human. Historically, all human societies have lived beside and have been based upon animals as commensals and competitors, helpers and predators. As an anonymous reviewer of a draft of this book noted, the following chapters discuss the non-human as complementary to the human at each analytic level: "the agrarian, military, and pastoral." Some animals were bred to work, some to fight, some to be killed for sport or food, and some represent uncontrollable symbols of the sacred, the abominable, and the alien. Their presence and their needs changed the landscape and thereby also human life.[42] The non-human includes the world of plants that, directly or indirectly, support all of life. I take account of the many products of tilled lands but also direct our attention to the often neglected theme of forest modification, of the cultivation of the spontaneous.[43] In the South Asian context, empires were uniquely founded on harnessing the power of a wild species, the Asiatic elephant. That choice created an ecosystem unique to this Old World region. Projects of empire focused on ruling and sought to know, consume, and shape their domains. Chapter 1 therefore moves from historiographic review to the consideration of state projects of control and exploitation. But no project of rule can ignore the features of that which it seeks to dominate. Empires made the first efforts to "know" the land in order to rule it. Reaction, or feedback, both denied and provided more information. Still, empires that connected suzerain and subject over featureless oceans had to develop forms of knowing distinct from those that ruled the land.

Chapter 2 concerns projects of empire in South Asia, from the founding of the Mughal (ca. 1526–1600) to the waning of the British (ca. 1900–1947). The former was emphatically a land-centered empire: alongside it, however, the Portuguese founded a seaborne empire, connected by the first truly global network of intensive maritime communication. Their presence on and perception of the land merits comparison with that of their Mughal contemporary. I will show how local knowledges remained opaque to the imperial gaze on land well into the era of British rule. It was only over decades that both the Mughal and Portuguese Empires were overshadowed by the British. I then analyze their novel efforts to map and manage their domains. Beneath the empires, however, were the seigneurial domains that co-opted or resisted them. Their presence shaped the knowledge that could accumulate at the upper levels of imperial hierarchy.[44]

Chapter 3 moves us one level below the imperial to the provincial and its elites; it therefore considers the seigneurial gaze and lordly intervention. Evidence from Marathi-speaking Western India is used to document the geographies made by production systems molded by elite consumption. Their effects upon the ecosystem are evident in how strong preferences for well-polished white rice, spices, and ghee among the elite of South India slanted tillage and land use toward certain products. This effect was strongest in the narrow humid belt of the mountains and the craggy, indented coastline of Western India. This is where landlord power most profoundly molded society and environment.

Chapter 4 begins with a survey of settlement patterns in a comparative setting and across South Asia. It offers an account of the effect of moisture regimes and kingly power in making the Indian subcontinent a land of villages. Avoiding the stereotype of the unchanging peasant in the unchanging village, I argue for a gradient between the tight cluster of houses that made a settlement and the mosaic of variously used lands that began at the edge of the last courtyard or threshing floor. These were interstitial spaces that included the abandoned shrubby field, the lopped and coppiced grove, and merged into the ungoverned woodland and craggy mountain. This last was from the village point of view, the remote wilderness. Those who used and traversed all of these are people rarely studied in the setting of "village India." Historically, however, the settled might wander and wanderers settle; forests replace fields and fields forests. Itinerant and transient communities saw the settled villagers from within their own different networks: as customers, as employers, as donors, or as prey. These itinerants included the villagers' commensals—seasonally visiting shepherds and cowherds and trading caravans of armed nomads, the religious singers and exhibitors of performing animals, and many others. Any understanding of the society of the time must include the itinerant and transient communities. Additionally, our understanding must encompass the mute subjects who outnumbered sentient humans in all empires: protected domesticates, reviled "vermin," venerated elephants, cherished horses, and so many more.[45]

Chapter 5 turns our attention to a neglected aspect of contestation: its effects on the ecosystem broadly. It therefore considers the passage of armies and their biotic demands and effects on the environment. It shows how people adapted, evaded, and resisted, and they changed the face of the land in the process. Elements of instability and conflict created their own ecotone of flight and resistance, with lands of refuge and terrains of resistance. Beasts of pillage and beasts of tillage were both deployed in the process. The chapter thereby widens an animal history of South Asia already begun when discussing elephantine effects on the distribution and composition of woodland. Chapter 5 concludes with the coming of the British Empire. The next chapter considers the British period in South Asia and finds both continuities and discontinuities from earlier regimes. Route itineraries inherited from the previous governments grew more complex and impersonal. New measuring instruments and more sophisticated mathematical methods were deployed down to the field level to generate maps of unprecedented uniformity and depth. A new, nautically derived mode of surveying led to a closer hold on the landscape and encouraged a deeper penetration of the market.

A Western imperial environmental consciousness emerged from the developed colonial apparatus of surveillance and record. I therefore examine how technologies of knowing combined with the military capacities of an industrial empire to permeate metropolitan understandings of the land and radically change it by the early twentieth century. The final chapter then shows how flora, fauna, and the land itself were irrevocably reordered in drastic ways. I consider how these imperial themes unfolded: the pragmatic navigational schemas of maritime empires, the enumerated landscapes of terrestrial powers, the lordly efforts to know and shape domains, the hard core and contested periphery of village communities, and the many kinds of wilderness and their inhabitants.

An increasing mass of data and the collaboration of immense numbers of diverse specialists have produced the successively disheartening reports of the Intergovernmental Panel on Climate Change. Yet at the same time there is a new possibility for achieving a synoptic and detailed scrutiny of landscapes. I, like anyone writing on environmental history today, am aware of this encompassing body of knowledge. Many experts are by now convinced of effects of contingency on ecosystems, our planet, and our cosmos. This has led scholars trained as ornithologists, lepidopterists, and oceanographers to write history.[46] I argue that historians are uniquely trained to study the unfolding of contingent events in past time and should make the effort to do so.

In this book, I apply my skills to one part of the world and its past. But the patterns found are illustrative of the inequalities of power and processes of resistance that have worked in environmental history worldwide. The book considers empires—those most unequal of governments—in order to uncover how their fluctuating capacity for domination was imbricated in the shaping of environmental knowledge itself. Their material presence is revealed on paper in lists and charts and maps and on the ground in landmarks and boundary markers, beacons, and survey baselines. This concrete engagement enables me to document how the resistance that imperial intrusion generated also shaped what was known. This book is therefore not only a history of empires but also a history of the imperial knowledge that ultimately produced the "common sense" of the educated person today.

Beyond that, I write of South Asia, a region where no other work to date has systematically compared the ways in which the exercise of power generated knowledge through two major empires, the Mughal and the British. I then show how regional elites both manipulated and resisted imperial power and how their "gaze" underlies imperial maps. This *longue durée* view breaches the Great Wall that historians of South Asia have frequently erected between the so-called precolonial era (a period of thousands of years!) and the colonial one that lasted less than two centuries. I can thus demonstrate the concrete diversity of the South Asian environment and tease out the changes that land, animals, and people all experienced through the centuries.

In conclusion, the research for this book has required me to trespass into many different disciplines and to digest their distinct knowledges. Specialists in each of these areas may find some of the arguments presented too elementary to bear repetition and others too simple to be accurate. My excuse is that this book is not addressed to specialists in any one field. The facts and arguments were novel and enlightening for me. I hope they may prove so for at least some readers. Furthermore, I believe that by the end of this book, the reader will have a deeper understanding of the historical roots of our modern worldview and appreciate the underlying structures of power that generate it, with all its costs and burdens. The following chapters lay bare the historical contingencies that have shaped the only world we have.

ONE

Inequality, Complexity, and Ecology

The exhibition of increasingly intensive and complex niche construction behaviors through time is a key feature of human evolution, culminating in the advanced capacity for ecosystem engineering exhibited by Homo sapiens.
NICOLE L. BOIVIN | 2016

THERE HAS INDUBITABLY BEEN AN EXPLOSION OF ENVIRONMENTAL studies worldwide since the 1970s, even if historians have been overshadowed by scholars from other disciplines. Most studies, however, do not investigate the structural basis of the information that they use. Sometimes, as with the oceanographers or ornithologists mentioned in the introduction, this reflects their sense that it does not matter for their narrative.[1] And indeed, it may not, as long as we speak of modern observational data that generates models that may be projected back and forward in time. An example would be the combined astronomical reckoning of the earth system's past and future location in the Milankovitch cycle, the precession of the equinoxes, or the seventeenth-century minimum in sunspot cycles. Laymen must depend on the self-regulation of the scientific communities. Their open and competitive structure may be assumed to safeguard us from misinformation, and if that fails, I am not qualified to detect it. That, however, is not true of information recorded as a precipitate of the political process, especially that generated as part of state building. Historians are equipped to scrutinize the motives of those who collected the information and how that inflected it. This is especially important when we consider the information collected by imperial establishments, institutions that are unequal by definition. We can ask if they entirely grasped what they presented, and we should seek the alternative knowledges of those who obstructed, resisted, or evaded the gaze and grasp of empire. Historical knowledge is fragmented, and different regimes fragmented it in different ways. Understanding these processes is what historians are uniquely equipped to do.

This chapter lays the groundwork by first considering how humans created early perceptual geographies before the emergence of major inequality. But these were habitats, niches adapted to their occupants. Cycles of life within them may be seen as a version of the French sociologist Pierre Bourdieu's concept of the "habitus." The emergence of empires changed perceptual and evaluative worlds of ruling elites. But their capacity itself changed through time and varied by surface. The trackless ocean long remained intractable: only on the London stage could Britannia rule the waves. Therefore I briefly consider how mapping the sea differed from ordering the land and suggest how techniques migrated from the one to the other in South Asia. But I also emphasize that power relations had to change before techniques could migrate.

MAKING MENTAL LANDSCAPES
OR HOW HOMO BECAME SAPIENT

Archaeologists have long recognized that early humans consciously modified their habitats to fit perceived needs even when organized in small communities or "bands"—well before they formed states. Indeed, the process began before we became entirely modern humans (*Homo sapiens*). Nicole Boivin and colleagues have reviewed the evidence worldwide and observe that "increasingly intensive and complex niche construction behaviors through time is a key feature of human evolution, culminating in the advanced capacity for ecosystem engineering exhibited by *Homo sapiens*."[2] Some historians now argue that humanity's cumulative effect upon the earth began with the use of fire as an instrument of landscape modification. Periodic fires helped hunters and encouraged specific plants long before agricultural fields were cleared by firing them. Such niche construction began some 400,000 years ago.[3] The archaeologist Graeme Barker's magisterial review of the beginnings of the Agricultural Revolution finds that humans specifically managed and modified landscapes to yield the products they desired for tens of thousands of years—a phenomenon traceable in some parts of the world to 50,000 years before the present. Humans had begun introducing new plants and animals and thus "cultivating forests"; in short, they were engineering ecosystems.[4] The productive phases of these habitats varied by location and through time. Their users had to visit them at the appropriate time and had to adjust plans after interpreting ever-varying signals from the weather.

Such niche construction was not limited to suppressing or promoting plants but inevitably included animals. Humans have manipulated animal species from the remote past to the present; they have also fitted them in their own ordering of the world. The anthropologist Claude Lévi-Strauss once explained animal totems by saying that they were selected not as good to eat but as good to think. Other animals were bred to be eaten and to work, as companions and as trophies, living or dead. But this does not exhaust the potentials of the many species that accompany, infest, and envelop humans. They have been auxiliaries in war, and landscapes have been changed to suit them as we shall see with the elephant and the horse. But oxen have also been vital to farming and transport, and many subspecies have been bred for specific conditions. Animals have also been incorporated into didactic fables such as the *Panchatantra* and religious discourses such as narrations of previous lives of the Buddha. No human ecosystem has been built without animal components in thought and in action.[5]

A developed "modern" version of the engineered anthropoid ecosystem may be conceived as what Bourdieu has termed the *habitus*. Bourdieu's work on the peoples of the North African mountains provided an early model of the coevolution of ecology and polity. It also developed the idea that ecology, polity, value, and affect ("feelings") all coevolved, with feedback loops reinforcing them.[6] Bourdieu's habitus was, however, a static one. Implicit in it was the idea that "traditional" life reproduced itself through time and shaped the people who lived it. This stable lifeway persisted until French colonial capitalism arrived to disrupt its balance. Bourdieu's study was thus structural, static, and fundamentally synchronic, or at best cyclical. That approach was normal for a sociological analysis completed in the early 1960s. This was a time when the field was recoiling from pseudo-historical and racist constructions of human societies that had been current up to the mid-twentieth century. But Bourdieu's work expressed a wider notion of humans evaluating, acting upon, and modifying their surroundings even as the changed settings reshaped them and their lifeways. All humans also have a perspective, whether extended or constricted, on the landscape that surrounds them. How humans perceived and lived in the intersection of symbolic and pragmatic geography shaped their habitus, but the habitus made them just as much as they made the habitus.

The temporal depth of this process is demonstrated in the work of Dwight Read and Sander van der Leeuw, who show that conceptual ordering and landscape modification indeed appeared early in human history. They demonstrate this by analysis of the geometry and material science involved in the production of increasingly sophisticated stone tools, a process beginning some two million years ago. By the beginning of the Mesolithic period (20,000 to 7,000 YBP), humans definitely possessed what Read and van der Leeuw term the "*conceptual tools to control the landscape.*" That is to say, they had begun to envisage manipulating nature through time to achieve some desirable end state. These tools were deployed to move from a resource-procuring (collecting ripe berries, for example) to a resource-producing (protecting and planting for future yield) mode of production. The shift was ultimately toward horticulture, agriculture, and animal husbandry. Such shifting also can be understood as "*long-term human investment in certain aspects of the environment.*" This then led "to a more extended conceptualization of space and time."[7] Viewed through deep time, the mental and the material aspects of humanity evolved together.

In the past few decades, archaeologists have come to interpret not just the making of tools but also their transport and caching by early hominins in the Paleolithic to be illustrative of expanded cognition and more complex social systems. Thus, construction of society and the mapping of landscapes expanded together. "Larger group sizes, extended effective networks, and, ultimately, extended 'social landscapes' require the storage of ever increasing quantities of information for longer and longer periods and the transmission of that information over larger and larger distances."[8] The transmission of knowledge enabled the exercise of power over the landscape and within the social network. Modern empires such as the British, which lasted into the mid-twentieth century, represent a culmination of a process with far deeper roots in history.

The history of the last five millennia is a story of increasing social complexity. Specialization and stratification—or bluntly, inequality—increased alongside increasing population. Concretely, that has meant the development of vast differences in power and wealth, as exemplified above all in the rise of huge global empires, the apogee of concentrated power. Some agents within these structures had great power and others very little. Elites could—and can—reach across the globe, modifying it to fit their state projects, transporting species across vast oceans, denuding it for recreation and consumption. This book is therefore focused on the age of world empires, from the fifteenth to the twentieth century—a short epoch but deeply consequential in human affairs. Empires desired but never achieved complete control of even their own subjects or the spaces those subjects inhabited. Divergent perceptions of the world and mutual struggles for control and escape nonetheless have deeply impacted the worlds in which we all live. It then becomes evident that the most impactful human action has been the result of struggles between humans as much as between humans and the non-human environment.

Human powers shape human horizons. Even at the beginning of the twentieth century, the little community, the face-to-face lifeworld, could not unaided even perceive its own global or continental setting, nor could its members effectively seize resources beyond their own little range. Lords and gentry, kings and emperors perceived larger worlds, and their acquisitive reach ranged far wider, over land and sea. But everywhere they reached, they encountered rival empires and local societies that contested their demands and responded to their presence. Conflict over environmental evaluation and equity also created fissures within each society.

Inequality within a population implies inequality in certain human powers—specifically, the evaluative gaze, the projective reach, and the pragmatic grasp. The anthropologist Paul Sillitoe has presented the idea that different evaluative gazes projected various pragmatic agendas upon the same landscape, such as a stretch of woodland. "A shifting cultivator will see potential swidden sites, assessing their value by a range of criteria such as species composition indicating fertility status, tenure rights at different locations and so on. A local entrepreneur might see a tourist location, perhaps a hotel with forest views and outdoor pursuits. A forester may see a mature standing crop, calculating its value depending on whether it is harvested sustainably or clear-felled with attendant erosion risks. A Western conservationist might see a beautiful natural environment that demands protection against any human depredation, as the habitat of endangered wildlife."[9]

Inequality of power also implies unequal capacity to reshape the land.

Terra firma was the contested domain of terrestrial kingdoms and empires, and their capacity to surveil and control gradually increased through time. Gigantic imperial projects—China's Great Wall and Grand Canal, Britain's Hadrian's Wall, and lesser projects that nonetheless transformed the earth—all depended on ignoring extant small-scale ideas of space and use in order to meet overriding sovereign goals. This required developing an empirical schema ("a mental map") of the land as it existed and then projecting what it should become. To succeed (and not all did), such projects also required an understanding of the allocation of human and environmental resources. Administrators had to determine how many work teams could be assembled and how much they could achieve in a day, a month, a year. A greater or lesser ability to comprehend these relationships and successfully alter the earth was an index of imperial power and knowledge. Only a realistic understanding of the combination of land and people that made up a village, a province, or a kingdom allowed the effective exaction of resources and allocation of tasks. Concretely this was manifested in the tax roll, the itinerary, and, above all, the representational scale map. The immensity of humans' collective impact on the world requires a historical understanding of how states and empires acted on the environment.

The greater ecosystem was, and is, a precipitate of conflict, shaped by a contested political ecology of perception and control. Historians understand our world as the product of many struggles. They deal not only with events but also with the changing and often conflicting perceptions that caused those events, perceptions that shaped intended and unintended outcomes. As historian Simon Schama writes, "Before it can ever be the repose for the senses, landscape is the work of the mind. Its scenery is built up as much from strata of memory as from layers of rock."[10] For the historian, it is impossible to see any one perspective as the only historically authentic one; we must layer them on one another as far as the evidence takes us.

THE COEXISTENCE OF SACRED AND PRAGMATIC GEOGRAPHY

Historical evidence is the surviving detritus of both natural processes and human actions. Tree rings are naturally occurring forms of historical evidence that may be "read" to reconstruct cycles of dry and wet years in, for example, the American Southwest. Archaeology enables us to review adaptive changes in lifeways of the Indigenous peoples of this region, which ranged from constructing irrigation channels to a reversion to nomadic foraging. We may infer from abandoned settlements that, after a succession of failed crops, surviving farmers decided to leave the sites. We may never learn how fourteenth-century Mesoamerican farmers explained the decade-long droughts they experienced, but tree rings they never saw tell us that such droughts occurred.[11] Conversely, four thousand years ago, diviners at early Chinese courts predicted events from the patterns of cracks in "oracle bones" taken from sacrificed animals. The cracks were read as omens and thus provide historical evidence of past interpretive frames. We may not know the fate of the Shang ruler at whose court the bones were interpreted 3,500 years ago, but we may infer his cosmological understanding, fears, and hopes from the questions scratched on the bones.[12]

There were many different kinds of minds at work in those complex societies of earlier centuries that have left us records of their thought. They were all dominated by what today's scientists characterize as a philosophical and religious outlook. The spiritual gaze came long before modern astrophysical cosmology and its encompassing vision. And it persists; Diana Eck has reminded us that we all live "in the mappings of our imagined landscape, with its charged centers and its dim peripheries."[13] All belief systems that we know of have mental maps of the cosmos, the earth, and humanity. The most influential have been the three expansive world religions—Buddhism, Christianity, and Islam. They all arose in what Karl Jaspers has called the Axial Age, the thousand years from circa 400 BCE that coincided with the appearance of great empires spanning the Old World. It has been argued that transcendently powerful divinities reflected the new political order and allowed the priestly intelligentsia to emerge as a permanent specialist stratum for the first time in human history. Imperial conquests, royal highways, and merchant routes by land and sea spread new faiths and shaped a new geography of centers and peripheries.

Beginning in the 1990s, the Center for the Study of World Religions, Harvard Divinity School published a series of volumes on ecology and world religions. The series editors write that religions shape attitudes toward nature "in both conscious and unconscious ways.... They shape the worldview of a society."[14] The collective lifeworld is expressed in sacred geographies, such as the Indic *mandala* universe of the past two thousand years. It depicted a tripartite cosmos, with heaven and hell framing the human world of concentric island continents. *Jāmbudvīpa* was the innermost. For the Jains, these were an infinite series of concentric circular bands, with humans inhabiting the innermost two and a half. That notion was shared by Hindu and Buddhist cosmology. For the latter, *Jāmbudvīpa* was also where the Buddha had lived.[15] Variations of that symbolic geography traveled along with Buddhism across Asia. Islam added the Arab holy centers of Mecca and Medina to the world map of pilgrimage. Meanwhile, at the western edge of Eurasia, medieval Christianity developed a view of a world centered on an imagined Jerusalem that few Christians had ever seen.

These cosmologies have, however, motivated vast numbers to arduous pilgrimages for at least two thousand years. But even the most pious traveled within what I term *pragmatic geography*. Sacred and pragmatic geographies coexisted. The two might intersect at specific pilgrimage centers, since important religious sites were shown on maps. These would guide pilgrims beset by touts and hucksters. Maps and sketches that guided pilgrims' physical journeys may also have served as devotional images or icons after their return.[16] Some Chinese maps of the world that aimed at realism were nonetheless influenced by the universal symmetries of Indian Buddhist cosmography. Chinese Buddhist pilgrims traveling to sacred sites in India knew of them from Indic cosmography. Getting there safely would, however, have depended on the pragmatic understandings of caravan leaders and sea captains, guides, and harbor pilots regardless of spiritual affiliation. These were the folk who knew the routes and seasons, changing tides, and shifting sandbars.

If the Chinese and Koreans knew of Buddhist centers, Vaishnava pilgrims within South Asia similarly knew the names and directions of major sacred sites such as Jagannathpuri, Dwarka, Badrinath, and Rameshwaram, for example. These were places perceived as framing the cardinal directions within the subcontinent with great shrines dedicated to the god Vishnu. A similar sacred geography shaped the world of the devotees of Shiva.[17] Then there would be regional competitors, such as Uttarkashi ("the Northern Kashi"), and also regional constellations, such as the "Five Kedar-s" (*pancakedār*) and the "Five Badri-s" of the Himalaya, which are regional arrays of important Shaiva and Vaishnava shrines. These were formerly linked by recognized paths and tracks with shops and temporary shelters at suitable campsites. These two culminated in the subcontinentally known temples of Kedarnath and Badrinath. The great shrines at Pandharpur and Jejuri in western Maharashtra in the western Deccan and Tirupati in the east played a similar role in regional configurations. Finally, there were village temples and small shrines in the fields.[18]

After the arrival of Islam, Muslims had to orient themselves toward Mecca to pray. Mosque architecture reflects knowledge of the direction where it lay. Pious Muslims also aspired to visit the two holy cities as pilgrims. The learned cartography that Islamic scholars had developed from the Ptolemaic tradition now intersected with the folk geography of pious villagers and townspeople.[19] Local burials with miraculous powers generated shrines and pilgrimage centers across the countryside of South Asia.[20] Finally, Christian communities in South Asia knew of Jerusalem and Rome and also developed many regional shrines. One of the most famous is in Old Goa, on the western coast of India, where the embalmed corpse of St. Francis Xavier sanctifies the great cathedral.

Economic geography had a different pragmatic vision that also intersected with the sacred. Bankers around South Asia sold payment orders (*hunḍi*) payable in places such as Banaras (Varanasi) or Ajmer to pilgrims and others, regardless of purpose. Commission charges varied with the demand for cash and each banker's network. The bankers would have a pragmatic understanding of time and distance, of risk and demand at different centers, regardless of confessional affiliation. The English East India Company's treasury would purchase orders payable in Banaras to remit funds to chronically deficit Bombay. Bankers in Western India would then draw on cash in Banaras to remit funds received from pilgrims traveling from that region.[21] Thus, the fiscal geography of the East India Company and the sacred geography of Hindu pilgrims could intersect over a single banking network.

Pilgrims and travelers followed guides but also used schematic maps of important pilgrim towns. Many of these are described or depicted in Susan Gole's unique compendium of Indian maps and plans.[22]

IRRIGATION AND THE DEEPENING OF EMPIRES

The rise of complex, hierarchical societies was everywhere accompanied by great increases in human population. These conjoint developments have, in the past four thousand years, consistently magnified humanity's effects on the global environment. Just as research has deepened our understanding of the effects of human use of fire and farming on the regional and global environments, so, too, has it intensified our comprehension of the potency of elite preferences and choices in shaping early historic landscapes. Rulers needed the mobilization—usually coerced—of vast numbers of humans and work animals to systematically change the face of the earth through their projects. The wealth extracted from their territories reached out far across the earth to enlist autonomous peoples as suppliers to their markets. As I have written elsewhere, the intensity of human environmental manipulation echoed patterns of authority and subjection within the human groups acting upon the environment.[23]

Artificial irrigation and drainage in Mesopotamia was an ancient practice that utilized the seasonal overflow and retreat of the many channels of the early delta. It was coeval with the beginnings of the mixed farming that emerged as the Tigris–Euphrates delta was still rising from the sea after the last Ice Age. Such projects were small scale and adaptable, and their builders were mobile. It was kingdoms and empires that pushed large irrigation projects to high levels of productivity. These needed coordinated labor on a recurring basis as well as great occasional mass mobilizations to recover from cataclysmic events. Strong political formations could achieve this but only at the cost of stretching system capacities to the edge of failure, thus increasing their own fragility. Mesopotamia, an arid land dependent on the management of runoff from distant mountains, has witnessed this cycle several times up to the present.

The apogee of ancient settlement and irrigation development in Mesopotamia was reached in the Sassanid period, ending circa 700 CE. It began to decline by the late ninth century, and the frontier of cultivation retreated as a result of political turmoil, salinity, and the spread of swampland. Efforts at restoring farming by building a transverse canal only worsened the problem of soil salinity. Political authority arising out of stratification had mobilized populations to intensify the use of land and water, but society thereby lost its resilience and adaptability.[24] The older, flexible agricultural system of shifting cultivation and allowing fallow periods returned. By around 1500 CE, the area's population dwindled, almost to levels that existed around 3500 BCE. Urbanism had shrunk back to a few cities, and cultivation was limited to their outskirts. Salinity resulting from previous overirrigation, however, precluded the reclamation of considerable areas. Another period of city growth came under Ottoman rule from the 1500s and ultimately stabilized through the exploitation of the region's petroleum in the twentieth century.[25] Thus, the regionally unsustainable exploitation of an extensive river valley is nowadays supported by the globally unsustainable exploitation of a fossil fuel.

The region where irrigation and empire truly meshed to change the face of the land was ancient North-Central China. The historian Yoshinobu Shiba has documented the complex, interlocking systems of water management built by imperial states in the Hangzhou Bay area between the eighth and thirteenth centuries.[26] These allowed the creation of large areas of irrigated rice fields. The environmental historians Mark Elvin and Ninghu Su have analyzed a thousand years of efforts to control the Yellow River and their consequences.[27] In this society, the massive capacity of the state to direct the energy and resources of its subjects was used for gigantic irrigation projects. Such powerful imperial societies are not passively captive to ecology, as Elvin laid out in detail in his pathbreaking environmental history of China.[28] Systems were resilient only if states were powerful.[29] The capital, Beijing, in particular, required massive environmental engineering to secure enough rice from the irrigated fields of the south to sustain a very large city in the arid, millet- and wheat-growing north. China's Grand Canal was built to ensure a steady supply of food and required constant attention; its very existence changed the hydrology of the coast.[30] Just maintaining the junction of the Yellow River and Grand Canal needed half a million workers and the expenditure of 800,000 ounces of silver in the year 1606 alone. The canal was the logistic lifeline for the imperial capital that had been fixed at Beijing in the agriculturally less productive north for strategic reasons. Almost a century ago, Karl Wittfogel developed a political ecology that connected water control with autocratic empire. He initially argued in orthodox Marxist fashion that the productive forces of an irrigation society generated the state superstructure that maintained them. By the 1950s, he moved to a more open view of the "man–nature" relationship. "Nature" itself changed in relation to new human technical capacities, social organizations, and "world outlook."[31]

The landscape effects of another empire—Vijayanagara city and its region—are available thanks to research undertaken by scholars of widely different disciplinary backgrounds. Like Beijing, Vijayanagara was a great imperial city pushed out into ecologically inhospitable terrain on the frontier of an imperial regime for strategic reasons. Recent studies have shown how deeply past imperial power was embedded in the landscape. Paleoecological analyses suggest that early land clearance on the hills removed most tree cover. The remaining woody material was depleted even further with the founding of the Vijayanagara Empire (ca. 1330–1565). Rice production occupied valley bottoms, and cattle would have grazed the hills, suitable parts of which would be used to raise millet and similar "hill grains."[32] This argument is supported by the work of Carla Sinopoli and her colleagues, which shows how elite preferences for white rice over the more nutritious millets shaped irrigation and water control projects far beyond that needed for functional adaptation to a semi-arid environment.[33] Archaeology thus shows how deeply the land was transformed by social stratification and the rise of states capable of mobilizing large labor forces. The effectiveness of these medieval irrigation projects was derided by British irrigation engineers and commented on by later scholars such as Kathleen Morrison.[34] And they certainly failed from time to time, but so do contemporary engineering projects, as Hurricanes Sandy and Katrina made amply clear.

It is important, however, to realize that while great projects might begin as imperial initiatives, the recalcitrance of land and water often led to compromises and adjustments along the way, even if they did not result in dam failure or reservoir extinction through siltation. Following a peace agreement with the Mughal emperor Jahangir (r. 1605–27), the Maharana of Mewar began the construction of a series of great reservoirs impounding runoff from the Aravali Range. This royal enterprise was intended for both display and utility, a sacred site and a royal pleasure resort. The works mobilized thousands of unskilled laborers but also the logistic and fiscal capacities of merchants and the pragmatic knowledge of elite engineers. British officials later judged it to be mainly symbolic because it had no adequate distributary network for flow irrigation. An outstanding combination of field research with literary and epigraphic analysis has enabled the historian Jonathan Seefeldt to show how the reservoir system in fact worked. He demonstrates that it operated synergistically with water-lifting by peasant farmers who would tap the now elevated water table. It thereby minimized the water needed for each unit of crop production even as it used more labor than flow irrigation would have done. It also extended the irrigation season, since water was lifted from constantly replenished aquifers not subject to surface evaporation. Cropping decisions were thereby decentralized in a way impossible with flood irrigation.[35] That arrangement would obviously economize water use and reduce the possibility of waterlogging and salinization. Paradoxically, therefore, the pragmatic success of a kingly project depended on merchant finance and peasant participation. "Thus, increased entanglements with water rendered polity formation in early modern Mewar a less linear, a less orchestrated, less Raja-centric endeavor than prior models of precolonial state formation have allowed."[36]

IMPERIAL LAND FRONTIERS

Even more complex relationships shaped the ebb and flow of life in all its forms across the steppe interface of Inner and East Asia, especially the lands equally suited to tillage as to grazing. Owen Lattimore deployed the richness of Chinese records and observations made during his own travels among the surviving nomadic pastoralists of Inner Mongolia decades ago to outline the pattern of borderland sociopolitical life. He perceived it as developing along the wide but fuzzy zone dividing lands well suited to pastoralism from lands well suited for wet-rice cultivation. His introduction to the 1951 edition of *Inner Asian Frontiers of China* generalizes this phenomenon to imperial frontier zones. Strong empires, he writes, expanded their power over "barbarian" peoples beyond the frontier. Yet such groups were also driven by a balance of opportunities and dangers into hardening their own political organization. Faced with strongly organized opponents, empires ceased to grow. That was when they could be blackmailed into paying off their borderers. At times, such groups could establish "overlord" regimes over much larger agrarian populations, but that structure would easily disintegrate and revert to a simpler tribal or war-band organization. The dividing line between the two lands with their sharply different sociocultural lives and subsistence systems did not, however, run along some hard environmental border; rather, it was the result of a long historical process in which different forms of society managed and controlled their environments. Each sociopolitical formation had to choose between agrarian life of a notably densely settled, labor-intensive form or nomadism of an especially dispersed form. Efforts at hybrid formations were caught between the hammer of the militarized pure nomads and the anvil of a fortified and densely settled agrarian order—and were crushed between them.[37]

The most famous social and political frontier in world history, that between the settled agrarian kingdoms of the North China plain and their pastoral nomad neighbors, was therefore not an ecological fact. Lands that grow grass can also grow millet, meaning that it was possible to farm in Inner Mongolia and Northeast Asia, and it was possible to pasture sheep and horses south of the Great Wall. Early states on both sides of the not-yet-built Great Wall grew out of a mosaic of farming-herding people ruled by chieftains. But those farther north and west were constrained by ecological boundaries from developing the kind of intensive farming possible in the Central Plain. They could not therefore concentrate resources and subjects in the way that more favorably placed early states could. They were soft targets for the expansionist urges of the increasingly more powerful kings. At the same time, fully nomadic pastoralists led by a horse-warrior elite pressed in on them from the north. As a result, borderland folk gradually abandoned agriculture to become full-scale pastoral nomads, adopting the techniques, equipment, and artistic motifs of the horse nomads.[38]

Archaeological research also advanced in the long-settled and well-documented landscapes of Europe. The Romans were the most persistently powerful of Western Iron Age empires at the granular level of human lifeways. They readily and obviously coerced the conquered into reshaping themselves into imperial subjects. An example of the lasting effect of their governance is the organization of farmland in Northern Europe, with its notable distinction between regions of hedgerow enclosure and regions of open field. In England, Roman-era fields had been rectangular and hedged, but the hedges were removed by the Anglo-Saxon invaders (fifth century CE onward) when they created an open-field system with individual landholdings marked off in scattered long, narrow strips. The Germanic open fields then came to be enclosed again during early modern efforts at rationalizing and capitalizing field structure after 1500. In England that process required the passing of individual Enclosure Acts through Parliament by influential political lobbies. Only then could the large common lands going back to the Anglo-Saxon settlements be broken into private property. In each case, the politically dominant community enduringly reshaped the landscape.[39]

MARITIME MAPS AND GLOBAL EMPIRES

Any abstraction from reality is oriented by the encompassing ethos of those who formulate it and the society that sustains it. It is also limited by available technology. Before the twentieth century, great overviews of the known world were chiefly the domain of established kingdoms and aspirant empires. Shortly after the discovery of the Americas, the kings of Spain and Portugal signed a treaty in 1494 that grandiosely partitioned the known world between them. It was to be demarcated by a line running from pole to pole at distance of 370 leagues west of the islands named Cabo Verde.[40] Communication routes carry the lifeblood of states: orders, reports, soldiers, officials, prisoners, tributes, and commodities. There was therefore a pragmatic geography inherent in their metabolic processes. New imperial states began to reach deeper into local society just as our species achieved its first true globalization. The most dramatic environmental effects came from the Iberian empires' transoceanic unification of the biota of the Old and New Worlds. Spain established a great empire stretching north along the Pacific coast at least notionally into today's California and south to Chile. Portugal recovered its lands from the Dutch and built a durable empire in Brazil. The Portuguese expansion southward and around the Cape of Good Hope also made them, for nearly a century, the major naval power on the high seas of Asia. Their military power created the "Estado da India" governed by a viceroy posted in Goa, to whom the king temporarily entrusted the totality of his powers, subject, however, to revocation at will.[41]

Transoceanic empires starting with the Spanish and Portuguese attained unprecedented sizes. Inequalities in consumption and access to global environmental resources ballooned. Formerly regional delicacies (tea, coffee, cacao, cane sugar, tobacco) became metropolitan luxuries—and then gradually common necessities. Humans spread new crops, animals, and diseases across the Atlantic and Pacific Oceans. International trade—most notoriously that in beaver pelts—drove entire species to the brink of extinction. Recently, some African elephant subpopulations, the black rhino, and the Indian cheetah have met the same fate, and in all three cases, the motivating force has been the international luxury trade. These trends did not begin in the twentieth century. They have a deep history. But the process has only intensified steadily since 1500.[42]

Before modern aerial photography, and before the satellites that sustain GPS were launched, oceanic navigation shaped a pragmatic geography quite different from that formed by land travel. The pragmatic and institutional geography of maritime empires extended across the trackless seas. Before the magnetic compass and navigational chart, pilots and captains relied on the sun by day and stars by night and by visual memory and experience of coastal skylines. Ship pilots, especially those of sailing ships, had to know the location of dangerous coasts and safe harbors. Knowledge of prevailing winds was equally important. This was easiest in a small, long-traversed sea such as the Mediterranean. Sailors away from land, but knowing the harbors to which they were bound, had long used the stars at night and sun by day to estimate their locations.[43] After the arrival of the Chinese invention of the magnetic compass in Europe, it was possible to combine the new device with sailors' knowledge of generally prevailing winds to sketch "wind roses" for future voyages. Coasts began to be traced out on paper or parchment in order to mark harbors relative to coasts. By 1300 CE, the small and much traversed Mediterranean had been represented in "portolan maps." These showed the shape of the coast and the shortest lines of constant compass bearing connecting origin to destination (rhumb lines). They were, writes the historian of cartography Tony Campbell, more accurate for this specific sea than even the Ptolemaic maps of the Roman period. They were also radically different from the *mappae mundi* of the clerics, which were maps showing a sacred geography centered on Jerusalem. Portolans enlarged over time as voyages extended nautical knowledge to the North Atlantic coasts of Europe. General geographical findings along the coast of West Africa also became known to European cartographers within a few years. The cartographic eye followed the pragmatic and shared its visions with the larger maritime public.[44]

Campbell shows us the perfect contrast between a sacred geography and a pragmatic one. Sailors taking pilgrims or crusaders to Palestine may have been devout believers, but they sailed by pragmatic maps, not divine ones. Not surprisingly, additional pragmatic visual representations were formalized and compiled after 1415 when Mediterranean kingdoms began systematically sponsoring transoceanic voyages beyond their familiar inland sea. Select inland features were added in later versions of portolan maps.[45] Many maps were commissioned for royal patrons and were artistic products enriched beyond functional use. But others were definitely used at sea, especially by mariners driven off course or when planning trading voyages.[46]

Maritime states and budding empires needed their captains to sail safely and swiftly across the featureless oceans beyond familiar waters. They encouraged the creation of institutional knowledge that would outlast the death or desertion of specific experts. Such knowledge was embodied through the compilation of pilot books and maps. We may take, for example, the decades-long effort of the Portuguese monarchy that resulted in the discovery of the sea route to India in 1497–98. It was part of a long-sustained and consistent effort that produced cumulative innovations in navigational technique and geographical knowledge. It then culminated in the successful domination of the Indian Ocean trade for a century.[47] Using maps and charts to navigate out of sight of land required the regular maintenance of "log-books" that captains could use to guess their approximate locations. These then added to the stock of geographic lore. Centuries later, these logs have been recovered and used to construct charts of past weather and climate.[48] The creators of maps and sketches and the authors of itineraries and travel reports all sought to represent the world. But as Daniel Dorling and David Fairbairn continue, the territorial map is a human construct, one that can be used to "order the territory itself as well as to order our knowledge of it." Particular projections suit specific needs. So, for example, the conformal Mercator projection was primarily used for navigation, a setting "where correct representation of bearings and angular measurement" are more important than representation of relative areas which are secondary for route-finding at sea.[49]

The systematic collection of information and its appropriation by the emerging early modern state thus gradually took it out of the control of the unlettered sailor. Efforts at the creation of compendia of geographic and oceanic knowledge were by the end of the sixteenth century being pursued by every European power. Cartographic and geographical information began to accumulate, and even if states were inclined to keep it secret, sailors and travelers profited from its sale. Books were quickly translated and reprinted in various vernacular languages, and readers developed a taste for these. The adventurous traveler Jan Huygen van Linschoten, who was originally from the Netherlands, traveled in various parts of Portuguese Asia in 1583–94. His narrative helped guide Dutch sailors into the Indian Ocean.[50] Of course, every need does not immediately call forth an invention. Thus, despite major naval disasters attributed to the incapacity to calculate longitude at sea, it was only in 1714 that the British Parliament passed an act offering a large reward for such an invention. It was to be many decades before an effective device was patented.[51]

ASIAN CARTOGRAPHIES

Asian kingdoms and empires also differed among themselves in what they chose to depict in graphic form and how this was done. Despite their agrarian orientation, imperial governments in China took the lead in cartography. This was perhaps because they were early concerned with the management of rivers and canals so vital to transport and agriculture. The more rugged topography of China's arable land meant that geographical features at the river basin level were relevant to water management, a major concern of Chinese regimes. Additionally, Chinese kingdoms early developed the need, capacity, and will for extensive environmental interventions.[52] All this, in turn, stimulated the production of maps that included long stretches of river and adjoining terrain.

Thus, a brief description of no less than 137 rivers of China was compiled between the first and third centuries of the Common Era. Diagrammatic charts of river courses and important terrain features such as mountains drawn in the Song period have survived. Grid maps began to be drawn, often at small scale. Joseph Needham remarks on one map that the "coastal outline is relatively firm and the precision of the network of river systems extraordinary." The genre became larger and more elaborate in the Qing period. Reclamation and protection of coastal lands motivated the preparation of works describing these lands. Coastal charts came later, Needham suggests, because of the need for coastal defense against Japanese piracy. The administrative function of mapping was also clear. In an order issued circa 1200 CE, villages were instructed to draw maps that would be joined into regional maps. "If there was any trouble about the collection of taxes or the distribution of grain, or if the question of chasing robbers and bandits arose, the provincial officials could readily carry out their duties by the aid of the maps." The administrative significance of records was illustrated by a tradition that the founder of the Han dynasty when plundering a captured city first took charge of the archive of ordinances, reports, and maps.[53]

Pragmatic geography thus depended on both knowledge and the power to use it. The two fed into each other. The decay of control meant also the loss of knowledge.

TRANSATLANTIC EXCHANGE AND ECOSYSTEM REVOLUTION

It is impossible to ignore the most dramatic example of the long-term environmental effects of concentrated power, that of the Americas following the Spanish discovery of the sea route thither. In 2004, Alfred Crosby followed up on his pioneering volume *Ecological Imperialism* with a more comprehensive consideration of packages of new biota that European expansion introduced into Australia and the Americas. The dramatic effect of Spanish-introduced sheep and cows in destroying the basis of Indigenous subsistence in Mexico has been illustrated by E. G. K. Melville's *A Plague of Sheep*.

Meanwhile, the intensification of global exchanges and the enslavement and transport of vast numbers of Africans to European colonies in the Americas had an even more complex relationship to fluctuations in power and anthropogenic changes in New World environments. After Spanish maltreatment and European diseases denuded the coasts and islands of their formerly dense Indigenous populations, large numbers of African slaves were imported to labor on colonial plantations. Local and immigrant mosquito populations began to spread yellow fever and malaria among elite and enslaved residents alike. But many Africans were resistant or immune to both diseases, and long-term local residents usually had immune responses that could suppress infections. There were, however, enough hosts for the transmission of both diseases to persist. Port towns and floating populations of seafarers proved to be excellent foci of yellow fever and malaria. J. R. McNeill has analyzed the complex dynamic between environmental modifications, changing demographic profiles, and climatic fluctuations, all of which played into this dynamic. One lasting structural change, however, was that foreign armies—not immunized by previous exposure—collapsed amid fever epidemics as soon as the wet season bred new vector populations. The Spanish and Portuguese Empires had been established before this disease wall was raised, and they suffered only marginal territorial losses from invasion until they were confronted by rebellions of their own subjects in the nineteenth century. The epidemiological dynamic also helped secure the ultimate independence of the former French colony of Haiti after great epidemics decimated Napoleonic efforts at reconquest.[54]

WESTERN COSMOLOGY AND THE RISE OF ENVIRONMENTAL THOUGHT

The Western intellectual tradition was comprehensively analyzed by Clarence Glacken in 1967. His work has not been superseded as a study of environmental thought from Greco-Roman times to the eighteenth century.[55] He noted that a vision of an Edenic past followed by anthropogenic decay has been a long-standing theme in that cosmology.[56] Glacken identified three fundamental ideas at the root of this notion: those of "a designed earth, of the influence of the environment upon man, and of man as a modifier of the environment."[57]

Enfolded in this structure is the biblical narrative of "Paradise Lost," which, secularized, has exerted a powerful influence on environmental thought to the present. We see it secularized in the early American environmentalist George P. Marsh's desiccationist theory. In a weighty volume published in 1863, Marsh narrated how human action had changed the earth and warned against the further imprudent waste of its resources by heedless civilizations. He declared that civilized man, alone among all the creatures of nature, had the power to act destructively upon the earth. "Savages," he claimed, possessed little such power. "Savage" peoples, Marsh thought, simply lacked the technological capacity to do much harm. But humans' destructive capacity increased with civilization. Hence it was the great civilization of Rome that had, in recent historical time, brought parts of the Mediterranean world "to a desolation almost as complete as the face of the moon."[58] Marsh gave the older argument of divinely designed harmony disturbed by human sinfulness a secular turn; it was civilization that brought knowledge and technical prowess. Wrongly used, that led to environmental degradation.

Strenuous efforts were still made in the early nineteenth century to reconcile the emerging science of geology with the Genesis narrative. Paradoxically, astronomers and philosophers had but lately rejected the earth-centric view for the heliocentric. This was linked to the old and widespread study of the unchanging heavens but applied now to the changing earth. The oceans, highways to empire, were the object of especially intensive study. A geographic cosmology based on secular sciences was by its nature an aspect of Western imperial expansion. In the next section, I will therefore take up the growth of the Western scientific narrative from the great systematizer Comte de Buffon onward.[59]

There was nonetheless a widespread assumption in secular Western thought that all living peoples were but a few generations removed from a long-stable traditional past. For many this carried a deep nostalgia. Major institutional changes that were separate from, and in great measure independent of, this scientific narrative were also changing the knowledge and management of the earth in Europe and its overseas colonies. In Germanic central Europe, the Enlightenment combined with the need for lordly domains and little kingdoms to recover from the devastation of the seventeenth-century wars. This produced a widespread, conscious effort to manage a state, small or large, on the model of the lordly estate. That, in turn, generated the "cameral sciences" in mainland Europe. Mercantile and military navigation intensified efforts to secure competitive technological advantages. Land management in an often timber-hungry economy was meant to produce sustainable harvests, including large supplies of usable timber.[60] The practical necessities of managing landed estates had parallel but distinct effects on the British elite.[61] But it was Germans who pioneered the sciences thought relevant to agriculture and forestry. In the nineteenth century, they exported their managerial approach and scientific experts throughout the British Empire and beyond.

Meanwhile, various damaging effects of human ecological innovation began to be felt, first on colonized islands and later on the mainland of the Americas and Australia. Buffon had already included such changes in his narrative of the history of humans and the earth. Fitting it into the short biblical chronology of less than seven thousand years meant that he had to adopt a climatic and dietary explanation for human variation. But the colonial islands of the Atlantic were also shaped by a novel political ecosystem: that of the slave-worked export-oriented plantation. Not surprisingly, Buffon's transatlantic critics had to espouse the idea of the fixity of inherited traits, independent of all environmental influences. The logical corollary would be some kind of theory of fixed human species or races.

The creation of a permanent population of African slaves required "race theory" to explain and justify that "peculiar institution" of permanent, race-based slavery. That is why systematic racial theory was born among European settlers in the Americas, men such as the plantation owner and colonial official Edward Long who expressed it in his *History of Jamaica* (1774).[62] The book was, like much racist writing, a justification of the enslavement of Black people. The rejection of Buffon's effort to explain variation by environmental settings was essential to the argument, since otherwise slave owners and slaves would converge biologically within a foreseeable period of time. A long footnote adduced various "facts" that supposedly refuted Buffon.

Buffon's evolutionism, however, had the intellectual advantage of explaining the diversity of human types without rejecting the short chronology (a seven-thousand-year-old earth) necessitated by a literal reading of the Bible. In contrast, Long managed to argue for the fixity of racial traits only by suggesting, but not claiming, multiple creations of humans by God.[63] Mainstream Western thought in his time (as Glacken shows) was still united around arguments from design that postulated a divine agency working though nature. The doctrine of the fundamental unity of the human species was not easily abandoned.[64] Christian orthodoxy could not deviate from sacred texts: Long could only suggest that God had created additional species of inferior humans as a supplement to the Genesis narrative.

It therefore took much of the nineteenth century for scientific racism to establish itself in the European world. The democratic revolutions of 1848 rallied the upper classes not, as before, against the "godless" revolutionaries of 1793, but rather against racially inferior plebeians. The French aristocrat Arthur de Gobineau published his famous racial theory in 1853, but the short-lived *Ethnological Journal* had preceded him in denouncing the idea of human equality.[65] The Anthropological Society of London was founded with the same agenda of establishing racial theory as a recognized "science." The great effort of John Hunt, its founding president in 1863, was to secure the recognition of racial anthropology as a scientific discipline. He therefore sought, but was denied, admission to the British Association for the Advancement of Science's Section E, where the older Ethnological Society was already ensconced. The gradual rise of race theory had however begun. It benefited from secularization and the quiet abandonment by many scientists of the whole Genesis narrative.[66] "Races of Men" were increasingly viewed as distinct and fixed rather than shaped by nature.[67]

RACISM, DESICCATIONISM, AND COLONIAL EMPIRE

But then, if the earth did not mold humans to their habitat, humans could be seen to change it. Race theory arose in the age of empires, a time when small elites felt the destinies of the world had been entrusted to them. There was an almost irresistible slide into assuming that the intellectually superior imperial rulers would change things for the better. Yet they also believed that the common people—at home or abroad—would if given the chance alter it for the worse. Scholars, though, were initially divided on whether civilized or "savage" humans were the true source of danger.

Although Marsh in 1864 had viewed "savage" peoples as largely incapable of inflicting any serious damage, the emerging body of professional environmental managers—often colonial "experts" and especially foresters—saw "primitives" and cognate ordinary peasants as the major agents of destruction. Vast destructive power was thus assigned to the activities of so-called primitive populations. In this discourse, it was only the authoritarian application of Western colonial science that could remedy the situation and stave off catastrophe. The transformation of small European bases into large territorial empires—most notably in South Asia—further stimulated this discourse.

By the time Marsh published, there was already a long tradition of environmental alarmism about conditions in Western colonies. It arose from the observed effects of a century of European plantation and empire on its early island bases such as Saint Helena, Mauritius, and the Caribbean islands. Three decades ago, the British historian Richard Grove traced how the formal "scientific" discussion of environmental concerns began as an imperial project. He described it as a consequence of the expansion of Western empires and their creation of specialized peripheral economies. The environmental effect was most evident on the plantation enclaves and islands around the Atlantic and Indian Oceans. The result was often catastrophic change. The idea that humans and associated invasive fauna could seriously damage island ecosystems was easily substantiated by a few decades of observation. It was then deemed to apply to all parts of the world. In these settings, whether in the Caribbean, South Atlantic, or Indian Ocean, denudation and desiccation were now seen not (as by Buffon) as beneficent processes, but as destructive ones. These ideas became part of the stock of geographical lore that fueled newer global syntheses of "natural history."[68]

This alarm was picked up by the "desiccationist" narrative that was spreading among the colonial officials in the various European empires. Grove shows how the expropriation of the native Carib populations in the West Indies was, by the late eighteenth century, being justified by the needs of the efficient environmental management of plantation agriculture. These projects were, however, delayed by Carib resistance through several decades. Grove argues that it was here that colonial "exclusionism" as a management policy began.[69] He then suggests there was a seamless transfer of such ideas to South Asia, where they inspired the various British personnel in the emerging Indian Empire. Officials were indeed inveighing against shifting cultivators, local farmers, and the Indian population generally in very similar ways some fifty or sixty years after their island-bound predecessors.[70]

The desiccationist argument was also made for nineteenth-century Africa—indeed, for much of the colonized world.[71] A striking and well-documented study of the western Sahel by James Fairhead and Melissa Leach illustrates the power of this paradigm. Steeped in the imperial consensus of the short-sighted destructiveness of their colonial subjects, early French administrators immediately perceived village forests and clumps of trees as the residue of vast primeval forests recently destroyed by native populations. The creation of institutional technocratic power to restrain the native peoples was a logical corollary of this doctrine.[72] Even in the United States, Marsh was alarmed by the activities of both small farmers and timber companies in the Adirondacks. Here his ideas shaped the demarcation of vast national parks viewed as "untouched primordial nature." This was achieved, however, through excluding the Native American populations and early settlers that had long used the lands.[73] Various parts of colonized Africa have also seen the application of variants of these desiccationist ideas under the aegis of colonial powers and now international expert agencies.[74] In Victorian India (as we shall see in chapter 6), these ideas acquired a hold over the public mind that endures to the present day.

MODERN COSMOLOGY

Scientists in the various fields connected to cosmology have, of course, long been aware that climate and vegetation have changed dramatically through earth's long history. Indeed, the identification of extinct fossil plants and animals in different rock strata has been a heuristic device among geologists from the inception of the science. Popular discourse gradually added parts of this geological knowledge to the "common sense" of educated people, though it sits uneasily alongside the vision of the stability of nature endangered only by man. The latest image of the universe is the world as constructed by contemporary cosmology. This is the most universal and totalizing so far. Geoscientists gaze upon our planet as a mediocre satellite of a waning star. Looking at earth from far beyond our planetary sphere, astronomers and geologists have collaborated in an extra-planetary perspective to trace the random interplanetary assaults of asteroids that have so fundamentally shaped the phases of life on earth. They also direct their gaze on its elemental fluxes—from the nitrogen and carbon cycles fundamental to life to the magmatic currents deep within its crust that yet produce key surface features. Regarding these fluxes, the magnitudes of carbon emissions and their contribution to global warming are well known by now. In addition, the twentieth century saw an enormous intensification in the nitrogen cycle. (All proteins are nitrogen compounds.) Vaclav Smil has calculated that by the 1990s "almost half of all N[itrogen] received annually by the world's croplands (46%, range 43–50%) comes from synthetic fertilizers."[75]

Dense forest is still an obstacle to the visibility desired by states and empires. Even after satellite surveillance replaced high-flying spy planes, forest blocks out the "eye in the sky" of most satellite remote sensing. It therefore has been an obstacle to the exercise of power. Great states are often hostile to woodland even as weaker ones exploit its defensive qualities. This book will consider how struggles around such uses of woodland might cause the frontier to shift dramatically over a few decades.

Over a span of three million years, humans became human. Mental maps of space and time began to be made as humans moved toward increasing control and manipulation of their environments. But their capacities varied widely. Pragmatic geographies and cosmologies intersected in sacred landscapes that shaped the goals of pilgrims traveling through them.

The subjection of the many to the few that culminated in the age of empires shaped the worlds of both. Modern representational maps—now coordinated via manmade astral bodies orbiting the earth—came from maritime origins before moving to land. But the availability of a technology is not sufficient for its deployment. The land had to be open to the integrative gaze of the state, whose personnel had to be able to move assuredly across the terrain. Great surveys—such as the Down Survey of Ireland begun in the 1650s—often followed military conquests. This was because they had to be backed by organized power. Landmarks had to be located, pillars raised, stone boundary markers laid, village by village. Then the survey offices had to juxtapose them to one another, and the new technology of the photozincographic press created the hundreds of copies we see today. The lists of halts and distances that had resided in the minds of guides began to be compiled into durable, impersonal books.

The possibility of wider domains of action came from and led to wider fields of vision for the ruling elites. These included the rise of "race science." Victorian self-confidence changed Marsh's early visions of the earth as damaged by technologically powerful empires into a vision of a global ecosystem endangered by the thoughtless many. The corollary was that it might yet be saved by the intervention of the enlightened few: the Western imperial elite. The next chapter will consider the legacies of empires in South Asia. It will especially focus on the political ecology, the environment-making efforts, of the Mughal and British Empires.

TWO

South Asia in the Imperial Gaze

"It does not yield wool, nor is it useful for milk or draught; its huge stomach cannot be filled with any amount of fodder. What an effort it would take to load a sack on that mountainous back! Who indeed would pay even a copper for this beast?" Thus do the peasants deride the elephant.
ANONYMOUS SANSKRIT POET | date unknown, *Subhāṣitaratnabhāṇḍāgāram* (Storehouse of elegant sayings)

EMPIRES WERE REAL. THEY HAD REAL POWER THAT THEY EXERTED on the world, changing it to make it legible to them. James Scott's 1998 book *Seeing Like a State* is a penetrating analysis of how modernist projects of state-making sought to shape people and landscapes. He begins with a discussion of German scientific forestry of the late eighteenth century—especially clear-cutting followed by the planting of pure stands of conifer—and then extends his vision to many other areas of state functioning. The gaze of the state, he notes, was not a passive one: it sought to survey and record but also to change landscapes and peoples into objects that could be surveyed and recorded. Efforts at control and efforts at escape clashed in contested terrain. Undesired outcomes were all too common. Working from European and other data, Scott developed a capacious understanding of the emerging early modern state and of the opacity of the world that it was seeking to capture and control in Europe or beyond. His is not merely a tale of imperial discourse in its hall of mirrors, where there is nothing beyond the text.

The administrative goal to which all modern states aspire, Scott writes, is "to measure, codify and simplify." In heavily agrarian societies, land records and maps were one such domain. "Land maps in general and cadastral maps in particular are designed to make the local situation legible to an outsider."[1] Such maps, he points out, were created slowly, imperfectly, ever behind the rush of changes—but they were created. Indeed, in the form of the now-ubiquitous GPS, such maps become part of pragmatic reality as perceived by most people worldwide. Similarly, the South Asian geographies used in modern climatology are connected to the historic origins of modern geographies at ground and planetary levels.

SOUTH ASIA IN MODERN GEOGRAPHY

Today, hot desert occupies the Sahara, much of the Arabian Peninsula, and also the lower Indus plains of Pakistan and the adjoining region of India to its east. The climatically and geographically adjacent arid steppe zone covers the Sahel Belt, much of Afghanistan, and northwestern India and extending south to the interior of its southern plateau region. Map 1 is a simplified climate map, drawn on the basis of the Köppen climate classifications.[2] In fact, most of the subcontinent, and almost all of the Maharashtra and Telangana states, falls in the semi-arid and dry sub-humid climate classes.[3] Much of the subcontinent is therefore relatively dry—even though the average twentieth-century rainfall for the Indian Republic is 119 centimeters (47 in.), 88 of which is contributed by the summer monsoon (see map 2). Western

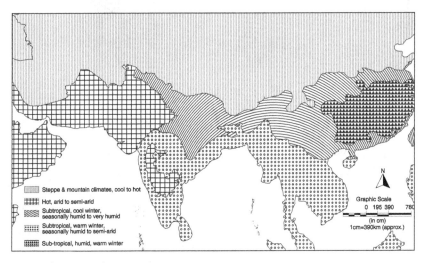

MAP 1. Asian agroclimates.

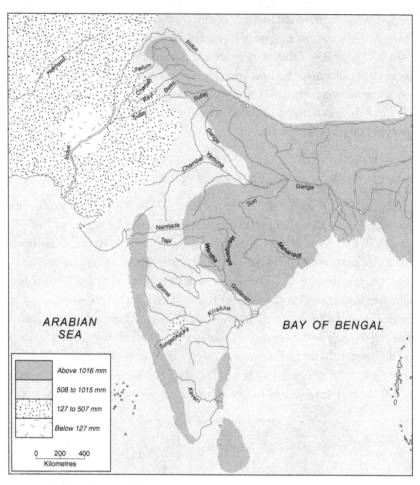

MAP 2. South Asian rainfall patterns.

Peninsular India, the special region of my study, has areas that receive both the heaviest and almost the lightest summer monsoon rains. The heaviest rain falls along the Sahyadri mountain range that borders the coast from South Gujarat to North Kerala—over 200 centimeters. The lowest rainfall measured in India is in the northwest plains regions (extending to the southwestern borders of Pakistan), but that is closely followed by the interior peninsular rain-shadow area, which includes much of central Maharashtra. That state thus has both some of the highest and lowest precipitation in the subcontinent. Low total rainfall is strongly associated with high variability and consequent high risk of drought. The converse also holds.[4]

Map 1 also shows us that South Asia overall is significantly more arid than what may be called "agrarian China"—that is to say, the lands east and south of the Great Wall. The Indian subcontinent thus lies southeast of the more arid Iranian world but west of the moister lands of mainland Southeast Asia. A significant portion of its northwestern region is hot arid desert, and much of its peninsula is arid steppe and tropical savanna. Aridity limits its primary productivity, despite its long frost-free growing season. Cereals and legumes provided most of the commoners' diet in every region and are still important today. Agriculture was largely rain-fed before the 1880s; significant areas still are. Except in the humid east and southwest, the success of rain-fed tillage depends on using the brief windows when the soil is moist enough to allow seeds to germinate.

Practically speaking, throughout the inhabited portions of the subcontinent, moisture—not sunlight or temperature—was and is the limiting factor for plant growth. This is especially true of the select set of domesticated plants on which humans have grown to depend. Intensive rice production was only possible in limited areas. Yet despite its comparative aridity, the subcontinent has sustained populations comparable in size to Chinese ones over considerable periods of time.[5]

THE BEGINNINGS OF IMPERIAL GEOGRAPHY OF SOUTH ASIA

The drive to power also imprinted imperial knowledge, its limits and its representation of the world. Valuation was embedded in understanding. We may see this most clearly in the "best" type of kingdom described in the compilation of early Indian political thought titled the *Arthashastra*. This text saw kingship as dominion over people, with the land as a necessary aspect of their life. This is embedded in the ancient Sanskrit name for a territory: *janapada*, "foothold of a people." The compilers of the *Arthashastra* had a wide view of the South Asian landscape and considered arid, semi-arid, and moist regions alike. It cited the region named Aśmaka as semi-arid and Avanti as moist: the west coast was accurately described as a region with immeasurable rainfall. It also considered micro-environments and their best use. "An area where foam strikes the banks is good for fruits growing on creepers; areas near overflows, for long pepper, grapes, and sugarcane; areas near wells for vegetables and root vegetables; areas near canals, for green herbs; and ridges for plants reaped by cutting."[6]

The next great description of an imperial landscape was prepared under the supervision of Abul Fazl, the grand vizier of the Mughal emperor Akbar (r. 1556–1605), around 1600 CE and is titled *A'in-i Akbari* (Administration of Akbar). It is interesting that the general chapter on agricultural geography in the Mughal-era *A'in* does not visualize agricultural failure as originating in dryness; when considering why land might fall out of cultivation, it speaks of excessive rain or flooding.[7] It is clear that the compiler of that section came from the northwestern part of the empire and was thinking of the practice of "overflow tillage." This was the late autumn cultivation of lands previously moistened by monsoon-swollen rivers, sometimes assisted by overflows from simple inundation canals. This was a farming system found in many riverain tracts, but it predominated in the arid northwestern plains—the middle and lower Indus Valley region. While it could not extend beyond narrow physiographic limits, it would also demand less investment in soil preparation and none in fertilization. These comments apply to the general chapter, but the provincial chapters in the same great compilation included details on particular crops, irrigation systems, and seasons. These presumably came from provincial officials, and the overview was not changed to accommodate this information. The imperial gaze may have aspired to universality but was nonetheless limited. In part, the limit might arise out of a paradoxical barrier to the imperial gaze in South Asia: the managed wilderness known in the Sanskrit tradition as "elephant forest" (*gajavana*).

ELEPHANTS, KINGS, AND FORESTS

Empires and kingdoms only existed because they had subjects. People—from coolies to courtiers to soldiers—provided the labor that sustained empires. It was universally admitted in early modern Europe that "population growth would contribute to agricultural production, industry, trade, state taxes, and military manpower."[8] But the farming population in South Asia also had to cope with another kingly demand, one unique to the subcontinent. This was the obligation to protect wild elephant populations and, if necessary, suffer their destruction of crops.

In addition to hundreds of millions of humans, South Asia preserved large populations of elephants (and other species such as lions and tigers) well into the twentieth century. In imperial China, conversely, animals of this kind were driven to the periphery or exterminated in almost the whole territory within the Great Wall. A comparison of the two areas by climate (and therefore biomass production) shows that China offers large areas of suitable elephant habitat. But its elephants began disappearing five thousand years ago and by the late Qing were confined to a few tracts in the far southeast. Mark Elvin's environmental history of China sees this "retreat of the elephants" as diagnostic of long-term anthropogenic trends.[9] The "retreat" of the Indian elephant was far slower prior to the nineteenth-century arrival of globe-trotting recreational killers wielding specialized "elephant guns." Over the nearly two-thousand-year span before that, the only South Asian elephant population that disappeared had lived in the northwestern part of the subcontinent. These elephants had inhabited a relatively arid region, and animals there had been long deemed inferior to the rest. This subpopulation may have succumbed to the extended droughts that characterized the end of the first millennium CE.[10]

Thomas Trautmann has offered the best explanation of the contrast in approaches to elephant conservation in East, rather than South, Asia. Elephants and elephant habitat were preserved in South Asia because they were sinews of military power. He points out that Indian states, especially emergent monarchies, were training elephants for battle by at least 327–326 BCE, when the Greek armies of Alexander encountered them in the Panjab region. Indeed, he makes a persuasive case that the large resources needed to tame and train sizable numbers of elephants for war could only be mobilized by emerging monarchies. That capacity, in turn, gave these kings a major military advantage over more decentralized polities (such as tribes and aristocratic oligarchies). To the east, the use of tamed elephants extended to the borderlands of the emerging Chinese imperial state, but, like the Roman, that great empire rejected this innovation.[11]

Trained and agile elephants could achieve surprising feats. When the army and camp were tangled up in thickets and mountains in Central India, the

English ambassador Thomas Roe noted that Emperor Jahangir (r. 1605–27) himself "gott bye on a small Eliphant which beast will Clime vp rockes and passe such streightes as noe horse nor beast that I know can follow him."[12] Beyond the utilitarian value, the possession of elephants became part of the Indian style of kingship. As late as 1792, commanders of the Maratha and the Nizam's contingents were invited as an honor to review the British Army in Mysore. They agreed to come only if they could ride their elephants along the lines; other steeds would lower their dignity.[13] Trautmann notes that the military use of elephants was emulated in West Asia and North Africa by the Hellenic kings and their immediate successors. Maintaining a large stable of royal elephants, however, required the protection of wild elephants and the habitat where they lived. As Trautmann puts it, "The relation of kings to elephants is in fact a four-cornered relation of kings, elephants, forests and forest people." The forest was therefore not the antithesis of the kingdom and its landscape of docile tax-paying peasants; it was an essential adjunct of the state itself.[14] But the resulting landscape was significantly different than it would have been under pure peasant farming.

Furthermore, Trautmann has also suggested that rather than view the protection of elephants in a religious frame, we should also consider how far kingship and its practices were integrated into religious thought. *Mandira* is the Sanskrit noun originally used for royal palaces and divine temples alike. Kingly protection could have meshed easily with popular worship of theriomorphic deities.[15] Buddhism contains a large collection of stories narrating the "previous births" of the historical Buddha. These are known as *Jataka* and include many births as noble animals, including an elephant with six tusks.[16] The powerful impression an elephant could make was narrated by the British official John Briggs in 1824. Upon his arrival among the Bhils living in an interior village, "they brought fruits, flowers and sugar cane, to propitiate an elephant which I had with me (never having seen one before) and they sang and danced round him."[17] In effect, the elephant was honored as a king or god might be.

What then were the environmental effects of military strategies that depended upon elephants? Elephants—unlike other domesticated animals—were rarely bred in captivity, because they were not ready for work until about age twenty. Instead, they were captured as wild adults and then trained to serve human needs. Elephants are, however, relatively rare animals; there are very few in comparison to other forest herbivores, and they are much slower to reproduce. Furthermore, large male elephants—prized in war, for hunting, for timber-working, and as status symbols—obviously make up only a fraction of the overall population. Within this subset, male elephants with certain traits—among them five or six toenails (not four), a tail with a full tuft, a red palate without a spot of black, large showy tusks, a pale face and forehead—were considered the most desirable.[18] These zoological givens and cultural preferences meant that Indian rulers who wished to build up troops of elephants had to make systematic efforts to prevent the killing of wild elephants and to preserve the woodland savanna where they bred.

It is noteworthy that the nutritional needs of the wild elephant have significant ecosystem effects. Because the elephant does not have the ability to synthesize amino acids during the fermentation process that ruminants (notably oxen) do, it needs a wider range of foods so as not to develop protein deficiencies. It also needs to forage for practically all its waking life: adult elephants need about 100,000 kcal of digestible energy daily from enormous volumes of low-grade biomass. Field observation shows that an elephant needs to consume between 1.5 and 2 percent of its body weight in dry matter equivalent daily. Grasses—especially new first flush grasses at the beginning of the wet season—contain high levels of protein, but both the protein content and palatability of grasses fall from wet to dry season.

Furthermore, wild grasses, especially their mature stems, have many defenses against herbivores. The British forest officer James Forsyth left a vivid description of the dry deciduous savanna in the Tapi valley. The early summer grasses, he wrote bristled "with a terrible armature of prickles, like needles of steel with the barbs of a fish-hook, which catch in each other and mat together into masses."[19] Even if unbarbed, mature grasses often contain high levels of protective silica that abrade animal molars. As a wild elephant that loses the ability to chew is condemned to a slow death, it seeks other foods at this time of year.

In the dry season, elephants usually uproot clumps of grass to consume the more nutritious root ball biomass, incidentally reducing the wear on their teeth. Browse plants (bushes and trees) are also less gritty and maintain more stable protein levels year-round. In some areas—such as the Nilgiri forests of South India—elephants eat large quantities of grasses, supplementing them with browse from trees in the dry season.[20] The leaves of the acacia, the most common savanna tree, are about 10–12 percent protein in the wet season and 8–10 percent in dry months. These percentages are much higher than those found in the basal portions of grasses consumed in the dry season. Trees might be slower to recover than grasses, though acacia seeds usually pass out undigested from most animals' intestines. Thus, the presence of large wild elephant populations would continuously modify the array of plants of all sizes. The ecologist Raman Sukumar states that extensive browsing by a large population of elephants converted African woodlands to savanna, as the number of more palatable trees was drastically reduced. He is, however, doubtful that elephant browsing was the sole cause in the period under study (since 1960s). The effects in study areas of South Asia were less striking. But Sukumar still notes that that tree frequency of favored browse species changed over time.[21] Elephants are prepared to eat a wide range of plant foods, but specific elephant populations can also develop strong food preferences, and their human keepers have to adapt, as a British officer discovered in 1803.[22] Selective browsing by large numbers of elephants will therefore modify the array of plants of all sizes available in the natural habitat.

An elephant-browsed woodland would verge toward savanna. The opening of the tree canopy by elephant browsing encourages wet season grasses that then provide fuel for frequent fierce fires in the dry season. Fires, in turn, kill seedlings and young trees and thus create and maintain savanna-type landscapes. This transformation of woodland into savanna "then favors the populations of grazing ungulates." Even if trees survive, elephants breaking branches and browsing on crown leaves help keep the trees in a stunted shrubby stage. That, in turn, allows smaller browsing mammals such as deer and goats to get at shoots and young branches.[23] These mammals would be prey for felines, wolves, and other canids. Large felines such as leopards and tigers have also long been known to prey on humans. They were (unlike elephants) frequent targets of hunting by villagers and kings alike, but preserving elephant habitat also preserved the coverts that sheltered large predators that attacked cattle and, on occasion, people. Thus, the kingly preservation of elephants through the centuries was also a major form of ecosystem management.

We can see the effects of this even today if we compare the lower Yangtze and lower Ganges-Brahmaputra river systems (now in Nepal, India, and Bangladesh). Both are humid, monsoon-pattern rice paddy areas, but nothing on the scale of the land reclamation and water management systems that developed in eastern China as early as the thirteenth century existed south of the Himalaya. Instead, the Indian subcontinent has retained a remnant population of tigers across large areas. Forest and scrub maintain populations of wild elephant and rhinoceros. All three animal species were abundant as late as the nineteenth century, though their current survival (barring perhaps the elephant) depends on active conservation and protection by the state. The same is true of the last surviving population of the Asian lion, now confined to a few hundred square kilometers in semi-arid Gujarat.[24]

Finally, elephants have always been turbulent neighbors for peasant farmers, whose blunt assessment of these beasts survives embedded in a Sanskrit verse cited in the epigraph. They raid human crops that have obviously been bred to lack the natural defenses that wild plants possess. Unlike patches of wild forage, field crops are available in great stands for bold raiders, who on occasion trample humans who anger them or get in their way.[25] S. S. Pokharel and colleagues have found that while crop-raiding is a "high risk, high reward" strategy, it may be optimal for adult and sub-adult males, the most common raiders. "Indeed, elephants can consume twice as much forage from cultivated millet and cereal fields (once they enter them at night) as compared to similar plant type (grasses) in their natural habitat." This study of stress levels found that crop-raiding animals experienced lower levels of stress than non-raiders. Crop-raiding may, the authors suggest, have enabled these animals to maintain a better nutritional status with corresponding body size and reproductive success.[26]

Paradoxically then, pockets of peasant farming within and around elephant forests might well have helped sustain elephant populations in South and Southeast Asia. Furthermore, as Trautmann pointed out, catchers, tamers, and drivers of elephants would come from farming and food-gathering communities that lived alongside wild elephant populations.[27] They would have known the habits of elephants, what plants they found unpalatable, and how to deter their attacks on crops and people. It is probable that they invented the techniques of elephant-proof fencing used for the timber and bamboo enclosures in which elephants were trapped in order to tame them for imperial purposes.

Not all vegetation favored by elephants suffered from their presence. The great beasts also consumed fruits as they became available and spread the seeds over wide ranges. The resulting tree vegetation would later provide future meals for themselves and other fauna.[28] Regions where elephants roamed thus became mosaics of modified forest, savanna, swidden, and settled farming—all of which might succeed one another on a specific patch of land over time. Protection of elephant forests necessarily changed the woodland and wider landscape for all other creatures, including humans. But, even if natural conditions had allowed, the premodern South Asian landscape could never be transformed into one covered edge to edge with cleared, continuously cultivated fields. Topography and climate would always have made it a "patchy" landscape, but the presence of protected but wild elephants added another element of geographic variability to an already variegated landscape.

This patchwork landscape was also adapted to many animal species that coexisted with elephant populations, such as the various ungulates that were food for tigers and lions as well as wolf and wild dog populations. Woodland also provided recreational hunting by the aristocracy; indeed, as late as the mid-twentieth century, a landlord's game reserve in Rajasthan sheltered wild pig that devastated peasant crops.[29]

KINGS, LANDS, AND TAXES

Great armies led by trumpeting elephants might terrorize opponents and conquer lands, but a functioning kingship needed resources of many kinds. It is impossible to even gesturally consider all the necessities and luxuries demanded by kings or the multitude of ways they were acquired. Ultimately, royal wealth and power came, directly or indirectly, from foods gathered and crops and animals raised by millions of humans in many difficult settings. These had to be known and measured in order to be controlled. Furthermore, to be efficiently deployed by an empire, wealth also needed to be mobile and fungible, to possess the qualities of money, and a functional money economy presumes the widespread existence of functioning markets. The *Arthashastra* certainly visualized a money economy, though taxes in grain and labor and other dues were also discussed.

Numerical estimations of territories were especially common in western Peninsular India. Historians have usually thought them to be numbers of villages in the relevant units, though some of the numbers would have to be conventional and exaggerated. Groups of sixty-six villages were frequent in the Shilahara kingdom in western Maharashtra. The village continued as a unit of tax valuation into the fourteenth century, when the scholarly Arab traveler Ibn Battuta was assigned the tax paid by two entire villages plus half that of a third, with an aggregate value of five thousand dinars, for his support by the Sultan Muhammad bin Tughlaq. These money reckonings were also aggregated by province. After 1500, imperial formations in South Asia had monetary conceptions of the worth of their dominions. There were even rough estimations of the ratio at which money converted into military force.

In 1526, after years of periodic raids on the borderlands, Babur, then ruler of central Afghanistan, embarked on the conquest of the Sultanate of Delhi. This he achieved in the last four years (1526–30) of his life. After Babur had overthrown the Lodi rulers and occupied Delhi and Agra, a quick inventory of his new conquests was prepared. This listed major provinces, their general orientation with respect to the capital, and their assessed revenues. (As was common with such data, they showed an exceptional, and very likely spurious, precision.) His "conspectus" or summary description of this territory was thus essentially a list of provinces with their reported tax yields. It began from the western trans-Sutlej region and extended east into today's Bihar. He recorded the aggregate at 520 million *tankas*. Babur also calculated that this revenue should have sufficed for the hire of 500,000 horsemen. But Ibrahim Lodi, the last Lodi Sultan of Delhi, could only (by Babur's account) muster 100,000. The importance of a money economy to the building of the Indian empires was thus already assumed by the Mughal founder.[30]

But a money economy depends on widespread presence of markets in which various products can be sold and also of a transport network to transport them thence. Agra, the city where the emperor Akbar and his successor Jahangir long resided, was strategically located at the hub of many routes. The Dutch merchant Francisco Pelsaert, who lived seven years in Agra, wrote that roads carried "indescribable quantities of merchandise."The fertile East (*Purop*) sent large amounts of food—wheat, rice, sugar, butter—up the river Jamuna or over land by oxen to supply the city and king's army. Pelsaert declared that without these supplies, "this country could not be provided with food, and would almost die of hunger." Shallow draft vessels took salt from the lake at Sambhar, opium from Central India, asafetida from Afghanistan, as well as select textiles back downstream.[31] The extent of bullock-borne commerce was confirmed by Roe. While on the high road from Surat to the

Central Indian city of Burhanpur, he saw many caravans of pack oxen, the largest of which had 10,000 animals in it. He cited this as illustrative of the fruitfulness of the land.[32] The production and transport of such quantities of goods over considerable distances would obviously change the agriculture and crafts of various regions. Furthermore, vast bullock caravans must have consumed much forage and water as they moved across the country.

Trading systems also depend on societal recognition of some goods as especially suited to function as universal stores of value (money). In the Mughal context, the empire began with money valuations in copper coins (*dām*). But the sixteenth century saw the opening of sea routes to India and the systematic Spanish exploitation of the gold and silver mines of the Americas. South Asia had no significant mines, but its export trade responded energetically to European demand. The resulting large balance of payments surplus meant that large quantities of bullion flowed in from overseas. The extraction of gold and silver in the Americas went a long way to destroying those local populations and contaminating significant areas there with toxic heavy metals, notably lead and mercury. In Asia, this enabled the Mughal currency system to move to a silver basis, with gold used for prestige coins. Local circuits functioned with copper coins, and lower value exchanges used currencies such as cowrie shells and bitter almonds.[33]

REPRESENTATIONS OF LANDSCAPE IN MUGHAL TIMES

Although much of South Asia was ruled by the Mughals through the seventeenth century, that empire (unlike its Western peers) had no interest in depicting its territory in maps, though its chancery officials compiled many statistical lists and textual descriptions. The Mughals therefore knew their domain through entries in lists, not graphemes on paper showing a two-dimensional surface. This began with Babur, founder of the Mughal dynasty through his conquest of Delhi, who took a keen interest in the flora, fauna, and general geography of domains that he conquered or raided. An educated man, he worked within the Islamic schema of the habitable world being divided into zones, or climes arranged from the torrid equator to the frigid arctic. Babur was a newcomer to the Kabul valley but soon developed a geographical understanding of the region, which lay, he wrote, in "the fourth clime in the middle of the civilized region." Many pages of W. M.

Thackston's translation of Babur's memoirs describe features of the small kingdom of Kabul. He also recorded the novel traits of his new empire of Hindustan—its seasons, plants, and animals, as well as its cities and agricultural system. But his synoptic view of his wider empire was, as described earlier, primarily numerical.[34] The tradition of descriptive and numerical geography continued during the empire that Babur founded and through the end of the seventeenth century. Animals—even the dodo birds presented as exotic gifts—had their portraits painted by skilled artists.

At the end of the sixteenth century, Babur's grandson Akbar created a more stable imperial structure out of the aggregation of tributary conquest domains that he had inherited. A great compendium of information and regulations on the government of this empire, the *A'in*, was compiled in the last decade of his reign (ca. 1600). Put together in the imperial chancery under the editorship of Abul Fazl, it records many geographical details of the empire from east to west. It declares, for example, that in Akbar's fortieth regnal year, the empire contained 105 major districts, with 2,737 subdivisions. Lists of village names also began to be compiled, and these were copied and recopied for centuries. The *A'in* achieved authoritative status and is still used to understand many aspects of the economic and political life of that period.

Enormously detailed in its textual descriptions and numerical accounting, the *A'in* includes no maps. Unlike transoceanic empires, whose personnel had to travel over vast featureless seas, the Mughals' couriers, officials, and armies moved along well-known navigable waters and over land. Even imperial hunting excursions went to fixed locations or began with locally supplied information of the presence of game animals. Great territorial empires such as the Mughals did not have vast stretches of ocean to navigate. They did not fear missing landfall or being wrecked on reefs or shoals. Mapping was not essential for their purposes; communication and control could be achieved without it. The Mughal camp was effectively a large traveling city of hundreds of thousands of humans and perhaps as many animals. Sir Thomas Roe described Jahangir's camp in 1616 as having a periphery of twenty English miles and yet being set up in the space of four hours. The center of the camp included immense bazaars: "wherin streets are orderly, and tents Joynd, are sort of shopes and distinguished by rule that euery man knows readely were to seeke his wants, euery man of qualetye and euery trade limited how farr from the kinges tentes he shall Pitch, what ground hee shall vse, and on what syde, without alteration; which as it togither may equall almost any towne in Europe for greatnes."[35]

Roe's wonderment at this phenomenon is obvious. But we should also consider how extensive market networks and urban stores had to be to keep this horde of men and animals supplied—however minimally—with all their needs. In 1610, the English merchant William Finch, who was in the region, described how the Mughal camp on campaign numbered five or six hundred thousand and that water had been so short that a single goatskin bag of it had sold for a rupee.[36] The English traveler Thomas Coryat reported a similar shortage of water in the emperor Jahangir's camp at Mandu (Central India). Two wealthy nobles had water fetched daily from the Narmada River, from a distance of twenty or thirty miles, and distributed it free. But small bags of water still sold at high prices.[37] The movements of this nomadic city would have drawn food and water from far afield, thus changing the face of the earth far beyond its own periphery. But the imperial power that could order this vast assembly did not create any cartographic representations of the terrain it traversed.

In 1974, Irfan Habib, an eminent scholar of the Mughal era, published an important article on the history of cartography. He succinctly laid out two forms of graphic representation open to premodern geographers: one was to plot loci according to their two-dimensional coordinates as determined by location vis-à-vis the sun and "fixed stars" (i.e., give the latitude and longitude), and the other was to show distances along a route without any effort to fit it into a larger frame. He finds the latter practice important in Arab mapmaking as early as the tenth century CE, when efforts were being made to space important places according to their relative distances. These route maps would have sufficed for overland movements. Even these linear representations were not always thought important; a list of names and halts would also do. This seems to have been for the pragmatic landscape of imperial power in South Asia and, as we shall see, continued into the early British period.

Habib's research, however, found a solitary Mughal-era compendium prepared by Sadiq Isfahani, a private individual in Shahjahan's time (r. 1628–58), part of an encyclopedic work titled "Shahid-i Sadiq." "Much of this work," Habib writes, "consists of wise counsels and apt anecdotes; but the geographical portion is extremely factual and detailed . . . lines representing degrees of latitiude [sic] and longitude form equal squares; and a town is put in each of them according to the co-ordinates assigned to it." It used the Arab graticule of latitude and longitude, with names of prominent towns inserted within the appropriate square. The map was completed at Jaunpur after three years of labor (1644–47). Habib also added that anxiety among learned Muslims over the determination of latitude and longitude arose from the need to cast horoscopes and also from the Islamic injunction to pray facing Mecca—something possible only if the worshipper's coordinates were approximately known. Detailed coordinates were unnecessary for the latter purpose.[38]

THE PRAGMATIC GAZE: COMMUNICATION ROUTES AS SINEWS OF EMPIRE

Empires in South Asia, as elsewhere, marched their armies and controlled their subjects through their lines of communication. That was how the imperial gaze was transformed into the imperial grasp. As successful, complex organizations, empires could not be viewed or managed from a single center; extensive political authority required that commands flow out from the royal center and information be sent back to it from its peripheries. Asian empires had recognized this from their beginnings. Greek scholars of the fifth century BCE admired Persian imperial highways and the unwavering diligence of the Persian couriers of the time.[39] The fourteenth-century Arab traveler Ibn Battuta remarked on the attention given by the Sultans of Delhi to maintaining teams of couriers on important routes, so that dispatches would cover a fifty-day journey in five days.[40] Postal stages were established along the routes by which each kingly military expedition advanced. Daily, or at least every few days, couriers would carry news of the army to the Sultan, and reassurance about his health would go out to key subjects. Even short interruptions in the flow of messages could threaten the integrity of an autocratic regime; rumors would fill the void and might precipitate an unraveling of empire. When no news of Sultan Muhammad reached the court at Delhi for several months, it provoked ministers there to place another ruler on the throne—a rash action for which they all paid dearly when the Sultan returned.

Regarding the empire's security, the *Arthashastra* emphasized the importance of observing and reporting movements along lines of communication, though not all rulers seem to have been vigilant in such matters. The governor of Kara, Ala al-Din Khalji, was able to mount a surprise attack on the Yadava kingdom's capital at Devagiri in 1294 and demonstrated how such surveillance might be circumvented. The Khalji sultans were particularly careful of communications, and their contemporary Barani wrote that runners were posted at short stages along the major roads.[41] Horse messengers were kept at longer intervals. At "every town or place where horses were posted, officers and report writers were appointed." The latter were probably nodes in the network of imperial power. They grew into small garrison towns that, in turn, grew into market centers and "service gentry" settlements called *qasba-s*. Ibn Battuta reported on the communication system in place in the 1330s when he visited India. Cavalry posts were located every four *kroh* [Hindi *kos*], while foot runners were every one-third *kroh*.[42] These men waited at sites along the road marked by small domed buildings, and, when letters arrived, they ran until they reached the next post. Similar arrangements were made by all other rulers of the subcontinent, such as the Bahmanis and Qutbshahis of the Deccan.

For the Mughals, as Deloche writes, "the route was an instrument of government."[43] As the court, the chancery, and the royal army could not be everywhere, much of what the imperial center knew came through intermediaries along established routes. It was also along these arterial routes that kings and courts moved to display and enforce their power. Quite often, of course, the center was not stationary but moved over its domains, displaying and enforcing authority, exacting supplies and subservience. When we speak of the imperial gaze, it should really be conceived as a conspectus of many views selectively collected through networks of communication—its existence was by virtue of this nervous system. Mapping the land was less important.

Merchants had private messengers of their own, and the early European trading companies followed their example.[44] In one letter, Roe proposed getting the news of Portuguese convoys departing from Goa by overland messengers fast enough to ambush them near Surat.[45] It is said that the news of the Maratha army's catastrophic defeat at Panipat in 1761 first reached the Peshwa, chief minister of the Maratha Empire, when a merchant's messenger was intercepted and his letters read. Indeed, as merchants, herdsmen, and guides all had stores of geographic knowledge that seldom made it into written form, these individuals could be recruited as spies and sent out to gain more information about a particular area.

STANDARDIZATION OF MEASUREMENT

Alexander of Macedon conquered the Persian Empire in 331–328 BCE. His armies were accompanied by "bematists" who counted steps to estimate and record the length of each day's march for future reference. His successor, Seleukos, sent Megasthenes as ambassador to the Maurya emperor in India. The ambassador recorded that in 300 BCE, a major royal road ran from the east bank of the Indus River to the Maurya capital at Pataliputra (modern Patna in Bihar). According to Greek accounts the road was measured to be 10,000 *stadia* of approximately 606.666 English feet each.[46] Of course, obtaining any such measurements depended on initially finding suitable guides who would locate the best routes, but once they had been recorded, this type of knowledge became a royal asset for war and governance.[47]

The measurement and recording of routes and halts was therefore an important part of the routine functioning of an empire. Knowing how long orders would take in transit and when tax remittances were expected would be an everyday function. The pomp and display of armies, the swift movements of spies and messengers, and the organization of supplies all depended on a ready knowledge of routes. Direction and distance were marked on *kos minars*—masonry towers at set intervals, usually along imperial highways.[48] Many rulers built and maintained caravan halts along well-traveled roads, although these *sarais*—walled, sheltered halting places for caravans or individual travelers—hinted at the limits of imperial protection. Off the highways it is likely that local knowledge remained under local control, and centralized topographical knowledge was equally limited. The vast entourage of a Mughal camp could not easily move off level ground and well-marked routes. In December 1616, Roe traveled with the emperor Jahangir through central Rajasthan. The road ran through thorny bushes, many camels perished, and the emperor had to halt two entire days to let the "Coaches, Carts and Camells" traverse the thorny mountains.[49]

It is notable that South Asian empires never achieved the geographic control and administrative tenacity needed to build highways or standardize units of measure along them as the Romans did. Despite repeated imperial attempts at standardization, the South Asian linear *kos* (like the South Asian land area unit, *bigha*) remained a variable measure, adjusted according to terrain. The limits of imperial power were reflected in the limits of imperial knowledge. Variations in the latter echo the limits of the former. The early colonial geographer James Rennell examined the size of the *kos* in North India extensively and determined that it did not vary much there. Minarets had been built along major highways to mark distances; British officials and spies moving over these roads found that the *kos* varied little. This is likely because the region had been firmly under the power of empires centered in Delhi and Agra for a century or more. We may contrast North Indian normalization of the *kos* along imperial highways that Rennell measured with its South Indian variability. Mughal power was never firmly established south of the Vindhya mountains. Lieutenant Edward Moor's military duties led him to march over much of the peninsula in the 1780s and 1790s. He found that in the peninsula, "the term koss conveyed to our mind no definite idea, unless we heard also to what part of the country it alluded. From Poona to the Kristna [River] this fluctuating measurement may be estimated at a mile and a half; sometimes more, sometimes less: from the Kristna to the Toombudra it increases, and is at the latter three miles and upward :—thence to Seringapatam it continues increasing, and we have in that part found a day's march of four koss, measure nearly twenty miles; at other times sixteen and less."[50]

Such observations were only possible because Moor, like most English officers on the march, generally had a simple device to measure the absolute distance traversed. If possible, they used the "perambulator" (pedometer), a simple wheeled device that mechanically recorded distance. Indian rulers were rightly suspicious of giving away too much geographical information. Even when traveling as a Maratha ally in 1792, Moor still thought it prudent to put away his perambulator when his party came close to Pune, where the authorities would understand his motives and perhaps confiscate his records.[51] The distances collected by Moor and many other English officers were then inserted to "fit" route observations between places whose latitude and longitude could be related to the astronomically coordinated maps that the navigationally minded British were preparing. Thus, a durable body of impersonal geographical knowledge began to accumulate in British hands and be disseminated through print.

LINEAR ROUTE MAPS AND PLANS OF STRATEGIC LOCALES

Maps should change as terrain changes. Yet textual maps and geographical descriptions of the medieval period often just copied earlier sources. By the twelfth century, Arab geographical works contained many inaccuracies, meaning that local guides with their personal knowledge would still be indispensable.[52]

Sketches of pilgrimage centers and some important regions certainly existed in South Asia. Forts were sketched for military purposes. Linear route maps were also drawn. One of the most detailed linear maps, prepared at some time between 1650 and 1730, encompassed the way from northwest India and into Afghanistan.[53] Information needed by a traveler—stages, halts, and some indication of the availability of water and supplies—was really all that was pragmatically necessary for officers planning marches or campaigns.[54] Lists of stages with names of halting places provided the information needed to plan longer marches, without urgent need to represent these graphically on paper. Where that was needed, simple representation could be used to sketch linear routes divided into stages. These can be viewed as topological diagrams such as are sufficient for movement along a linear route.[55] Essentially then, the dimensions of the empire were "visualized" as a list of cities and provinces.

Irfan Habib, the leading authority on the Mughal Empire, nonetheless attempted to "map" Mughal statistical and descriptive information onto the graticular visual representation of India created by the British Empire. The result of his project was published in 1982. Habib, however, did not inquire why the earlier empire did not seek to map its own domains using the already extant European (with Arab contribution) technology for measurement and mapping. It is striking that the one geographically accurate map from the Mughal period discovered by Habib was not state sponsored. It mapped the surface of the Indian subcontinent into the classic graticular frame used in marine and terrestrial maps of the West and was created (in all probability) to orient worshippers toward Mecca at prayer time. It did not guide their peregrinations across South Asia. The absence of similar administrative and military maps indicates the limits to the reach of the Mughal Empire. There was a wide gap between the paper representation and real terrain over which officials rode and messengers ran.

In fact, Habib's own notes on sources reveal how Mughal officials initially visualized—or rather verbalized—their territories. In his source notes for the map of Bengal province, for example, he writes of the *sarkar* (district) named Bāzuhā that its name is simply the plural of the Persian word for "arm" metaphorically used to mean "direction of." He adds that a large number of subdivisions in that district, as well as some elsewhere, contained this word. I would argue that this reflects that the name was merely an indication of direction: "on the side of, towards" some named place.[56] Presumably the local guide would be expected to know how to get there. Posts and stages thus marked arterial roads, and territory would be known by such stages. These gave rise to the linear maps drawn under the Mughals that showed major stages as well as aggregate route distances.

Several examples of linear maps dating to the Mughal period are published in Susan Gole's *Indian Maps and Plans*. A late example of this class was described by the historian R. H. Phillimore: "It records the stages and distances between these [great] towns, the crossings of the great rivers, and the main passes through the border hills; and it gives notes on the nature of the country that would be of greatest value to a military commander."[57] Of other examples, Gole penetratingly observed that they were "really little more than tables abstracted from the textual itineraries" with some logos indicating walled campsites (*sarais*).[58] Even the long-established peninsular Sultanate of Bijapur (ca. 1500–1687) did not or could not accumulate detailed local knowledge. A selection of its Persian administrative records were studied many years ago by the Japanese historian H. K. Fukazawa.[59] He observed that Arabic loanwords were used to label fiscal-administrative units: *samt, tarf, qalah, qaryat*.[60] Each is revealing of the geographical understanding of royal officialdom. The first and second names denote (in this context) a direction: that is, toward. Like *bāzū* in Mughal records, these indicate simply an orientation toward which the tax collector or commander and his entourage were to march. The third word, *qalah*, means a "fort"—that is, a defensible administrative center—and *qaryat* means a town. When these last two were used to signify a cluster of up to two hundred villages spread over a considerable area, it again indicates that exact geographical boundaries were not known and perhaps were not functionally important. This was because taxes were collected and brought to the fortified center, and its name therefore was used to label the group of actual settlements that paid into the local treasury there. We find it common in many areas that the installments of tax were brought in to them by a village headman and one or more attendants.[61]

The situation did not change under the Marathas who successfully campaigned across much of South Asia in the eighteenth century. Vast amounts of information of many kinds were gathered in their capitals and secretariats, but their maps are confined to fortified towns, a few regional landscapes, and battlefields. More realistic sketches of forts, cities, and some important battlefields have survived, and their military value is obvious. The Marathas were familiar with European maps and plans—and rightly suspicious of the motives of their makers—but there is only one Maratha map that I know of that tried to move from the enumeration of stages to sketching of global maps. The cartographer, however, was reluctant to abandon the sacred cosmology of the puranic tradition.[62] The map is now in the British Library's collection, and is the frontispiece to this book; the information it contains resembles that found in a geographical memorandum from the Menavali Daftar belonging to the Maratha potentate Nana Phadnis (d. 1800). It depicts an ovoid earth surrounded by oceans. A triangular land mass in the southern sea is labeled Lanka, connected to the mainland by a rectangular *śvetu* (Sanskrit *setu*, a bridge or causeway)—clearly referring to Rama's famous bridge in the Sanskrit epic. The southern mainland (from west to east) contains the labels Maṁglūr (colonial "Mangalore"), then Malyāḷa deś, two ovoid clusters of mountains labeled Malayagiri and Mahendra Parvat, with "Keramaḷa [*sic*] deś" between them.[63] Rameshwaram is a large area placed on the coast east of the bridge. The river Kaveri correctly originates in the western edge of the peninsula but is shown as flowing almost directly east, with different towns placed on either side. The rivers of Maharashtra, the Krishna and Godavari, are more elaborately outlined with several tributaries shown for the former. Mumbai and Dwarka both appear on the shore of the Western Sea. Later Western knowledge is incorporated, too, with two oval islands in the ocean northeast of "Kalkata" (modern Kolkata) labeled "China" and "Greater China." At the extreme west of the map, three small D-shaped boxes show the lands of the "ṭopikār [hatwearers], Dingmār, Valandez, Pharāsīs, Purtkāl and Ingrej [Danes, Dutch, Portugal, English] Vilāyat."[64] No one could effectively travel by either land or sea using this map. Its real purpose remains obscure. But the whole sketch illustrates how irrelevant realistic cartography was for practical statesmen and soldiers, even those who traveled and warred over the symbolically mapped terrain.

BRITISH MAPPING OF SOUTH ASIA

The British government in India, however, was well versed in European mapping techniques and actively developed impersonal, bureaucratic forms of knowledge. Like their predecessors, they recognized the value of itineraries for planning travel and war. But they went further and standardized them in "stage books" or tabular sequential statements of routes that could be used by other members of the English-knowing elite.[65] Measuring distances and providing a frame for maps and plans were part of much official travel. Emissaries and officers such as Moor often recorded rough estimates of route distances and other information with the avowed objective of filling in gaps in colonial maps (see map 3). Some also recorded passes, defensible sites, and the strengths and weaknesses of such strongholds as they could inspect.[66]

The Madras Presidency early raised a "Corps of Guides" who were on the establishment of the quartermaster general, the senior military officer who oversaw logistics. Route information came to be systematized in his office. A compilation guide of 1853 proudly noted that sixteen thousand miles of road had been added to this latest edition. The basic source is revealed by the discussion of place-names: "The mode adopted to prevent error was as follows—the Original Field Books in Tamul or Telogoo, constructed by the valuable little Corps of Guides and Surveyors attached to the Quarter Master General's Department, have been read to the Compiler by the senior of that body, and the most scrupulous care has been taken both to have the names accurately pronounced, as well as to represent the sounds as closely and naturally as possible in the English character." Thus, speakers of Indian languages were assumed to be the primary source of the knowledge now translated, standardized, and made independent of individual experts and guides. Furthermore, regiments on the march were required to report the features of the roads and campgrounds they encountered. The quantity and quality of water was especially important, and its sources were noted.[67]

Itineraries along major routes were therefore gradually compiled by British authorities and printed largely for military and official use during the nineteenth century. These listed possible daily marches, either for military units

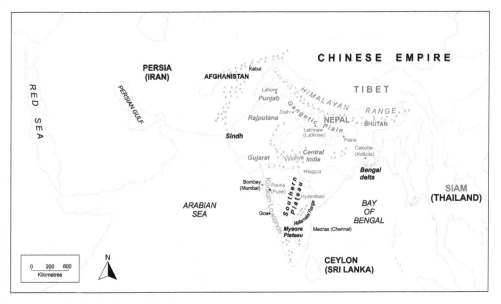

MAP 3. Asian geopolitical regions, ca. 1800.

or touring officials. It was presumed that local guides as well as the villagers usually conscripted to carry baggage would know the best paths connecting one place to another eight, ten, or twelve miles away. British dominance had by now allowed the routine use of the pedometer or other devices on all routes. The tables all therefore listed distances in English miles and furlongs (eight furlongs make a mile). So it was possible to write, for instance, that the distance from "Bahmunwarra" to "Nimgaong" was eleven miles and four furlongs. But simple distance meant little. The reporter added that the road was generally hilly and "indifferent," meaning somewhat difficult. Water had to be fetched from a seasonal watercourse, the "Kirpa Nullah." The fact that there was only one shop where a traveler might buy supplies is noted. Indeed a column titled "Supplies" in every table specified if shops existed and if so, how many. At another village, "Pavannah" in modern Nashik district, there was plenty of water to be found by digging two feet into the bed of a seasonal watercourse. But the only ground for encamping a battalion was on the right bank, and that very confined and rocky area lay between the river and the hamlet of Aujun. The latter was surrounded by a mud wall that was

SOUTH ASIA IN THE IMPERIAL GAZE | 67

in very good repair and about twelve feet high, which hints at the place's capacity for armed resistance, or perhaps safety from bandits.

Seasons mattered: if the description did not specify the months when it applied, then that omission was noted by the compiler. Water for drinking and washing obviously varied with time of year. At Pavannah, seasonal ravines were quite dry in January, but there were two good wells nearby and others within a short distance that were normally used to irrigate wheat fields. The compiler (and his colleagues) would feel free to disregard such peasant needs. The military origins of the publication are evident not only in remarks about the size of campgrounds but also in notes specifying if a route was passable for artillery. The road through the "Wasseyra Pass" was "steep, winding and difficult." It took much labor to enable the "Poona Division" and its guns to cross it in 1818. A special note warned officers taking troops from Asirgarh to Mhow that they should minimize wheeled vehicles as some stretches were too rough for anything less sturdy than a gun carriage.

Beyond monsoonal variations, military and civilian travel had to be mindful even of the phases of the moon that affected tides. This was particularly true in western Gujarat. A special note remarked of the road to Dundooka that the first part crossed a firm and not unfrequently rocky soil, but beyond that town, it entered a low and flat tract of country, clearly "exceedingly marshy, during and for some time after the rainy season." Then came two small creeks, flooded with seawater during the high tides at new and full moon. That left a "considerable quantity" of deep mud that made crossing difficult. Much well water in the area was saline and unpalatable. At the important harbor of Goga, English visitors halting at the government rest house had to get water fetched from a hill two miles away and paid two pice (1/32 of a rupee) for each pitcher. Neither reporters nor compilers show the romantic sensibility that rhapsodized over rugged hills and deep ravines. These were simply obstructions to the passage of transport carts and gun carriages. The contributors were also suspicious of jungles—one guesses because they might shelter guerrillas. They approved "open country," and they wrote approvingly of campsites where groves of trees afforded additional shelter.[68]

As quartermasters compiled and printed such works, English-reading officers no longer needed to depend entirely on guides or informants. They could plan out itineraries on paper before embarking on a march or expedition. They could also check if their guides were misleading them, whether out of ignorance, laziness, or malice. A century of effort by the British Empire in India brought mapping to a level of detail only exceeded by today's satellite-enabled and digitally processed data streams. It radically changed landscape and record across South Asia by deploying powerful instruments of demarcating, mapping, and recording on unprecedented scales, large and small. It accompanied and enabled the exertion of imperial power on a granular scale never previously achieved, with lasting effects.

PAPERING OVER THE CRACKS IN EMPIRE CA. 1600: THE *A'īN*

The *A'īn* was a key document that framed imperial South Asia long after its composition. It was valorized for centuries, and legends about its encyclopedic quality deeply impressed the early British when they began to grapple with land administration after the 1750s. They were introduced to the *A'īn* by Persianized Indian subordinates. Indian and British alike thought that all aspects of the Mughal Empire—its farms and marts and cities, the quality of its horses, and the diet of its elephants—had once been equally transparent to the imperial gaze and carefully written down by myriads of clerks. This was reminiscent of the idea current among "free-market" economists of the twentieth century that information was perfect (or that, at any rate, imperfections made no difference). A number of future Nobel Prize winners began to deconstruct the latter idea in the last decades of the twentieth century. They introduced the important idea that information is routinely imperfect, slanted, and incomplete.[69] Collecting, processing, and compiling information was and is costly. This is especially so if the information is being collected to tax, regulate, or govern.[70] I argue that the same logic held even more strongly for Mughal-era accounts and, in general, for all tax records from imperial periods.[71]

The conventional and stereotypical nature of some statistics was tacitly recognized by emperors such as Jahangir as well as by imperial officials. Historians have found that statistical information from the *A'īn* was routinely cited to describe the condition of the empire decades afterward, when conditions on the ground could scarcely have remained unchanged. Starting with the later part of the reign of Akbar, the empire was divided into territorial units called *sarkar*, each containing a delimited territory usually defined as a number of villages. A group of these subdivisions constituted a province, or *subah*. Imperial administrative lists contained the names of villages located in each *sarkar* as well as a tax statement, including assessment and, sometimes, past collections. All transfers of power began with a copying of lists and registers. Sometimes they also ended there. Other information was recopied as much as a century later when it would look perfect on paper but have no administrative value. To give an example: eastern Bengal was nominally added to the empire under Akbar. The fractional values of ungoverned lands were carefully listed—and even allotted to particular commanders as pay.[72]

These practices, however, meant that what the authorities actually had was a roster of villages—or rather of tax-paying units—with a money valuation attached to each. It was out of such lists that village-by-village compilations (*deh-ba-dehi* lists) of the kingdom of Hyderabad (founded in 1724) were prepared.[73] I have demonstrated elsewhere that the empire, "like South Asian governments before and since, was a regime whose gaze exceeded its reach and reach exceeded its grasp."[74]

But the imperial gaze was not a cartographic one. As previously discussed, the *A'in* reflects an imperial statistical outlook in which painstakingly detailed accounts of Mughal provinces are accompanied by no cartographic representations. The historian A. J. Qaisar confirmed that the "study of geography in Medieval India appears to be largely literary-descriptive rather than practical or cartographic."[75] The new geographical synthesis rising in the Renaissance West was certainly known in Southern Asia, but it remained a curiosity. Globes, for example, were sometimes visually appropriated for the symbolic representation of Mughal power. The cover image shows the emperor Jahangir using a globe as a footstool, or standing upon one. Likewise, his successor Shahjahan was painted bestriding a featureless globe with cherubim hovering above his head.[76]

TOTALIZING DOCTRINES, PRAGMATIC IMPROVISATIONS—MAURYA TO MUGHAL

It is difficult to believe that the great structure of administrative control and record that the *Arthashastra* and the *A'in* envisage could have emerged except by the subordination of extant regional domains and the incorporation of their administrative elites into the state. How much autonomy local domains and chiefdoms retained in periods of imperial rule cannot be determined for early periods, but it was very considerable even in the most prosperous days of the Mughal Empire.[77] It is, however, noticeable that chiefdoms, small kingdoms, and tribal confederations all survived Maurya and Kushana Empires or, alternately, reemerged by the fifth or sixth century CE.[78]

Central power obviously did reach down into the locality from time to time and install favorites as land grantees and, in effect, representatives. Such grants constitute much of the historical record of the first millennium CE. In the case of temples and Brahmans—and, later, Islamic functionaries and other holy men—these grants have left durable records. Accountants and record keepers appeared across the countryside at the behest of central authority. But literate men of various origins who performed scribal functions at the capital and provinces soon founded castes and subcastes. They often used their control of records to create small hereditary appanages and caste and lineage monopolies.[79] Indeed, the Delhi sultans had established a system of village valuations and *pargana* (village cluster) record-keeping in the fourteenth century when Ibn Battuta visited that kingdom in the 1330s. At least near Delhi, each village had a headman and an accountant, and villages were grouped into sets of a hundred (evidently parganas).[80]

The imperial chancery believed that local officials could, if pressed (sometimes literally so), produce considerable and detailed information about the taxable capacity of their locality. This was clearly the working assumption of Akbar's finance ministry in the late sixteenth century. A published document detailing that emperor's creation of tables of yield (and tax) rates for the province of Panjab describes how those rates were estimated. It states that every town and pargana should send a member of the hereditary accountant (*qanungo*) family to the court. He was to reside there a year to provide this information for the imperial records. After a year he would return and another representative of the family should be sent out. His interrogation would presumably be a way of cross-checking the accuracy of the first.[81] The rationale seems to be either that family rivalries would induce the second informant to reveal what the first had hidden or that discrepancies would be exposed by separate testimony.

But the overall assumption was that these men would in fact know the average or normal yield of a variety of crops grown under ever-changing conditions over tracts of dozens or hundreds of villages. The latter is improbable even where such appointees were inserted from the imperial center. Central appointees often ensconced themselves in local patronage and landholding, and holders of tax allotments sought to penetrate more deeply into village society in order to most effectively squeeze it. But that itself would result in corresponding efforts at compartmentalization and concealment of information from superiors and rivals. The suspicions thus generated then led to the use of imprisonment and torture to extort taxes. The historian Iqtidar Alam Khan wrote that "evidence on this point is literally unending, and it is full of sickening details of torture perpetrated against the persons of the officials and their families."[82] This low-information, high-suspicion setting would make securing accurate information of ground conditions such as are needed for a cadastral survey inconceivable. It proved immensely difficult for even the vastly more powerful and ingenious British. Their early experience of revenue surveys was little more successful than that of the Mughals whom they sought to imitate.

Nonetheless, the Mughal Empire was the most durable and persistent subcontinental political formation until the British Empire. Whatever its limits, it is clear that the empire knew more than previous regimes had known. At minimum it created permanent posts for record keepers. It even gradually began seeking data on actual collections as distinct from assessments. These efforts increased during the intensification of "military fiscalism" through the eighteenth century. The Mughal system was founded on the allocation of much of the empire to its major commanders as *jagirs*, or lands valued as equivalent to their pay. It thus allotted taxes in lieu of pay to commanders, who therefore became interested in enforcing tax collections. These allotments were supposed to transfer to another officer every few years. The system therefore introduced men with military followings, large or small, into areas removed from their home territory. But it also often required commanders to serve far from their allotted lands. One result was the common practice of "revenue farming," in which a moneyed man would advance money and reimburse himself by collecting the taxes as they came in. These men quite often sought to acquire permanent rights as hereditary landholders. Sometimes they came from the local gentry, sometimes they originated in the clerical bureaucracy, but all sought to employ their local power and information to solicit continued imperial patronage.

Mapping the exact location of villages vis-à-vis other places was not important. Tax collections, tax partitions, and tax exemptions were what rulers were interested in and were what district records would contain. Therefore, the subdivisions within which villages were grouped were quite often not contiguously located. We have seen that the first colonial view of the landscape was a collection of routes and itineraries that were gradually fitted into maps looking inland from the coast. Early British annexations initially secured only lists and valuations—and not maps.

Even under the totalizing rule of the Mughal emperors, several major Bengal lordships were created by men of the clerical class who originally entered the state system as accountants. This happened even in the Awadh district of Unnao, an area that lay close to the imperial and regional centers of power. In the course of time, the revenue officer Charles Elliott wrote, "the Canoongoes [hereditary accountants], taking advantage of their opportunities for cajoling or frightening the villagers, and supported by the Amil's [tax administrator's] influence, managed to become land-holders themselves."[83] When the centralized state fell apart, as it regularly did, it left a stratum of local authorities over the land. Some were old and some new. The social role, if not the specific lineage, persisted through the centuries.

The Mughal secretariats labeled all these intermediate lords, as well as still powerful subordinated rulers, *zamindar*. The historian S. Nurul Hasan also noted how the empire strove for conquest by nomenclature: before Mughal rule, records recognized powerful chieftains under the names of *rajas, rais, thakurs*, and so on, with different titles for smaller intermediaries. The Mughal Empire, however, labeled all hereditary landholders, from tributary kings to petty landlords to hereditary officers and village heads, *zamindar* or *bumi*.[84] That was an example of conquest by nomenclature, one in which modest village headmen and self-conceived kings were all grouped into one class, all equally far beneath the imperial gaze. Powerful heads of militant clans might also be accommodated in the imperial structure by being enrolled as commanders or auxiliaries in the imperial military bureaucracy.[85]

Much power resided in localities and regions, though Mughal rulers would rarely acknowledge this. Babur, founder of the Mughal dynasty, inherited the Timurid ideology that all subordinate rulers held by virtue of royal grace. He therefore wrote that at the time of his conquest, some 80 or 90 million *tankas* of the assessed value of his North Indian domain was the value of districts awarded to *rajas* who had submitted and were awarded these "for their maintenance as of old."[86] We may notice the assumption of complete dominion in the phrase that regional rulers exist by imperial sanction rather than by their own capacity to withstand central power.

Concrete information on terrain, production, and taxation existed patchily at lower levels of the power hierarchy, in the hands of powerful regional lords—variously termed chaudhuris, deshmukhs, and gowdas, among other names, in different parts of South Asia. The civil servant W. H. Moreland described the functions of the Chaudhuri as prescribed in Mughal documents. But he cited Elliott's pragmatic observation that the post was generally held by a prominent landholding family of the subdivision, or *pargana*.[87] The term was inherited by the early colonial administration. Pelsaert wrote that the country was broken up by many mountains and the people who lived there recognized only their own *rajas*, who were very numerous.[88] A major historian of the Mughals accepted Pelsaert's view and added that even in regularly administered areas, "practically the entire country was under the jurisdiction of one or the other types of intermediary zamindars."[89]

More recently, R. P. Rana's fine-grained study of the Mughal core territories around Agra shows the ubiquity and diversity of men termed *zamindar*. This was "a broad-spectrum category that encompassed an array of entities stretching from the ruler of a large kingdom to the holder of a tiny share in the village produce." These chiefs and kings were of diverse origins. Some were heirs to regional kingdoms, others successful leaders of peasant insurgents, yet others immigrant soldiers or officials who turned local office or temporary tax assignment into permanent domain. Sometimes powerful neighboring kings used these modest titles to expand their effective domain. In one striking instance, the powerful kings of Amber (Jaipur) took what were ostensibly temporary subcontracts for tax collection and then forcibly transformed them into extensions of their kingdom. They then settled military retainers in allotted villages to subdue them and draw their own pay thereby. These developments in the closely governed lands near imperial capitals help us understand the logic of record-keeping as a strategy of control. The holders of these military fiefs "surreptitiously" transformed them into their own hereditary domains in defiance of the king who had installed them. It is striking that all this went on in the vicinity of the imperial city of Agra.[90]

Great kings and emperors could not track misconduct or default through personal presence. They needed records and reports as instruments of control: they were blind without them. But most rulers were fiscally overstretched, so such local record keepers had to be paid by the communities they administered. The collection of such perquisites was, in any case, difficult to restrict. Records then became family patrimonies. Special scripts and writing conventions made it difficult for outsiders to understand them.[91] These intermediaries became powerful by blocking the royal gaze, even as they used the threat of kingly power to reinforce their own dominance.[92]

Mughal prescriptive documents made impossible demands for individualized field assessments for every crop in each season, from cumin seed to water chestnut. No apparatus of surveillance existed to enforce such claims. I have shown elsewhere why both Mughals and the British claimed to be collecting a fixed harvest share even though they rarely had the information and agency to achieve this. It was an ideological statement, tantamount to the assertion that the entire surplus above subsistence belonged to the king. Imperial information came from and through layers of local elites—local lords (zamindars), patrimonial scribal elites, and, at the lowest level, "writers" of accounts. Commands and exhortations whose implementation assumed individualized knowledge of each field and farmer could never have been fulfilled by Mughal appointees, who had dozens or hundreds of villages to supervise. These appointees were also of uncertain tenure and would spend spells in prison when their accounts were being verified.[93]

Imperial authorities were really only asserting that they had the degree of control exercised by lords of small domains, one whose agents could be present at every threshing floor through harvest time. In practice, these would have been very small holders. In North Bihar around 1900, for example, the average "estate" in areas where rent in kind predominated was 40 acres in one subdivision and 77 in another. Where the average size increased to 285 acres, landlords found supervision too difficult and did not enforce produce rent paid in grain, preferring to take cash plus a range of perquisites.[94] In other cases, these harvest time enforcers would have to be supported by the peasants through a share of the crop, as was done in the central Rajasthan estate studied by Ann Gold and Bhoju Ram Gujar.[95] The problem facing an emperor in Agra who sought to actually enforce share rents can only be imagined.

Kings and emperors in South Asia had to deal with a dense layer of intermediate lords. Some dominated a single village; others were kings over hundreds. But all were localized potentates, closer to the land. The Mughal

Empire was a new and exceptionally stable formation. It was culturally as well as politically powerful; it inspired emulation and competition among regional rulers. It was also statistically driven to a novel degree and prescribed measures to reach and control not just villages and towns but also individual fields and threshing floors. It not only sought to achieve the granular control exercised by small local lords. It also sought to enumerate the results on a standard numerical template. These features also appeared in regional regimes. A specialized apparatus of record and account already existed, but the intensification of administration caused that to reach more deeply into village and district society, enlarging the clerical classes alongside the older nobility of the sword. The *A'in* declares that the *patwari* (village accountant) "is a writer employed on the part of the cultivator . . . no village is without one."[96] In early nineteenth-century Gujarat, the *patwari* was termed *talati*; Thomas Marshall described this functionary who was paid out of the village collections as "strong in the interest of the village, or rather of the Patel [headman]."[97]

Verification of the accountant's declarations never seems to have extended further than seizing and translating his papers. C. A. Elliott, who saw the records of the late Mughal system in North India, commented that even this must have rarely happened.[98] Nonetheless, the effort to attain such detail was made by the first long-sustained imperial regime to appear in second-millennium South Asia. It meant a heavier footprint on the landscape. The accompanying imperial propaganda convinced later British officialdom that their predecessors had in fact achieved it and caused them to emulate the model. Viewed from below then, the Mughal Empire developed from a conquest state to a domesticated giant like Gulliver in Lilliput, a creature to be feared and manipulated.

The persistent drive for information and control alongside the incapacity to create a true ground-level bureaucracy meant, however, that officials such as Qanungos or Deshpandes endured through many changes of regime. But their records, if they were not merely an abstract of local gentry's reports, came up from the *patwari*. In Eastern India where big landlords were powerful, these men were simply the landlord's servants, often sitting in his local office.[99] His role as landlord's representative, wrote one experienced officer, made him "the most important of the village officials" in every Bihar village.[100]

When the British sought to revive Mughal administrative usage in Eastern India following the Mughal cession of the region in 1765, they found the pargana record keepers (*qanungo*) firmly established as the sole sources of information on conditions in their districts. The British official R. B. Ramsbotham wrote retrospectively that these functionaries alone "possessed the statistics on which any form of land revenue assessment could, with any pretence to accuracy, be made."[101] I would argue that even they knew less than they claimed. Locally differing usages also complicated matters; opacity, however, helped such subordinates become indispensable, until they were displaced after decades of effort by current information gathered through the Survey of India and the local revenue surveys that operated alongside it.[102]

The East India Company nonetheless made a series of strenuous efforts between 1765 and 1793 to secure independent access to information about land and what it produced. One frustrated official attempted to reconcile the Mughal model with facts on the ground. He wrote from Chittagong (Chatgaon) that no single pargana or subdivision was held by a single zamindar—they were all divided. Collections were therefore made at various places depending on where each pargana's officials sent their taxes. It was also impossible for any collector "to ascertain the true and actual collection of any one zamindar's district or pargana." Measurement had been tried and failed because (he believed) the surveyors were corrupt. Another measurement "would not only have been expensive but of little or no use, had the Collector himself not been present, for venality would have made the same progress as in the last settlement."[103] Dependable measurement to detect unreported land or even ascertain the boundaries of any zamindari was thus impossible.

The East India Company in Bengal and Bihar finally abandoned the effort at replicating an imaginary Mughal system. They took the extant ad hoc tax assessment and made it permanent in 1793. Essentially, therefore, the new colonial regime abandoned the effort to recapture a knowledge of the land that they believed their predecessors had possessed. But the British were ultimately more powerful and more efficient: the mapping and evaluation of lands down to the individual farm plot was ultimately achieved at considerable expense by a staff of thousands, on the very brink of the final retreat of the empire from South Asia.[104] We can now understand why mapping was not a high priority for the Mughal Empire: they could never achieve a consistent presence on the ground. It was many decades before British offices realized that Mughal knowledge was larger in reputation than on paper and existed more on paper than on the ground.

This chapter began by framing the ecology and geography of South Asia in the contemporary frame of scientific cosmology. That geographic vision has been naturalized by satellite-based GPS as well as the pragmatic geography of the modern smartphone. But historically, different frames of reference and bodies of geographical understanding existed. Today's "educated commonsense world" is the product of centuries. The chapter considers the past knowledge of Indian empires. It shows how keystone animals such as the elephant molded the political ecology they willy-nilly created. It thus traces how the needs and capacities of earlier empires limited their perceived world up until the enthronement of maritime geographies begun by the British Empire from 1800. The new geographic understanding came allied with an unprecedented capacity to dominate and control the land. That capacity was enhanced by devices for mechanical measurement, such as the theodolite for angles and the perambulator for distances. But their systematic deployment depended on military power to traverse the land and the bureaucratic capacity to compile the information. That knowledge could then be preserved and diffused through centralized, bureaucratically organized printing. If the limits of Mughal knowledge reflected the limits of Mughal control, the enlarged power of the British is reflected in the amplitude of the geographical and statistical knowledge that they could accumulate.

THREE

Imperial Gaze, Lordly Grasp

> Adilshahi sultans, Nizamshahi sultans, Mughal emperors
> all conquered these countries. But in those domains,
> all the peasants remained under the control
> of village heads and accountants, of district chiefs.
>
> RAMACHANDRA ANANT | 1694

THE RAVELING AND UNRAVELING OF EMPIRES WERE PROCESSES THAT worked themselves out on a subcontinental scale. But because of the immense diversity—ecological, linguistic, social, and political—of the subcontinent, environmental histories are best written at the regional level. The limits of imperial power constrained the imperial capacity to secure actionable knowledge. The Dutch merchant Francisco Pelsaert reported during the reign of Jahangir (r. 1605–27) that while the emperor's name meant "holder of the world," much of his own territory was outside his effective grasp. The emperor Jahangir, Pelsaert wrote, was king of the "plains or open roads only," as travelers had to either have a strong armed escort or pay heavy tolls to rebels.[1] It must be evident that people who did not even recognize the authority of the emperor were unlikely to submit statistical information to him, even if they collected it. The remaining chapters of this book are devoted to the recent (historically speaking) political ecology of an Indian macro-region, one that now constitutes a large fraction of the Indian states of Maharashtra, Madhya Pradesh, Chhattisgarh, and part of Gujarat. No single part of the subcontinent can replicate the social and environmental diversity of the whole, but this area (which I shall usually term Western India) displays a considerable range. However, even at regional levels such as this, the inheritors of Mughal power knew no more than their imperial suzerains.

LANDS KNOWN AS LISTS

The Nizam of Hyderabad surrendered his claims in the province of Khandesh to the Peshwa Madhavrao I in 1760. It had been under Mughal rule since about 1600. The Peshwa sought to resettle and repopulate the area. His administration began with no more than a Mughal-origin list of districts, subdistricts, and villages. In 1769, it entrusted one Balaji Nilakanth with the task of resettling specific abandoned villages in the region. His charge was clearly not based on any field survey; instead, its baseline was a list of villages obtained in all probability from the offices of the hereditary accountants of the areas concerned.

The Peshwa's memorandum was to the regional administrator, who was directed to take a declaration from the lower-level tax collectors as to which villages and towns had paid anything. The remaining listed villages within the specific subdivisions were assumed to be deserted. They were the ones to be repopulated by Balaji Nilakanth. The document does not state how the latter list was created, but it was probably done by deducting tax-paying villages from the complete list. This is evident from the separate mention of two districts (Sarkars Bijāgaḍ and Hāṇḍīyā) and a pargana (Khargon) for which no list of subdivisions was available. Finally, there was a subdivision (*tarf*) named Pāl in Raver *pargana* reported to contain seventy villages, without further detail. The tax farmer was instructed not to draw tax-paying peasants from other villages to the abandoned ones as that would lower the aggregate revenue. He was, however, permitted to induce the headman and Dalit watchmen and village servants (Mahar) of any abandoned village who were living elsewhere to return. Clearly, their presence was perceived as an essential core of any viable village.[2]

This pattern of knowing through lists persisted into the nineteenth century. Thus, W. H. Sykes, who served as a statistical reporter for the Bombay government, found in 1826 that he could not calculate population density for even a single pargana. His population returns had been assembled from village accountants according to the administrative division to which the villages reported. His area calculations came from a topographic survey by the military engineer, C. H. Jopp. Sykes found that there were many instances of villages belonging to one pargana being in fact sited "inside" another. He added that similar considerations applied even to the large assemblages the British termed "Collectorates" (modern districts). Even the town after which a subdivision was named might not administratively speaking be in that subdivision itself. So, twenty villages administratively grouped as *turuff* (subdivision) Mandugaon under taluka Ahmednagar surrounded the two towns of Mandugaon and Mirajgaon, yet in the list sent to the British surveyor, John Jopp, the former was under taluka Jamkhed and the latter under subdivision Kadevalit. Sykes also observed that the entire subdivision was simply not to be found in the British government list in his possession. Some of its actual villages were located in another list that had been supplied by the Hyderabad government in order to work out an exchange of select villages with the Bombay government.[3] In effect, therefore, some local officials and village heads considered themselves under British rule even if the government had no exact cognizance of it.

The British-appointed temporary governor of the Nagpur kingdom, Richard Jenkins, commissioned an Indian subordinate, Vinayakrao, to conduct a statistical survey of its territory in Central India. The latter evidently set out with a list of villages in each district and soon discovered its imperfections. For example, the village list for the Umrad district contained 268 villages; in 1821, but only 120 of them had resident cultivators, and a few fields in one hundred more were cultivated by commuting or shifting cultivators. Eighteen were "long abandoned," and even the sites of thirty others were lost in the great forest.[4]

REGIONAL LORDS AT THE INTERFACE OF IMPERIAL AND GENTRY POWER

As the title of this chapter suggests, an important obstacle to imperial domination and total knowledge lay in the resistance of small, usually hereditary regional lords. They appear in Mughal and British records under various names.[5] The imperial gaze sought to reduce them to insignificance by terming them all *zamindar* (literally "landholder"). The word never took root in Western India, where the term *deshmukh* (meaning "head of the country") was current. *Desai* was the corresponding title northward along the coast into Gujarat and *Gauda* in Kannada-speaking areas. These emerged in the Sultanate period, after circa 1300 CE. S. N. Vatsa-Joshi, however, pointed out that they had a functional equivalent in the *vishayapati* (lord of the region) of earlier grants. Local power and knowledge would reside in such offices. The text on statecraft written by Ramachandra Pant Amatya in 1716 warned the monarch not to confuse them with other subjects; they were small but independent territorial chiefs (*deshnayak*). Even Mughal commanders newly arrived with the emperor Aurangzeb (r. 1658–1707) after 1682 sought to acquire such offices. The hereditary holders of the Wai *deshmukhi* were the Pisal family. A fierce dispute within the lineage led to it being taken over by the emperor. His regional governor Nyahar [*sic*] Khan Ghori then had the estate recorded in his own name. Upon the Mughal retreat from the south after 1707, the incoming Maratha king Shahu acquired the post and duly fulfilled its duties. Joshi noted how even two decades into his reign, Shahu signed a judicial verdict not in his capacity as sovereign but rather as one of the *deshmukhs* who decided the case.[6] What I see as important in this entire episode is how outsiders were anxious to ensconce themselves at this intermediary level; even Mughal regional governors were quick to do so as opportunity offered.

The struggle for control nonetheless led to the growth of records. That was the result of the parallel rise of a clerical elite as state formation intensified. In South Asia they formed a cluster of castes known as Kayastha. The creation of durable charters (often stone or copper-plate records) was intended for later verification by other Kayasthas, thus providing a durable source of income for the brotherhood of scribes. The obloquy heaped on this profession in the Sanskrit literary canon is perhaps evidence of how these bureaucrats deployed their power over the comfortable sinecures of the literary elite.[7]

Kings and lords alike wished to see a fully cultivated landscape producing the most valuable and most highly taxed crops. Thus, the *A'īn* exhorted the tax collector to encourage cultivation and not allow any land to turn into "waste." He should therefore ignore the pleas of any farmer who wanted to reduce the area cultivated and should also stimulate the increase of valuable produce rather than inferior crops.[8] This was a widespread kingly understanding. Afzal Khan, minister and general of the Bijapur Sultanate, reproved the hereditary *deshmukh* of Shīrval in 1655–56. He was charged with collecting his own dues but neglecting his other duties. The *deshmukh*'s duty, Afzal Khan wrote, was to tour his district and not allow a finger's width of land to "fall" out of tillage. The Marathi *Paḍ* can also mean "fallen" in the sense of "dead." Persian has an analogous usage, also deriving from the root "to die."[9] The hereditary lord, the command continues, should arrange for temporarily reduced tax rates and the supply of plows and oxen so as to bring the land under cultivation. He should make the tax collections increase from year to year.[10] This last imperative endured into British times until challenged by the birth of the Forest Department.

VILLAGE RECORDERS AND SUPERIOR POWER

The emperor Akbar's system assumed that village accountants were found in every village by 1600. But when had they been installed? It is unlikely that the largely illiterate village community would voluntarily install and pay a clerk whose records could only be useful to tax collectors. Even in landlord-owned villages, if all major claimants on village produce were locally present, it was possible for taxes to be taken directly as money, labor, grain, fodder, vegetables, shoes, basketwork cloaks, and so forth without any written records being created at all. But larger domains and centralizing authorities could—and did—compel the creation of records and offices charged with maintaining them. The exaction of money tribute or deliveries of set amounts of specific grains then led to the establishment of record keepers over clusters of villages (termed *qanungos* of the pargana). Thomas Marshall, who saw the system at the beginning of British rule, observed the role of *majmudars* (the regional equivalent of *qanungos*). He described them as part of the hereditary establishment but presiding over "a small canton" and noted that they were not members of the village community but rather agents of the state *against* the village community.[11]

In seventeenth-century Western India, we find such divisional officers controlling records themselves and not appointing village record keepers until coerced into so doing. Therefore, if royal authority reached down to the village, accountants appeared at that level too. They were paid directly by the villagers. In Western India, they were largely royal officers who claimed a property in their office.[12] Once they were created, however, all functionaries had an interest in perpetuating their own offices. They set up claims from below contradicting those being asserted from above. This was especially true in humid lands where intensive labor produced things the elites valued, such as rice, coconuts, areca nut, betel leaf, and others. All along the humid coastal lands, villages and village clusters were dominated by gentry landlords known as *khot*. British officials generally saw these hereditary rights as usurpations, as though their own empire was not. D. C. Graham thus labeled them mere temporary tax collectors who had transmitted the office to their descendants and were left undisturbed because of native "anarchy and misrule."[13]

Another body of information came from land- and privilege-holders, old and new, who also existed at the interface of village opacity and imperial intrusion. The Mughal Empire sought to incorporate them into a service hierarchy and, failing that, to eliminate them. The Maratha Empire emerged out of members of the local gentry and willingly permitted the transformation of state office into family patrimony. Patrimonial lords participated in "state" functions. Only the British bureaucracy that emerged from the unrelenting pressure of the British Parliament on an ossifying trading corporation succeeded, after a century of effort, in reducing these intermediaries to a service bureaucracy or eliminating them altogether. But that was achieved only in those parts of directly governed British territory, such as the Bombay Presidency, where tax administration penetrated down to the individual holding.

Therefore, for at least three centuries before 1900, hereditary accountants had stood as gatekeepers of local knowledge. It often made them the direct superiors of peasant populations. Much of Western India had long established hereditary officials, such as the Adhikari family of Cheul (near modern Mumbai). Such functionaries worked with lists of tax domains (*mahāl*), each of which was usually, but not always, a village. All higher units were "perceived" through lists of villages belonging to each pargana and then of parganas grouped into larger divisions. Such hereditary officials had a strong incentive to accumulate and manage information. After his kingdom was nearly overrun by a Maratha military campaign in 1731, the lord of Janjira signed a treaty with the Peshwa dividing the district of Cheul between them. As they had long done, the hereditary Adhikaris managed all of the subdivision and allotted the collections to whichever potentate had established control.[14] The Company official John Briggs wrote from Khandesh in 1819: "When I arrived in Candeish, I found the [hereditary officers] possessed of unlimited powers; they had been the agents of extortion made use of by all the plunderers."[15] Yet it might be argued that they had made the best terms possible to preserve the locality in the face of overwhelming power. Managing information was an important method of manipulation. William Chaplin, after several years' tax assessment work as commissioner in the Deccan, declared of local record keepers that "those who can show no ancient records are never at a loss to furnish either a fabricated set, or to give a traditionary account of the old rates."[16]

Fabricated records certainly appeared when the new collector of Khandesh, the aforementioned Briggs, made impossible demands for detailed crop and field information from the hereditary officials he had summoned to his headquarters in Dhule. Less than twenty years later, the settlement officer H. E. Goldsmid discovered what had actually happened. His informants described how Briggs summoned the hereditary officials of the district to his headquarters. Once gathered, they were ordered to produce a record of the types and areas of land together with a calculation of the rates of tax needed to yield the amount collected in previous years. "At a distance from the villages themselves, and without there being a single document extant which could throw light upon the subject, it is evident that the Zemindars could not possibly supply the required information. Desirous however of leaving a place where the cholera had broken out, they lost no time in giving a statement."[17]

ELITE GEOGRAPHIES OF MARATHA OFFICIALDOM

The Mughal Empire certainly widened the opportunities and ambitions of elites across South and West Asia. Foreign adventurers embedded themselves in localities where the empire had temporarily posted them. Local lords who joined Mughal service enlarged their holdings at home and added lands across the subcontinent. Within the Mughal Empire, the Marathas emerged locally as gentry of the sword and pen and grew into a power elite across the subcontinent. These processes changed the horizons of elites who might otherwise have limited their knowledge to the locality or, at most, the circuits of pious pilgrimage.

Consider the inventory of incomes held by the important functionary Chinto Vitthala in 1777–78. As a participant in the expansion of Maratha power, he had acquired hereditary posts as Phadnis (auditor-accountant) in several widely scattered divisions. He then secured grants of tax-free lands and villages in several places where he held the Phadnisi office. He thus possessed the entire village of Ahīre in the Mawal region tax free and also the military salary grant of another village in the same area. He held unclassified land estimated at 85 *ruka* (a traditional money value) in Hingni, a hill village where he held an irrigated garden that was measured at fifteen bighas. Coming to smaller holdings, he had an irrigated field of five bighas in a third Mawal village and thirty bighas farther north in today's Nasik district, as well as an unmeasured field in a village in Aśer pargana (location uncertain). Furthermore, he also possessed a village remote from Maharashtra, in the Makḍāī subdivision of Central India. He could not be present at all these, and they were mainly administered by salaried deputies he appointed.[18] Chinto Vitthala would have had a strong understanding of regional geography as well as of individual villages with which he was connected, and this would have enabled him to understand—and possibly change—the assessment geography. Such specialized knowledge would be found at many levels of the Maratha administrative hierarchy as it expanded patchily across the subcontinent.

In 1743, when they were important participants in political affairs across the subcontinent, the Peshwa lineage nonetheless took the opportunity to purchase a half share in the headmanship (*patilki watan*) of the village of Garade near their new capital at Pune, for 1,200 rupees.[19] Major potentates—most famously Mahadaji Shinde—continued to use the title of Patil, or village headman, to signal their ancestral status in rural society. But even if great potentates might possess considerable knowledge of how local society managed its lands, their own management of political loyalty depended on the grant and suspension of benefice and office. If these rewards and punishments were to have any value, overlords would not completely dispel the veil of secrecy that protected local hereditary bureaucrats via a thorough-going inquisition such as began under colonial rule. Many of these local officials were also tax farmers or connected with tax farmers who would have an obvious interest in disguising collections from inquisitive fiscal officers, often by buying them off.

Thus, even though the Peshwai emerged from the clerical classes, their attempts at accurate recording could be frustrated by their own kind. The Konkan coast was also the original home territory of an important group of Brahmans who migrated across the peninsula to occupy secretarial as well as governing office through the eighteenth century. The Peshwa dynasty originated here. Their government surveyed the coastal districts around

1780 and fixed a government demand in kind on each field, notionally as a fraction of the produce. Some decades later, many cultivators were found paying one and a half, two, or even two and a half times that grain share to a landlord who would deal directly with the tax collectors.[20] It is obvious then that either the area or the yield of the land had been underestimated in the 1780 assessment, otherwise such enormous shares—fractions equal to or exceeding the entire harvest—could not have been paid for decades on end.

Sacred personages and institutional grant-holders were another class that straddled the village and the regional court, but they also listed their lands in the same way as peasants did. An example is found in the list of confiscated temple lands gifted to the newly built Catholic church in Salsette in 1568. Here the property of the old temple as well as the perquisites and gifts formerly received by its servants had to be attested by sworn depositions from the villagers. The inventory lists fields by name and by their immediate neighbors. For example, "a paddy field (varzea) named Eporset which is bounded by the field named Aodi and by the river Arny and the paddy field Pomdu Jaõho, the drainage channel (valado) and the areca grove of Māgu Sinay."[21] This was, of course, in the early years of Portuguese administration; almost all the signatures on this document were in old Kannada script with only three written in Portuguese (i.e., Roman) script. There do not seem to have been any paper records extant, and inscriptions might have been demolished along with the temple. So the new government fell back on sworn testimony. Such village geography had to suffice for terrestrial administrative, fiscal, and judicial purposes for several centuries. It is especially noteworthy because the Portuguese administration was always anxious about the accurate recording of the king's taxes and territories. Edicts on the subject were issued as early as 1519–20.[22]

We can see this again in the island of Bombay, which came under English control in 1666 after a century of Portuguese rule. Most inhabitants and property owners stayed, and royal dues were simply transferred to the English East India Company. Yet the tax record of the island under Portuguese and early Company rule was essentially in the same form as that found in Goa in 1568. It described parcels of land by their uses and the names of adjoining property owners in the cardinal directions. These evidently relied on local knowledge of land use and ownership. So, in 1728, the Company granted "a parcel of waste land called Degouree, situate in the Backbay, whereon is newly planted or about to be planted one hundred twenty-five Palmeiras, [palm trees] having for boundaries East, the oart [grove, from Portuguese 'orto'] Dassoury belonging to Jegee Moody and the oart Carvell belonging to the said Antonio de Silva; West with the highway; South with a passage and the oart Ranoury belonging to Jessing Ransor and Pondujee Posjee."[23] Local knowledge of local ownership and boundaries may have also served to conceal encroachments or usurpations, or was at any rate suspected of doing so. The Company sought to reclaim lands for which no clear title was to be found. Resident landowners agreed in 1674 to pay 20,000 "xerafins" annually provided this inquiry was ended. They would, they declared, work out the contributions due from individual property owners among themselves.[24] Once again, local potentates were anxious to screen their ownership titles and incomes from inquiry.

Many other documents show that the specification of four landmarks, or of adjoining owners, was usually sufficient to demarcate a piece of land.[25] The formula ordering demarcation itself was often that the officer addressed should literally "make (demarcate) the four boundaries" and place so-and-so in possession.[26] Landmarks themselves might be more or less elaborate, but sometimes just listing the immediate neighbors would suffice. All such property arrangements depended on the concurrence of villagers and testimony of neighbors. Landmarks were often such as would only be known to people in the immediate locality. For example, a typical land sale deed translated by W. H. Sykes was written in the presence of fifteen village officers and leaders. It recited that one Kusaji Thorat was to receive one *cavar* measure of land from the field named Sandus, the four bounds of which were defined as follows:

> On the east the field called Juwadee cha Mullah; on the west . . . the limits of the hamlet of Gurkol; on the south by fall of water from the hill with the milk bush on the rock in the field called Urdurruh; on the north by the . . . watercourse where it forms an island, separating into two streams: these are the limits. The line of your Chowar runs from the nullah outside the garden, dividing the field into two parts and terminating on watercourse of the upper well. . . . We have resolved that the Malee of the garden before mentioned shall permit you without impediment, to water two Beegehs of your Chowar.[27]

External authority was thus unable to "see" the pattern of ownership and authority, and individual landholders had to rely on the testimony of neighbors. Local geography was socially constructed.

THE FOLK GEOGRAPHY AND GENTRY ECOLOGY OF MAHARASHTRA

It is a truism that South Asia is shaped by the monsoon and its regional and local variation. The greatest part of the subcontinent's carrying capacity, its habitability, is determined by the minimum dry season availability of water. At their worst, famines were aggravated by the diseases transmitted through scarce and contaminated water.[28] Even in normal times, precipitation and runoff are largely determined by regional physiographic features. The geography of Western India is dominated by the high mountain range that fringes the coastal plain and separates it from the east-tilting plateau that gradually slopes to the Bay of Bengal. This region therefore exhibits every type of land use practiced in the Indian subcontinent.

The seasonal moisture regime was central to agricultural and pastoral life, to travel and pilgrimage. But kings and their advisers were especially aware of how terrain and the three major seasons—wet, cool, and hot—controlled the possibilities for the use of force. The *Arthashastra* discusses the muster of armies suited to particular seasons—classed as hot, wet, and cold (the familiar summer, monsoon, and winter succession)—and terrains.[29] Gentry and peasants alike, however, shared a regional geographical understanding of the land—a folk geography.[30] The major regions of the Maratha country that will figure most prominently in this work have long been named from west to east as Konkan, Mawal, and Desh.[31] The first is the rugged coastal belt with limited areas of level cultivable land and heavy rainfall; second, east of it, is the mountain belt that rises in tiers from the Konkan below; and third is the Desh, the open valleys widening out to arid plains east of the mountain tract. The latter was the Maratha homeland often simply referred to as *desh, the* country.[32]

In modern terms, we may see these zones as grading from the abundant moisture and high primary productivity of the coast and mountains (Konkan and Mawal) to the intermediate ecotone where level terrain and secure precipitation encouraged farming to the arid east (Desh) that became known as the "famine belt" of the Bombay Province. Harold Mann, an agronomist with long experience in the area, wrote in 1917 that east of a line running north–south and about fifty miles of the mountains lay a zone of low and uncertain rainfall. Cultivation depended on moisture from local storms that came in September and October.[33]

The western valleys and eastern plains were the home of peasant farmers organized in tightly knit village communities grouped into village clusters. The tract was depopulated by the political and climatic catastrophes of 1801–4 and still little cultivated in 1819. South of the Neera River lay arid lands where horses were bred for the Maratha cavalry and recruits for Maratha armies were drawn.[34] By 1880, horse breeding had declined, but the region was still seasonal pastureland for the cattle of the richer valleys to the west.[35] Even in the 1920s, the arid region was home to a large community of shepherds. But for up to half the year they migrated in search of pasture and water. They also sought to earn money by folding their sheep overnight to fertilize farmland. Thus, nutrients collected from untillable land went to enhance the output of the sown.[36] Between the semi-arid and per-humid lie narrow transition belts. In these, landform dominates climate. This area contains many natural strongholds, and these hillforts and their garrisons were an important feature of life in western Maharashtra, keys to dominating the widening valleys and increasingly arid plains to the east.

The Sahyadri mountains (sometimes called the Ghats) drain monsoon winds of much of their moisture before they proceed farther east. The headman of Vihire, a village on the eastern edge of the mountains, had an unromantic view of the mountain region. When Sykes asked him where he considered the Mawals commenced, he "humorously said 'They commence where men are six months up to their knees in mud and the other half of the year are shivering with cold.'"[37] Wading in mud was needed for wet-rice cultivation. Also, as viewed from the plateau, the Konkan was a land where coconuts were so abundant as to be almost free, where people ate rice but also where local gods were fierce.[38]

The emerging European romantic view saw the area differently. Editing his notes after his return from India at a time when military concerns were less pressing, the retired Colonel Sykes apostrophized the mountain region: "Stupendous scarps, fearful chasms, numerous waterfalls, and perennial verdure, complete the majesty and romantic interest of the vicinity of the Ghats."[39] On hilly land whose topography prevented the formation of stable planting beds, cereal and other crops were raised by burning the vegetation and sowing in the ashes. Rice and nagli (*eleusine coracana*, also known as finger millet) were the most important cereals, but a range of legumes, vegetables, and tree crops were also raised. Wild produce was collected, and large areas were unfit for rice farming except as an unirrigated cereal. Shifting cultivation and gathering were still very possible, and the sea was a resource to many. Moist slopes suited *ragi* or *nachni*; as the *Kolaba Gazetteer* described it, "on hill slopes the soil is cleared of brushwood and the brushwood burnt as manure. The surface is smoothed, and, when sufficiently wetted by rain, the seed is thrown into the mud. Beyond watching that animals do not destroy the field no trouble is taken until the crop is reaped by plucking off the ears." If fresh brushwood to burn on the land was unavailable in the second year, it would be fallowed for three or four years.[40] Even the rice paddy land depended on woodland materials to prepare the seedbed, and most peasants were also heavily dependent on shifting cultivation of hilly lands and on a range of forest products. The forest was not "wild"; in some respects it was as closely farmed as the embanked rice paddy that depended on the steady flow of resources from the hillside woodlands and pastures.

ELITE TASTES AND THEIR ECOSYSTEM EFFECTS

The most striking example of the power of elite tastes to mobilize resources and change ecosystems is the case of rice cultivation.[41] Rice, of course, has a long history across India as an item of prestige consumption. Its prehistoric beginnings in the subcontinent in both wild and domesticated forms have been traced in the archaeological record and in later Vedic texts. Rice has been found at most archaeological sites in the prehistoric and early historic periods.[42] Sanskrit prescriptive texts on offerings to ancestors often include cooked rice in the offering. The distinctive culture zone of Iron Age South India also valorized rice. All four cist graves in a Porunthal complex dating to at least 500 BCE contained unhusked rice in four-legged pots as well as disarticulated bones in clay pots.[43]

Recent work by Dorian Fuller has shown that Indian rice strains were domesticated from *Oryza nivara*, a variety adapted to monsoon wetlands that grew and shrank seasonally. Domesticated rice (*Oryza sativa*) originated in Northern India, probably in the Gangetic plain as early as 4000 BCE. But cultivating rice was economically optimal only in limited regions where harvests could be managed by foraging communities that visited the wetlands seasonally. Bengal was the most important such region. By the 1600s, it was a major exporter by water, sending grain as far as Aden by sea and Agra by river. Rice spread to less ecologically adapted arid peninsular India by the Iron Age. Irrigated rice in an arid zone required the tight control of labor and constant management of water. It is likely that this reflected the establishment of more rigid hierarchies that in turn valorized elite food preferences and stabilized elite control of labor.

All over the subcontinent much rice came to be grown under carefully managed conditions. That, in turn, enabled highly productive rice fields to be created and tilled year after year. Thus, "it was the social changes towards hierarchy and new means of labour organization that were the turning point in the development and expansion of rice agriculture." Inland, South Indian rice farming was thus generally associated with the spread of tank irrigation under elite management. It developed with the rise of stable early states in the Iron Age.[44] Reservoirs were therefore often built in difficult locations where they eventually had to be abandoned.[45] The valorization of white rice as a status food in the mature Vijayanagara era (1400–1560s) was accompanied by enormous efforts to reshape a near-desert landscape to accommodate irrigated rice farming. Kathleen Morrison has shown how South Indian elites and their institutions—notably the great temples and courts—valued and demanded the products of irrigated paddy cultivation, compelling rural society to change its patterns of production and consumption.[46] This was not only true of the Vijayanagara empire; at the end of the sixteenth century, the mountain valleys of the western Tapi basin were densely settled and famous for fine aromatic rice raised by damming small torrents and leading them to cultivable fields. However, much of this area reverted to forests in the eighteenth century and was still thinly peopled in 1880.

White rice became an essential part of an upper-class diet. When the treasonous noble Tulaji Angre was arrested and sent as a prisoner to the fort of Daulatabad in 1767–68, he was to be given food as befitted his noble status: wheat and fine-grained white rice as well as lentils, salt, ghee (clarified butter), and sugar. Additionally, he was to receive a cash allowance of

5 rupees a month to purchase pan-supari and vegetables. He was attended by two women servants, who only received the normal plebeian rations of millet, lentils, and salt.[47]

Rice was not all that elites demanded. Ghee was an essential addition. If the rice paddy depended on a large resident population, much butter was produced by seasonally mobile cowherds who migrated across the peninsula following the rains and new grass. They were proverbially consumers of buttermilk, which is the residue after cream has coagulated on soured milk and been churned off. The cream would then be boiled to make ghee—in Maharashtra associated with Brahmans.[48] Even in the 1840s, D. C. Graham found that much ghee was produced by nomadic Dhangars. They lived in the forests, moving with large herds of cows and buffalo in search of fodder and water. Their ghee was exported mainly to coastal towns after it had passed though the hands of special refiners who removed its rancid odor. Within the kingdom of Satara, ghee consumed was locally produced by peasants who had two or three buffalo and brought their ghee to the bazaar. Only the upper classes could afford it, and others used oil.[49]

Many spices flavored and augmented the rice of the upper classes. Areca nut fragments and their leaf wrapping leaf were enthusiastically consumed across the subcontinent and adopted by new elites, including the Mughals. Specialized castes and forest foragers managed the horticultural-woodland complex that produced these. The upper classes also sought other products of humid hill forests, such as sandalwood and cardamom. Peasant farmers adjusted their irrigation devices, cropping patterns and personal consumption to the pull of these affluent consumers.[50] Lesser elites also emulated these patterns. We shall illustrate this in the Maratha lands later in this chapter.

ECOSYSTEMS AND AGRARIAN SYSTEMS: THE WESTERN COAST OF MAHARASHTRA

Humid zone farming thus supplied the most important commodities consumed by the elites and emulated by middling strata across the Maratha country. The major social divide between landlord-focused and peasant-held lands followed the humid-arid transition. This coastal belt was shaped by water—the salt waters of the Arabian Sea that surged perilously onto the shore and the heavy monsoons that broke on the mountain walls some twenty or thirty miles inland and gushed in torrents to the sea. Early British officials provided a succinct view of Konkan geography in 1880, before the rise of Bombay/Mumbai as a megalopolis dramatically swallowed most adjacent territories. Agricultural systems had not changed for centuries, and so we may use this evidence. The coast was a relatively narrow belt studded with well-built villages among carefully tended palm groves, yielding many things, including food, drink, and cordage. Landlord-dominated areas included the coastal lowlands—pocketed with labor-intensive rice paddy, much of it financed and held by non-cultivating owners. The Konkan coastal belt from south Gujarat to Kerala has historically been dominated by an important class of landed Brahmans. It was also a region where rice and coconuts were important features of local agriculture.

Rice, originally a swampland grass, might appear a "natural" fit in a region of superabundant water. However, rice needs not just water but carefully managed water. Zones of coastal rice were intensely hierarchical. Unlike most of the subcontinent, the area was not deficient in fresh water but deficient in level land where soil would hold firm against running water and allow edible plants to grow. Apart from landlord mansions, larger villages contained the homes of skilled workers. Strongly corporate castes of toddy tappers and palm tree farmers grew up along the coast; careful manuring—including fish and fish refuse—was essential for their sustenance.[51]

These were folk who could clamber up tall palm trees and knew their care or who could navigate the storms and tides of a dangerous sea. As is often the case on coastlines shaped by Holocene sea level rise, lower land lay behind the coastal barrier upland. The *Kolaba Gazetteer* described the interior coastal lands as "tracts of salt marsh and rice land, ugly and bare in the dry season, and, except the raised island-like village sites, without trees." Inland from this, major watercourses ran through narrow, winding valleys, "well tilled and thickly peopled. On either side of these valleys . . . [were] rolling lines of low bare uplands, cropped with coarse grain or used for grazing." The valleys were relatively short and ended in the Sahyadri mountains that fed short, west-flowing streams. They separated the Konkan from the plateau beyond, a sloping plain whose long rivers flowed east to the Bay of Bengal.[52]

The interaction of gentry power with local topography produced a rice paddy and palm orchard (coconut, areca) commercial agricultural complex. It was established along creeks and on relatively level ground. Its tillage needed large areas to supply biomass for the pockets of intensive agriculture, particularly by affording grazing to cattle and supplying small branches and other biomass to prepare seedbeds for rice. The material was known locally as *rāb*. E. C. Ozanne, the director of agriculture, demonstrated its value by actual experiment in the 1880s. This was a time when the Forest Department was seeking to minimize the use of tree loppings in order to enlarge its own revenue-yielding domains at the expense of peasant agriculture. It claimed dung and other material would suffice. Ozanne measured the monthly dung output of a full-grown buffalo (it was 270 pounds dry weight) and showed that all the cattle in the district would only supply enough to prepare one-fifth of the seedbed area needed for local agriculture. He went on to show that grass also had to be supplemented with tree loppings, regardless of Forest Department fiat about the latter being unnecessary.[53] Thus, rice land—like spice, betel leaf, and areca gardens—drew heavily on upland and forest. Small-scale reclamation of the shallows was gradually pushing rice land out to sea. The cultivation of salt-tolerant rice strains assisted that process.

Rice tillage, therefore, was enveloped in and sustained by a more diverse peasant and forager economy that provided vital subsistence to the working population, seasonally to some, year-round to others. The extensive rugged uplands were unsuitable for rice but spontaneously generated grass and shrubs. These could be periodically burned to prepare the land for crops of millets and lentils. Nutritionally speaking, these were much more important for the majority of the population. Wild lands also yielded much food and drink, with the wild date palm and mahua fruit a valuable source of both. The caste most famous for tilling "salt rice" drank liquor, "chiefly country spirits distilled either from mahua flowers or from cocoa or brab-palm juice."[54] Coconut husk provided ropes for many purposes, including ancient ship-building techniques that did not use nails to hold the sheathing planks together. Reclaimed rice paddies and coconut or areca nut plantations all needed initial capital investment and continuous care through the years. The Indian peninsula was shaped not only by sea level rise during the Holocene and the fluvial action of rain and tide but also by still active geological processes. The craggy west coast has been less vulnerable than the fluvial Bengal delta where land rising from the waters might also be capriciously reclaimed by them.[55] But both up-thrust and subsidence—and accompanying earthquakes—are marked features of western India into the present. Even if rice fields were not damaged by warfare, storms and storm surges might overwhelm embankments, flood fields with salt water, and make laboriously shaped fields unusable for many years. They might also blow down carefully nurtured palm orchards and destroy the homes of rich and poor alike. The Adhikaris of Cheul were a prominent landed and office-holding family through two centuries. Their everyday book or journal recorded major storms and earthquakes as well as political changes and reorganizations of the tax system.[56] In 1596, Sudak Thakur Adhikari appeared before the Sultan's tax assessor and reported that the ravages of the Portuguese in the previous three years had depopulated the region. Some people had been enslaved, some had fled to other provinces, and some died. Presumably as a result of the resulting lack of maintenance, three inlets of the sea had breached embankments, destroyed sea gates, and inundated the fields. A large expenditure would be needed to reclaim the now saline soil. The violence of man combined with the wrath of the sea had overwhelmed the small defenses around laboriously reclaimed rice fields. The petitioner's request for a temporary reduction in taxes was granted.[57]

The Adhikaris' power ended after the British survey and assessment of the Kolaba district was completed in the 1860s. This survey began the process of opening the land to standard measurement and taxation. The contrasting value of rice and other crops was exemplified by the fact that 140,000 acres of "rice land" were assessed at 4.40 rupees an acre (totaling 616,000 rupees), while 329,000 acres of "dry crop" land were rated at 0.26 rupees an acre (86,000). Garden land—that is, palm groves and special crops such as betel leaf—covered only 3,282 acres, or less than 1 percent of the taxable total. (But the groves would additionally contribute heavily to the alcohol excise.) Rice was evidently the most valuable crop, and the best land was devoted to it. Hardy and nutritious grains such as nagli and kodra were by comparison carelessly cultivated. Finally, an escape into shifting cultivation was generally open until the mid-nineteenth century. We shall see in chapter 5 that there were times when political turmoil made it an essential recourse for many settled villagers.

Elite consumption also directed elite investment. Landlord tenures were widely prevalent in rice-growing areas. On the one hand, the labor-intensive rice land encouraged and required a dense population. On the other hand, the long-term investment needed for the creation and maintenance of rice land and slow-yielding coconut and other palms needed financiers with both political power and money capital. Much rice was grown in artificially protected wetland that needed considerable initial investment. Important personages sponsored such works. So, in 1721, Tajuddin Ali Khan, the finance minister of Janjira state, sponsored the reclamation of a field in Ashtagar named "Meḍhe" that was no less than 450 bighas in area. These were not the only such instances. We have listings such as the "salt marsh in Parhā, the holder of its quit-rent, Habaskhan Paul, bought it from the Portuguese for 400 lāhārī; recently Tajuddin Ali Khan, tax collector of Ceul, made it more prosperous by building a stone embankment at the water's edge [to keep out seawater]. The reclamation was therefore named *Dīwānkhār*."[58]

Other such reclamations are also mentioned in sources. The *Kolaba Gazetteer* believed that most reclamation in that district (near Mumbai) was done between 1755 and 1780. Reclamation needed two dams: an outer and an inner. The outer dam had sluices that were kept closed in the dry season to prevent the entry of seawater but opened in the monsoon to allow excess fresh water to flow out. Land adjoining creeks was easiest to reclaim but still required high, strong embankments using stone, earth, and timber. "Two years after the embankment is complete, rice is sown in the reclaimed land in order that the decayed straw may offer a resting place and supply nourishment to grass seeds. As soon as the banking is completed, the reclaimers sublet the land in plots, but five years generally pass before any crop is raised."[59] In the aggregate, such investment meant vast expenditures of plebeian labor on the fields and reservoirs were what made rice production possible, whether on the semi-arid plateau or the humid coastal landscape.

Even if water could be had more easily, rice demanded constant field labor, usually performed by teams of servile workers, bound by debt and marginalized by caste. J. A. Mollison of the Bombay Agriculture Department noted that rice cultivation in 1900 extended across humid and arid environments alike. He was aware of the labor involved in its sustained cultivation. In almost all rice fields, he wrote, "the original surface required a certain amount of levelling and digging out . . . the excavated soil was used in filling the hollows, or in forming the embankments. On and under the ghats [mountains] on the gentle slopes of valleys and on the steeper slopes at the foot of the hills, rice beds have been formed in terraces with great ingenuity and at considerable cost."[60]

In the aggregate, therefore, adoption of a rice production system meant vast expenditures of labor on the fields and reservoirs that made rice production possible in both zones. Furthermore, the semi-arid regions of South Asia have long been known to experience much greater oscillations—sometimes decades-long—in rainfall. Dams and aqueducts built on the basis of recent experience might dry up or burst during extreme weather phases.[61] Another study was a farm in the relatively humid western part of the Deccan plateau, near Kalghatgi in 1885–86, and shows concretely how land use and marketing were driven by the demand for rice. The farm consisted of 9.5 acres, but 2.5 acres were either grass or patches of uncultivable land. The director of agriculture commented in 1885 that the holding provided the entire subsistence of the farmer and his wife. His daughters had been married out. He owned a harvest cart and four bullocks but no other cattle.

> The land is ploughed with the large 4-bullock plough (*ranti*) as soon as the crop is removed. In the hot season it is harrowed with the 4-bullock harrow (*harago kunti*) and then on the first rainfall again ploughed. The seed at the rate of 17 sers (= 47 lbs.) is drilled with the 4-coulter drill (*kurgi*) drawn by one pair of oxen at the end of April and seed covered with the *halaki* or seed harrow. When the crop is about 4 inches high it is bullock-hoed 4 times or oftener with the *yedi kunti*, between the rows to kill weeds. The rows are hand-weeded by hired labourers 10 or 20 at a time.... The late coarse grass on the headlands and embankments was cut at an agreed cost of 40 sers of paddy. One very important operation was omitted, *viz*. the mud-rolling (*hodata*). It consists of rolling the standing crop with a broad bar of wood hollowed on the lower side in the direction of its length, before the stems have hardened, while the field is full of water. Its object is two-fold. It checks the natural tendency of the crop to excessive growth of straw at the expense of the grain yield and thus corresponds to the transplantation of seedling raised in a nursery, and also keeps down weeds which have grown up since the bullock-hoeing and hand-weeding. The hodata cannot be done unless the rain is sufficient to flood the field with impounded water. In the case in point it was unavoidably omitted, with the natural result of a low proportion of grain to straw.... The rice crop is manured in alternate years.[62]

Thus, a few acres of paddy absorbed large amounts of labor: it required the constant availability of landless work teams that could be mobilized at peak season. It also needed significant animal power deployed at times when feeding oxen also needed special attention.

Landlord power endured as long as the production system was centered on the capital-intensive cultivation of rice. Tenants came to prefer the presence of a *khot* who was both landlord and moneylender. By the 1830s, the Government of Bombay found that in areas where it had ousted these *khots*, ordinary small farmer refused the permanent tenancy from the state that was common in the *desh*. "Small farmers have generally declined to accept it and prefer living under a capitalist, who can advance them the petty sums they may require for present expenditure and assist them in their cultivation."[63]

A resource—and, if needed, a refuge—for poorer farmers also lay in the stony upland and dense forest that formed the largest part of the region. Poor men who had no oxen could still till these lands by axe and fire. Near Suvarnadurg in the Konkan, one farmer surrendered his independent tenure to the village lord on the introduction of a fixed assessment by the Peshwa's government in 1810–11. He said he feared being unable to pay a regular tax because he had no plow or oxen.[64] He would presumably live by swidden and the collection of wild foods and perhaps join the landless labor force when extra workers were needed.

Even with the high grain prices around World War I, a merchant in the Pune district told an officer that "no *savkar* [banker] would sink money in even the best rice land in the West owing to the risk of damage to the land from excessive rains."[65] But peasant farmers did not make that calculation as they pursued farming as a way of life. They laboriously rebuilt channels and terraces because tax collectors could best be satisfied by growing what elite tastes demanded. "The assessment-paying crop in Azra taluka is rice, farmed for its superior quality and aroma which is eagerly purchased by merchants for export."[66]

A farm studied under colonial rule gives us a vivid picture of peasant life's adaptation to elite power mediated through the market. A small masonry reservoir at the edge of one village's lands irrigated just over six acres that formed the sole support of two Lingayat brothers and their wives. They possessed two bullocks and two buffalo. They husked their own paddy at home. It yielded 59 percent clean rice and another 12 percent broken rice and less than 9 percent bran. The family sold all its clean rice and purchased sorghum or other millet to supplement their broken rice. They even sold the bran.[67] Another rice farm was also studied in 1884–85. Most of the land (6.43 acres) was rice paddy irrigated from a reservoir. The holder considered 4.5 acres of it also capable of yielding a second crop, usually lentils. He was keenly interested in preserving the half acre of earthen berm that supported the masonry wall of the tank. He declared that he was happy to pay the land tax on it and deliberately kept it under grass for his cattle.[68]

Even in areas with a substantial, dependable rainfall, such as in Gujarat, rains usually ended before the rice crop was ready. So it was important that the soil retain water as long as the rice was likely to need it. This required the laborious capture and regulation of water supply. Embankments were built and the surface of rice beds carefully leveled so that water could be impounded and kept at a height that was adjusted as the crop grew and no more than two-thirds of the plant was ever immersed.[69]

Other important elements of elite consumption also came from humid zone plants such as cardamom, vines such as betel, and tree nuts such as areca. A whole caste of farmers came to specialize in such luxury horticulture in the heavy rainfall belt of southern Maharashtra and northern Karnataka. The Havig, a Brahman subcaste, raised cardamom, which was grown alongside areca (betel) nut palms. A fully stocked betel nut garden could have 300 to 400 cardamom plants per acre. A well-grown, healthy plant might yield up to half a pound of dry cardamoms. But the cultivation was beset with dangers, and Mollison thought the average yield was much less, often not over four *tolas*, perhaps two ounces, per plant. Spice gardens needed considerable investment to set up and a great deal of labor and attention to manage. They also drew heavily on the woodlands around them because farmers would only use carefully processed leaf mold for manure.

> They have never used manure of any other description, and have no faith that ordinary cowdung manure, oil cakes, or other concentrated manures would serve their purpose equally well. They consider that the best leaf mould manure is got from the green leaves and small succulent branches of certain trees which during the monsoon are used as litter under the feet of cattle tied during night and the greater portion of the day in sheds. This litter is freely used, five large headloads being brought daily for about twelve cattle. The litter, having absorbed the urine and dung, is removed daily or

every second day, and put in square pits which are generally about 8 feet deep. These pits are dug in situations where they catch the whole direct rainfall, which is very heavy, and possibly also a good deal of drainage water from higher levels.[70]

Cultivation of these special crops was all done manually, but so essential was manure processed by cattle that animals might be hired and fed through the monsoon season solely for the manure they would yield.

Like imperial centers, regional and trans-regional elites also generated monetization and the flow of resources across regions. Consequently, they reached more deeply into the locality. In Maharashtra, the movement of coastal Brahmans into the offices of the Peshwa and his lords in Pune led to annual caravans of oxen bearing loads of rice from their home farms to sustain their households. In 1788–89, for example, permits exempting these from the usual duty were issued to 154 persons for 3,380 ox-loads of rice.[71] There are records of feasts and ceremonies consuming tens or hundreds of thousands of *pan* leaves—doubtless with their accompaniments of lime and areca.[72]

BEASTS OF TILLAGE, BEASTS OF PILLAGE

In contrast to rice or cardamom, millets, the food of working people, rarely received much attention. Indeed, for the upper classes eating such grains was deemed equivalent to fasting. Mollison wrote of one hardy and nutritious millet that it is "ordinarily a poor man's food grain. It is also used on fast days by the middle and richer classes." Nagli was carefully tilled and transplanted only in Gujarat. Yet it could yield heavily if given resources: "a really good crop from a fertile, liberally managed field, 2,000 lbs. per acre." It was widely grown as a peasant food elsewhere and had the great virtue of staying edible after long storage. "*Nágli* will keep good if stored in underground pits for a very long time. It is recorded that it has been stored safely in Mysore for half a century."[73] That made nagli ideal for subsistence farmers of rain-fed crops for whom bountiful harvests came infrequently and unpredictably. But the elite disdained it, and such crops were wherever possible replaced with rice paddy. Peasants whose labor grew quality rice raised their own millets on hillsides tilled for three years followed by three or four years of fallow. Sometimes they sold their own good rice and bought cheaper and, as it happens, more nutritious cereals. On steeper land, brushwood was cut and burned, but it needed eight to ten years' fallow after three crops had been raised.[74]

The backbone of Maratha armies was light cavalry, which was made up of acclimated locally bred horses and peasant soldiers drawn predominantly from the *desh*—the plains of the plateau. The idea that South Asian village communities had little to do with superior power beyond the payment of taxes is false. In much of the subcontinent, horses drew on the same foods as humans: domesticated cereals, many key oilseeds, beans, and lentils in addition to grass and straw. Cereal crops were also valued because their by-products (straw, bran, oil cake) were essential food for work animals, almost entirely oxen.

The latter were essential to peasant sustenance in regions where the low-moisture regime meant low plant density per unit area. Subsistence production then required the tillage of larger areas. But plowing and harrowing was seriously constrained by narrow windows when soil would be moist enough to permit germination and maturation. It was impossible to get the land in good tilth in time to catch an unpredictable monsoon without late-summer and early monsoon tillage. That, in turn, depended on the muscle power of plow animals. This was ritually recognized in Maharashtra with a special festival in which the oxen were ceremonially worshipped with their owners prostrating themselves before them. The oxen were then ornamented and taken through the village, with those belonging to the village headman leading the procession.[75] Peasant vocabulary reflected their importance: Lakshmi (goddess of wealth) was a synonym for cattle.[76] In the 1930s, the Agriculture Department began recommending wider spacing of field sorghum in order to increase grain yields. But many farmers would not follow their advice because it made the stalks thick and woody, so that cattle refused to eat them.[77] In rice-growing lands, oxen were universally needed for "puddling" rice beds before transplanting in heavy rainfall areas. Crops were not raised solely to feed men; the reproduction of farmers needed the reproduction of their farm animals.

Village needs therefore conflicted with the demands of the great for fodder and water. Immense numbers of animals were needed for elite transport and consumption. These were predominantly ruminants that needed fodder and water daily. The former could not be transported across great distances and had to be secured locally. One area where royal and lordly power overlapped in their demands on the rural population was therefore grazing and fodder. In dry seasons, this could extend to water. For example, 1778 had been preceded by two years of drought. The only water to be found near the village of Kaloli was in a gully in the borderland with the adjoining village of Naloli. A brawl ensued when allottee of crown land in that village prevented Naloli villagers from taking their animals to drink in the gully.[78]

As vegetation depended on rain, there were periodic dry season shortages in an economy so profoundly dependent on animal power. The crop mix was adjusted to yield fodder as well as human food. One result of shortages was the rise of a market in fodder; another was its inclusion in state taxation. In the 1740s, the administrator of two districts near the city of Pune was required to deliver 20,000 bundles of grass annually as well as 5,000 bundles of jowar stalks for fodder. He was also commissioned to purchase another 25,000 bundles for 1,200 rupees.[79] It must be evident that there was already an active market in fodder resources, implying that the regime of scarcity was already in place. The buyers included peasant farmers. For example, in the month of Kartik, Shaka year 1709 (September 1787 CE), we find nine landholding peasants of the village of Pimple, Chakan subdivision borrowing a total of 10,000 bundles of millet stalks (*kadba*) valued at 250 rupees from Balaji Shankar Sonavani of Pune with the undertaking to repay in kind within Mrugshirsha, that is, within two months. They were required to deliver good quality fodder to the lender's store in Pune city. If this refers to the village of Pimple Saudagar on the Chakan road, then this involved cartage over about fourteen kilometers.[80] But then, as the acute physician and vaccinator Thomas Coats observed a few years later, "the riches of the cultivator, nay his existence, depend on his cattle, he always nurses them with great care." He also wrote that toward the end of the dry season, "grass is always scarce, and if the rains are late in falling, as seldom any provision is made for this, the cattle become extremely thin and weak, and a murrain not infrequently gets among them at this time, and destroys many; which reduces the cultivators to beggary." Coats noted that, as in the 1740s, the superiority of jowar straw as forage led to it being more widely cultivated near the city. All the uncultivated land of the village he studied was used as a common pasture. It was clearly land unfit for tillage, for Coats noted that nowhere in the common land was the soil more than a few inches deep. A few decades later, the forest officer Alexander Gibson reported that in the western mountains nachni straw was purchased by those who valued their work oxen, as it was more nutritious than other plant stalks. The grain had to be kept for human consumption.[81]

Inequalities of power affect the control of biotic resources. Chapter 2 discussed the ecological impact of the elephant as a central appurtenance of kingdoms in South Asia. However, elephants were not the only animals deployed. Vast numbers of oxen and smaller contingents of camels transported and supplied armies and formed part of royal entourages. Horses had always been important, but by Mughal times cavalry was the key arm of all armies across West and South Asia. All these beasts were also fed out of the resources of the countryside, both wild and cultivated. Some products could, of course, be provided from far afield—cereals, for example. But fodder and water could not be moved over great distances. They had to be secured locally, even at the expense of the farming community.

The small needs of local villagers and townspeople could be met under a regime of locally managed commons, but closure was necessary when the kings and lords appeared on the scene. War horses and elephants and the panoply of animals that enforced and displayed royal power often preempted resources. One result was the creation of special reserves for grazing and firewood from which peasants were excluded. William H. Tone, an officer in the Peshwa's service, also tells us that cavalry contingents had portions of jungle (meaning uncultivated land) allotted to them where they normally maintained their animals. Such preserves were known under various names in the arid parts of the subcontinent. I suggest that the reason behind the absence of fodder production on arable land was the difficulty of preventing the rights of free pasturage and princely purveyance from being exercised in it. Grass and hay meadows were conserved in the eighteenth century but not by the peasants. This use of land was the preserve of powerful families, whose reserved lands were termed *kuran*. When British administration asked noble houses in Kolhapur to list their lands, many included income from grass fodder cut on special reserves. The Nimbalkar family even kept two bighas of good land under grass and secured 6,000 bundles annually from it. The royal physician Mirkhan held land in various places and listed the cash, grain, or fodder received from each holding.[82] Ruling houses also held such lands, and many were subsequently taken over by the colonial regime and came to form the core of Forest Department lands on arid plateau of

Western India. I now illustrate the expedients that might culminate in the formation of such permanent reserves.

Ibrahim Khan had charge of a unit of the Peshwa's cavalry. Anticipating shortages, he issued an order to all village headmen in the tract east of Pune, demanding that all meadow lands should be reserved for his needs. Cavalry units would obviously claim priority over local requirements. In another news report of that period, we learn that men from a nearby military camp simply came and cut down all the standing crops, both rain-fed and irrigated, in the village of Karathi in Khandesh. The villagers then thought of abandoning the village and settling elsewhere. Troops on the march not only trampled but also grazed large tracts of arable land. Encampments exhausted or monopolized local water sources.

Such closures might be temporary, or they might become permanent: in that case, these lands would become the above-mentioned private or government meadows. Many of these formed the core of Forest Reserves in the nineteenth century. The creation of one such reserve was ordered by the Peshwa Bajirao in 1758. The order noted that the court often marched through the district of Karde-Ranjangaon and needed wood and fodder. So the local officer should find a village (preferably a partly cultivated one) assessed at four or five hundred rupees in tax, knock down most of it, allow a little cultivation to remain, and convert the remaining lands into a *kuran*. In other cases disputed lands were taken over. So, for instance, the villages of Kale and Nandgaon quarreled over a piece of land, and it lay untilled for some forty or fifty years. Thereupon the Peshwa simply turned it into state property and appointed a manager, warning the headmen of both villages not to trespass into the government *kuran*. Both the Peshwa's government and leading gentry families possessed numbers of meadows of this type, all probably created by excluding local villagers in the way described above. Apart from supplying grass, wood, and bamboo, such areas sometimes served as hunting reserves or parks . Villagers in the vicinity of such reserves would be called up for compulsory labor in them—so, for example, the peasants of several districts were required in 1763–64 to cut and supply 484,000 bundles of grass; those in other districts were exempted from their obligation to provide 1,247,500 bundles but required to pay 4 rupees per 1,000 bundles in lieu of the service. Sometimes these reserves were made available to the peasants as well—for example, after the Nizam of Hyderabad's army had burned many villages in the Junnar area, the peasants were allowed to take 100,000 bundles of grass as well as wood and bamboo from the Randhervadi *kuran* to rebuild their homes.[83]

This regime persisted into the nineteenth century. Arthur Wellesley (later Duke of Wellington) moved out of Mysore to the conquest of the Marathas in early 1803. His military papers show him to be constantly concerned about logistics. Apart from rice, meat, and arrack for the soldiers, which his unlimited supply of funds from the East India Company's treasuries allowed him to buy, he was also always concerned about the sustenance of the oxen and horses of his military establishment. For example, preparing his movement into lands that had already been plundered, he instructed executive officers and the officers of the detachment in general, "to urge their followers to cut the roots of the grass upon which alone the existence of the cattle depends." There was clearly a common practice by which military units would post guards in particular villages and requisition all the fodder that could be found. Wellesley sought to prevent this and ordered that if there was any dry forage anywhere near the camp, the manager of the government draught cattle was to have it first. All other guards should withdraw when his were posted. Arriving in Pune at the end of April, Wellesley immediately purchased fodder from the stores of the Resident (English envoy). The grass-cutters accompanying the army, he explained, were still on the road. In this region, fodder was cut at the beginning of summer in the hills some thirty miles away. It therefore sold at high prices.[84] This was not a new development: Harji Naik, headman of a troop of scouts and messengers, moved to Pune with his following circa 1763. They brought one cow with them, only to discover that no fodder was available. Harji petitioned for hay from the government store, but none was to be had. Instead, he was given a warrant to demand 500 bundles of hay from any meadow within ten *kos* (about thirty miles) of the city but for one year only.[85]

On the dry plateau, therefore, military establishments competed directly with peasant needs. Villagers lived by raising crops in a harsh and unyielding environment. Monsoon rains might fall short or be maldistributed. Blights might strike the crop. Illnesses could destroy the essential work animals or incapacitate the workers themselves. Only through a deep understanding of local geography and the ever-changing dynamic of plants and soils was it possible to grow enough to survive. In almost all the subcontinent—and especially in its semi-arid lands—oxen were central to farming and to survival.

Indian agriculture, and indeed Indian society, has long depended on the locally domesticated zebu (*Bos indicus*). Before the advent of the tractor, this species was the major source of power for agriculture and transport, and agrarian life would have been difficult to sustain without it. The monsoon was scanty and unpredictable. Rain-fed crops had low yields per acre, so farmers needed to prepare large areas for tillage. The fields had to be prepared to receive the rain by plowing in advance and seed sown in the short period when soil conditions permitted germination. If the seedlings withered or were washed away by heavy storms, then the land had to be resown. Oxen were also used for sowing, sometimes for weeding and always for threshing out grains and seeds. Irrigation from wells again needed oxen to draw up the water. Bovines recycled cellulose indigestible by man into animal power, plant food, and human fuel. Apart from grazing, they consumed the inferior parts of domesticated plants. Thus, residues such as cottonseeds, the "cake" left after oilseeds had been crushed for oil, and so forth were the only supplementary feeding they usually received. Their flesh was eaten more often than admitted, and their hides were essential for footwear and as components of farm and military equipment.

The greatest part of overland trade was also carried by oxen (supplemented by camels). Road conditions usually precluded wheeled vehicles; such goods as did not move by water were carried overland by droves of bullocks. While the dairy yield of the village cattle was small, professional herdsmen reared both cows and buffalo for milk and durable products, such as clarified butter. The fodder and grazing needs for all these beasts made (as we shall see) significant demands on the environment and led to active contests over its control.

As is well known, field armies of the time were assemblages of contingents raised and disciplined by individual commanders. Their provisioning was similarly decentralized. Commanders still recruited and managed their men and arranged for their maintenance at their different stations. Maratha military organization was even more decentralized. Lands were parceled out among various commanders. Writing in the 1790s, Tone observed that a large part of the Maratha armies was composed of groups of cavalrymen who brought their own horses. Each of them had a certain portion of jungle allotted to him "where he pastures his cattle: here he and his family reside; and his sole occupation when not on actual service is increasing his pagah or troop by breeding out of his mares, of which the Maratta cavalry almost entirely consist. It is by no means uncommon for a silladaur [cavalryman] to enter the service with one mare and within a few years to be able to muster a very respectable pagah [cavalry force]."[86]

But in all cases, armies and camp-followers drew on the biotic resources of the peopled countryside and the villages they moved through. It was here that the lordly gaze and peasant eye surveyed and grasped for the same objects. The most precious of these were water and fodder. Demands could fall heavily on peasant localities. We have a plaint from the village of Kadus written in 1736 when several powerful Maratha commanders were posted in the area:

> The honourable Rajshri Senapati's camp-followers go daily from the main camp to Talegaon. They turn elephants and camels into the fields, and they get into the irrigated lands and steal. The Lord (Peshwa) may [should] command on this matter. Rajshri Mahadji Govind has been granted the village of Turakdi. He has just reserved its grazing lands; he beat (our) cowherds; to the north Rajshri Mahadji Govind has reserved the grazing, and that of Sayegaon is reserved by Rajshri Tryambakrao Mama. Where will the people of Kadus take their cattle to graze, from which forest will they fetch their wood? It is not possible to carry on the life of the settlement without touching the border tracts of the adjoining villages. The Lord is able to command.[87]

In this milieu, even the powerful had to exercise a constant vigilance to ensure the conservation of their demarcated reserves. For example, a meadow had been reserved for the state elephants near the village of Vade, Vandan subdivision. The bold headman of that village, Sakhoji Navlage, not only turned his cattle into the meadow but assaulted its keeper when he protested. Sakhoji was summoned to the court. Another village headman was found to have plowed up meadowland allocated to the royal herdsmen and had to be warned to desist.[88]

The extent to which this affected productivity may be seen from a document prepared in 1773–74. This year saw major factionalism within the Maratha political system, with the consequent assemblage of huge armies around the capital. Probably in order to preclude the destruction of the tax base through depredations on the peasants, the Pune government ordered Balaji Krishna to take charge of all meadowlands, government and private, "within 15 or 20 *kos* of the city," to arrange for the cutting of 300,000 bundles of grass, store half of this supply, and send the rest to the city. In addition to this, he was to supply a large quantity of both firewood and charcoal. It is noteworthy that the order prescribed the target yield of fodder and fuel but was hazy about the extent of the lands from which it might be procured. This was not a "map view" of the terrain.

The scheme recognized that influential owners, powerful men, could not be denied all access. The order declared that if they took more than their domestic consumption, they were to be charged market rates for it. Biotic resources were therefore eminently seen as quasi-property, open to arbitrary seizure and use. It seems that the supply within this radius was estimated equal to 50,000 bullock rations or 37,500 horse rations, giving us some idea of the limited extent of meadowland protected and available; 300,000 bundles would be 675 tons of grass. If we follow Sykes in estimating the *kos* at two English miles, or 3.2 kilometers, a radius of fifteen *kos* would include an area of over 7,000 square kilometers. Less than half could possibly have been under cultivation. Yet the surplus grass available was only equal to the total yield of perhaps 2.5 square kilometers (250 ha) of good meadowland cut and carried. Even this limited yield was to be achieved only by hiring 175 guards for a year to control these lands.[89] It is clear that there were limits to the power of overlords. The persistence of the many and poor and the defiance of the few and powerful could never be permanently suppressed. Continual contests for biotic resources shaped the environment.

This chapter showed how empire builders needed gentry participation in extracting and sharing the agrarian surplus. But the presence of these essential elites also proved a barrier to imperial surveillance and control. I then demonstrated how the creation of local record keepers formed part of an information strategy imposed from above but subverted from below. In addition, the tastes and needs of these intermediate elites changed the face of the land by slanting production to their fulfillment. Finally, I considered how subalterns developed alternative subsistence strategies that evaded elite control.

FOUR

The Village and Its Inhabitants

We are not a global village, but a globe of many villages.
PAUL WARDE | 2018

THE VILLAGE COMMUNITY IS OFTEN CONSIDERED AN ANCIENT traditional feature of South Asian life. But I will show that the organized village was not an unthought result of rural life or of the functional needs of agricultural life in thinly populated countryside. Rather, it existed as a dynamic balance between external power and internal cohesion. In some areas, only the persistent princely and imperial gaze into and demands upon the countryside created an administrative village with little internal coherence. Elsewhere subaltern cohesion from below emerged from defensive resistance and was co-opted for elite manipulation. In such regions—and Western India was one—village cohesion often proved more durable than royal authority.

In the twentieth century, there were large areas of British India where the village existed only as an administrative unit. Actual settlement, or even the unit of collective action, could be larger or smaller. The social anthropologist McKim Marriott used printed sources to estimate the difference between what he called the "Effective village"—meaning a socially interacting unit—with the "Census," or administrative village. But none of these might exist visibly on the ground. Households that lived near one another might not function as a community: households scattered over the land could still work cohesively for common needs.[1]

HUMAN SETTLEMENT AND VILLAGE SETTLEMENTS

Two thousand years ago, the early imperial statecraft of the Sanskrit *Arthashastra* already normalized the South Asian village and its headman. These forms of residence and organization have been axiomatic ever since, yet the nucleated village settlement is not always a spontaneous organization. In some areas, it was a result of the pressures of state organization. Human settlements are limited by environmental possibilities and sociopolitical needs. Foragers must move to their resources, and pastoralists must accompany their flocks to seasonal pastures. But tilled fields require attention and protection. Even so, agriculture does not always require settlement in nucleated clusters of houses or "villages." Minimizing travel time between home and field is one rationale for dispersal. Indeed, sometimes rugged terrain, thick woodland, and the need to periodically fallow upland swidden fields led to houses scattered singly or in clusters as needed to guard and till the fields.[2]

But apart from optimizing access to the fields, settlers must allow for human and animal threats too. When Thomas Motte traveled west through central Odisha in 1766, he was struck by the layout of small villages on the way. The houses, he wrote, "were placed in a regular street, close to each other." They had no door or window except in front. At each end of the street was a fence of bamboos knit together. "This serves to protect the inhabitants and their cattle from bears, wolves and tygers" that came down from the mountains nightly in search of prey.[3] Yet the location and harvest season in farming areas was easy to discover. Raids could be planned in advance. Babur records the decision in his council that they raid one Pathan region earlier in the season when there would be grain to plunder.[4]

Where human predation was the major concern, mobility and concealment by scattering allowed the exploitation of micro-environments and opacity to aggressors. Pastoralists were adept at this. For pastoralists, an optimal strategy might be seasonal concentration where and when water and plants for grazing were abundant, followed by dispersal as resources ran down. This was the subsistence strategy adopted by the Baluch peoples who inhabited the arid borderlands and lower Indus plain but also ranged far into southwestern Iran.[5] The legacy of such patterns of life is the several important towns named simply "Dera," meaning encampment, found on both banks of the Indus River.

In the early twentieth century, the Government of Bombay sought to install a village police system in the lower Indus province of Sind. J. W. P. Muir-Mackenzie, then commissioner of Sind, pointed to the large number of very small settlements as an obstacle to having a village-based police. Hamlets could never sustain one, and the village in Sind was just a tax-collecting unit imposed from above. These units consisted "of a cluster of hamlets rather than villages." For every settlement with a hundred or more inhabitants, he added, there were twenty smaller ones. Likewise, P. R. Cadell, collector of the Sukkur district in 1903, explained the settlement pattern in Sind through a combination of natural and social factors: "In Sind, the village is less the unit of administration than in perhaps any other part of India. The pastoral habits of the people, the nomadic character of the Baluch tribes up to recent times, the liability of large areas to floods, the desire for privacy of the higher families, the desire of leading men to be the eponymous founders of their own villages—all these reasons have caused the number of villages and hamlets to multiply and have prevented the growth of the village community."[6]

At the other ecological margin, one marked not by aridity but humidity—the Ganges Delta—the village had an equally fleeting existence. The periodically flooded terrain meant that many settlements were clusters of houses built on patches of artificially elevated land, surrounded by trees and separated by ponds, rice fields, and wetlands. British officials had discovered by 1800 that the *mauza*, or tax village, in Bengal was merely an administrative unit. "It answers to the word parish more nearly than to any other English term; for several villages or hamlets may stand in the same Mauza; and on the contrary the same town will sometimes include several Mauzas." The autonomous village organization found in the western half of the subcontinent did not exist in the landlord-dominated rice-producing lands of the east. The only vestige of it that the civil servant Henry Colebrooke in 1804 remarked in the lower Gangetic plain was in Bihar. There the post of headman had sometimes become hereditary and conferred a permanent tenure of some land as a perquisite. The real sociopolitical unit was the house of the superior landlord, or zamindar. Village record keepers (where they existed) were the zamindar's appointees. This was probably the situation wherever a superior lord existed. These men were also dependent on the latter for their pay and perquisites. It is therefore not surprising that the landlord's agent was the most important functionary in the typical Bengal or Bihar village.[7]

Thus, in both areas, the landlord, chieftain, or "little king" governed without creating the "traditional village."

Whether in the densely populated humid lowlands of Kerala, or Bengal, or in arid upper Sind, the British administrative village was imposed across functional patterns of sociopolitical life determined by the interaction of ecology and power. At another extreme, in the Bhil-inhabited upland areas of southern Rajasthan, houses were widely scattered along the forested hills but united politically to face external authority. The anthropologist G. M. Carstairs wrote that to a stranger, houses appeared to be scattered at random all over the countryside, but they were usually on a hilltop or rising slope that commanded an extensive view of the approaches to it. Bhil villages in southern Rajasthan were identifiable not by residence but by affiliation to a headman, *Mukhi*. In the 1950s, he still represented "the village in all dealings with other villages or with the Ruler's representatives."[8] That would include the management of crime, the provision of labor, and the collection of taxes. Thus, the village was universally a British-imposed political-administrative entity and not invariably a co-residential community.

In the open plains of the peninsular plateau, or Deccan, the need for collective defense might, however, require the creation of nucleated and walled villages. Clustering was sometimes needed for the collective provision of water. The government statistical reporter Thomas Marshall remarked in 1820 that in eastern Karnataka, extensive arid plains with fertile soil could only be permanently inhabited by digging masonry wells at enormous expense, with cattle having to be driven five or six miles to the nearest river to drink each day.[9] Villages would then be centered around the wells whose construction and maintenance was essential to the life of the community.

KINGSHIP AND THE IMAGINING OF VILLAGES

The idea that a monarchical domain was composed of people ordered into villages had a deep genealogy, yet kingship was in reality overlaid on a diversely settled countryside. Indeed, the village was more ubiquitous in thought than on the ground. Its apparent universality as a unit of rural life is in great measure an artifact of colonial and precolonial governance. The idea of the village as part of a perfect hierarchy of nested governance had appealed to ruling elites long before the British *Imperial Gazetteer* was compiled. Would-be emperors had, from the *Arthashastra* onward, dreamed of a perfect hierarchy, with obedient peasants at its base ordered in identical units. Secluded from entertainment and distraction, they would produce "treasure, labor, goods, grains and juices." Each would have an official in charge who would be paid in minor dues in kind by the villagers.[10] That last clause betrays the nature of this entity. This official was clearly a local chief who was drafted into the imperial hierarchy; alternatively, he might be a royal appointee who entrenched his position into a village domain.

I argue that the need for such a social position arose because agents of empire lacked the information to penetrate each individual household and tax the multiple activities of each farm or workshop. If the village did not exist, it was necessary for the state to invent it. But the village as an autonomous entity at the lowest rung of kingly governance represented an administrative failure. It was an intermediate authority needed to obviate administrative ignorance by the imposition of collective responsibility. In many parts of the country, crops had to be brought to a central place, a collective threshing floor. It was this that enabled the overlord's agent to estimate the output and insist that his master's demands be met before any of it could be taken away by those who had grown it.[11] Collective responsibility for crimes and taxes was functionally necessary because the apparatus of governance was unable to reach down or to identify the individual culprit or taxpayer. As political scientist James Scott observed in 1998, "the modern state, through its officials, attempts with varying success to create a terrain and a population with precisely those standardized characteristics that will be easiest to monitor, count, assess, and manage."[12]

This culminated in the records of the high British period, when exactly 728,605 villages were enumerated as extant in the British Empire in India circa 1909. But the compilers of the *Imperial Gazetteer* were constrained to add that only some were actual named units of residence, while others were merely areas demarcated by government survey. They were no more than administrative units.[13] The village cluster (pargana) and then the village had been opaque nodes in state information networks for millennia, but the tenacious colonial regime was seeking to open it to gaze and record.

VILLAGE AND PARGANA (CANTON) IN WESTERN INDIA

Extensive records of taxation, both in cash and kind, have survived from the eighteenth century when regional states had partly penetrated the structures of rural life. Accessible higher authorities could draw money and information out of the locality. The tussle between superior power and local tenacity was manifested in the making of hereditary post or *watan*, a term best translated as patrimony. These existed at the level of the village cluster or *pargana* where the superior *deshmukh* served as equivalent to the village headman.[14] Claimants to specific hereditary rights might petition seeking the exclusion of outsiders. Finally, the village was composed of people, but people combined with rights to land and its usufruct. Villagers feuded over their claims; itinerants contested one another's rights. Thomas Coats noted that boundaries might be indistinguishable to strangers but yet carefully watched by each village community. Village headmen knowing that divine displeasure would strike false witness yet might undertake solemn ordeals to defend their village's claim.[15]

In 1950, the historian R. V. Oturkar published a rich selection of documents that bear on rural life at many levels. The documents in Oturkar's collection originated in the office of the hereditary registrar and accountant (*deshpande*) of Saswad subdivision and reflect the tensions and disputes in local society.[16] Saswad subdivision lay a few miles south of the important city of Pune, occupying the plains of a small valley, closed off by the Sahyadri mountain range to the west and opening into the flat open lands of the Dakhan plateau to the east. The strategic hillfort of Purandar was located in the hills overlooking the plain, and Saswad was a subdivision of the lands dependent on Purandar. The stable monsoon climate permitted the unirrigated cultivation of millets, oilseeds, and wheat. Vegetables, cereals, and a little sugarcane might be grown under irrigation, either from hill streams or from wells. In 1825–26, when a comprehensive census was taken at the instance of W. H. Sykes, Saswad reportedly contained 7,088 inhabitants, living in 1,541 households; 747 of these were classified as "cultivators"—meaning landholders directly assessed to tax. There were also 106 households of shopkeepers and traders, and 59 households of weavers and various other craftsmen. Though this was primarily an agricultural economy, trade was not an insignificant activity. There were 1,748 plow bullocks but also 312 pack oxen. Apart from the fixed shops, periodic markets and fairs also offered opportunities for trade. These linked the villagers with regional market networks. The political economy of the pargana framed the life of the village.[17] But Saswad's hereditary officers were incorporated into the larger structure of the Maratha government. It was possible for authorities there to demand statistical details—for example, a nominal roll of artisans and tradespeople such as cloth merchants, weavers, jewelers, money-changers, and sweetmeat makers was demanded overnight by the Peshwa's government.[18]

THE MAHARASHTRIAN VILLAGE IN CULTURE AND ECONOMY

The idea of the village as a social and agronomic unit in India can be traced back to the first Indic theorists of empire. When the British began to consider the government of their new conquests in Peninsular India, they thought that the whole country was divided into monadic villages whose borders met so that the entire habitable landscape had been occupied. Mountstuart Elphinstone declared in 1821, "In whatever point of view we examine the Native government in the Deccan, the first and most important feature is the division into villages, or townships. These communities contain in miniature all the elements of a state within themselves, and are almost sufficient to protect their members if all other governments were withdrawn. . . . Each village has a portion of ground attached to it, which is committed to the management of the inhabitants. The boundaries are carefully marked, and jealously guarded."[19] The idea of well-established village governments also served their idea that India possessed a well-structured native society that only needed sound British governance to function harmoniously again. The limits of this concept were discovered early, but such caveats were ignored. It was a powerful and administratively convenient idea. The new imperial regime set about realizing it on the ground, at least in areas where it had not retreated from the locality (the Permanent Settlement areas).

The first step in the making of a village as a territorial unit was the demarcation of boundaries. The *Arthashastra*'s demarcation of boundaries clearly drew on extant folk practice. It recommended that junctions of village boundaries should be marked "a river, a hill, a forest, a band of pebbles, a cave, a dike, a Śamī tree, a Śālmalī tree, or a milk tree."[20] Several of these are obviously impermanent, and their renewal would depend on the tenacity of community memory. The author was clearly prescribing folk practice. More importantly, the compilers recognized that the details of the land were unknowable without local concurrence. While the grant might endure as long as the sun and moon, landmarks would have to be renewed through the generations. The knowledge of local inhabitants was decisive. The *Arthashastra* stated that elders, or those knowledgeable about the boundary, should declare what the markers were and then point out the entire line. The king had no other record.[21]

So the top-down grid had to build on the bottom-up one, the local geography known only to residents. The humble had pragmatic geographies too. These adequately enabled people who had to traverse the earth in their localities operated by tracks, signs, and landmarks. Their knowledge was also all that was available to higher authorities before the British trigonometrical surveys and permanent boundary markers of the mid-nineteenth century.

I illustrate my argument by a comparison of two records. One is a donative record from peninsular India in the late eleventh century that I traced through the reference in Gole's *Indian Maps and Plans*. The boundaries of a village granted to Brahmans were defined by natural features and landmarks. I quote part of it to show how it clearly depended entirely on local knowledge provided by the inhabitants: "The eastern boundary is clearly discerned; on the south-east is the stream well known as the Imguṇī; then is the southeasterly bank of the tank called Gōpāla, which is altered with stones; next is the southern bank of the Gundi tank and thence the stone-heap; then, on the border of the boulder called Jambaka is the Kadamba tree; then on top of the raised spot, are two banyan trees with their roots intertwined" and so on.[22]

This type of mental map seems to have persisted to the last years of Maratha rule. My second example comes from the collection of documents titled *Sanadāpatreñ*. This contains a long eighteenth-century document recording a bitter boundary dispute between three villages that lasted for at least a century under three different governments. The boundary was finally described and marked at twenty-seven places, of which the first is partly illegible. Omitting the first and starting from the north, the second marker was a memorial stone on a mound, the third a large rock next to the road and so on. The twenty-seventh was the sandy spot under the *sami* tree where three paths met.[23] Very clearly, only locals would have been able to identify these landmarks. Therefore, whether in the coastal lands of the Portuguese or the Maratha-ruled uplands, the administrative gaze looked through local eyes.

Locals also invoked kingly authority. Villages quarreled over boundaries, lineages feuded over hereditary posts, cousins brawled over small slights, village servants neglected their duties, and individuals insulted or injured their fellows—all these issues were frequently carried up to the district administration or even to the Peshwa's court at Pune.[24] When complete outsiders received lands, they might demand stronger local attestations and more permanent markers. In 1776–77, the assembled gentry and headmen of the village of Kadni, today's North Karnataka, gathered to attest a grant made to Mukund Tirko who had saved the village from an army preparing to plunder it. The Peshwa then granted him the right to display an ornate umbrella and a portion of land to support the honor. Then all the villagers and village servants gathered to mark the hereditary allotment from the field to the south of the road to Tavarkheda and marked it with boundary stones. They promised that it would endure as long as the sun and moon shone. Muslims, Lingayats, and Brahmans were all sworn to respect it.[25]

VILLAGE SITE AND VILLAGE COMMUNITY

The pargana or canton such as Saswad was a self-conscious, organized cluster of villages.[26] I now turn to its constituent units. T. N. Atre was raised in a village setting and joined the subordinate civil service in the Bombay Presidency in the late nineteenth century. He rose to the senior rank of *mamlatdar*, officer in executive charge of a taluka, a subdivision of a British district. He clearly acquired a reputation for understanding regional conditions. Some time after 1910, he was selected to assist R. E. Enthoven, an officer who was then preparing a three-volume ethnographic compilation on the tribes and castes of the Bombay Presidency that appeared in 1917. A man of scholarly interests, Atre also began writing his own ethnographic study. This study was published in 1915 under the title *Gāñv-Gāḍā*—roughly translatable as "village wagon." The title sought to capture the metaphor of the village as a sturdy, slow-moving vehicle with many specialized parts.

Atre's book has been reprinted several times and is widely recognized as a classic of Indian rural sociology. Its most striking feature is that although he was obviously thoroughly conversant with British-style statistical knowledge, the book addresses the village as essentially a human community of specialized occupational castes. He cited the English conservative thinker Edmund Burke to argue that schemes of social improvement had to originate in indigenous institutions and not from the utopian schemes of the intelligentsia. He added that in India, this required an understanding of the age-old village community. Pointing to the small number of Indian cities with more than 100,000 people, he proclaimed the village as *the* major component of Indian society in his time. Succumbing to a bias that most scholars experience, he also assumed that the strongly self-conscious Western Indian village was typical of the whole country.

Atre is an excellent source for his own region and for the outlook of the substantial peasants with whom he identified. For him, the village was centrally a community of farmers. The village's rural and agricultural characters are frequently mentioned but only in the context of the actions of groups or individuals. We may contrast this with the earlier pathbreaking study published by Coats in 1823 in *Transactions of the Literary Society of Bombay* and subtitled "In illustration of the institutions, resources &c. of the Marratta cultivators." Coats began by describing the boundaries and surface area of his village and its division into arable and pasture viewed by a visitor coming toward the cluster of houses surrounded by a low mud wall. This clearly mirrored his own arrival and was perhaps a visualization intended for a European reader who had never seen Western India at all. Marshall, another contributor to the same volume, began his geographical account by describing the shape of the pargana of Jambusar in Gujarat. It was, he wrote, an "irregular square" with an area of perhaps "240 or 250 square miles."[27] Both Coats and Marshall evidently had a map notion of the world, even if they did not possess actual maps of their objects of study.

Atre, however, had a *social* understanding of what made a village. He began by quoting a Sanskrit verse defining a village as being a settlement of affluent farmers with many farm laborers and located on fertile land. He then went on to describe the two major parts of a village as the core settlement and the borderland (*śivār*). The latter often described farmland that shaded into woodland. Borders were not linear, as they were for Coats or Marshall; rather, they were zonal. In this respect, Atre was closer to the villagers' view of their landscape. The village core, often walled, was sometimes termed *pāṇḍhrī*, the "white," in contrast to the "black," which referred to tilled land.

Tilled land, Atre wrote, had several synonyms: "the black," "mother-black" (suggesting that the black earth fed the village as a mother would), *rāṇ* (also used of woodland or waste land), and borderland (*śivār*). The continuity of field and woodland is shown by a secondary meaning of *śivār* in Molesworth's nineteenth-century dictionary: it was "a trip into the jungle to bring wood."[28] I have seen many historical documents in which *pāṇḍhrī* refers to the village community as a whole.[29] Atre, however, also saw it as originating in the selection of water-repellent "white" soil for the village sites because it did not become muddy in the rains, unlike the absorbent black soil that is suitable for farming. Atre was also aware of caste identities as shaping residence; thus, Dalit village servants such as Mahars were often required to build their huts outside the village wall. Less impure tribal communities were usually settled near the village gateway, or even outside the wall altogether. But having an allotted house site anywhere was a marker of permanent membership of the village community. Many deeds granting a share of village office included a specific house site as part of it. Important personages resided in fortified citadel at the core of the village site.

It must be obvious that villagers had "mental maps" of their village and also, by default, of neighboring villages. Such maps were based on landmarks, both human and natural just as the field boundaries and property maps were.

While the village site was perceived by authorities and its residents as a specifically human community, the lands outside its wall or boundary shaded into the "wild," but in a more graduated way. This was where crops were grown, cattle grazed, minor produce was gathered, villagers went to defecate, and itinerants camped. Worthy visitors might enter the habitation area and stay in the village "hall," or *Cāvaḍi*, or in the village temple. The village bounds were also defended by its local gods. In a valuable sociological study of extra-village communities, Prabhakar Mande emphasized the enduring importance of its boundaries. "Even now [1983], a wedding party that is traveling in bullock-carts breaks a coconut as offering to the gods of the village before crossing the boundary into their land."[30]

H. E. Goldsmid, G. Wingate, and D. Davidson attempted a new survey of parts of Maharashtra in the 1840s. They began by trying to mark out village boundaries before surveying and assessing the individual fields. But they found that disputes between adjoining villages were numerous. Their existence prevented the cultivation of extensive and often valuable tracts of land. Many disputes went back to time immemorial, so that the land in dispute only served as contested grazing ground for the cattle of neighboring villages. "The occurrence of cases of disputed boundaries in the course of the detailed survey of the village, has caused more interruption to the work than perhaps all other sources of delay combined." The survey's superintendents therefore hoped to settle these summarily and install durable boundary marks that would prevent disputes from arising in future.[31] This was a radically new mapping of landscape, one that excluded local knowledge for the future.

Boundary disputes such as those Wingate encountered could be violent. Lower-grade land was often used in common by adjoining villages. In 1702 CE, the prosperous little town of Saswad sent its cows to graze in the woodlands (*rān*) of other villages in the month of Sravan (at the beginning of the wet season), and Saswad town officials were ordered to pay an appropriate grazing fee.[32] There was a long-standing boundary dispute between the town and the adjoining village of Bhivdi. When Saswad cattle were found grazing in woodland claimed by Bhivdi, its villagers came out and impounded the animals. Saswad's farmers came to recover them, whereupon the Bhivdi men came out armed with spears and swords. The men of Saswad, alarmed at this show of force, invoked the authority of the Padshah (then Aurangzeb) and, more pertinently, the nearby fort commandant Khanchandji. Nonetheless, the Bhivdi men assaulted them and inflicted a sword cut on Dharma Mahar.[33] His presence was probably not accidental: a Mahar Dalit usually held the post of village watchman. Their evidence was the most authoritative in boundary disputes between villages.

Nor was Bhivdi's pugnacity unique. Thus, there was a long-standing boundary dispute between the village of Pargàu and Kaḍegàu. Finally, the latter offered to undergo an ordeal to prove their claim. Babrata, son of Janka, *virtikar*, or hereditary watan-holding Mahar, underwent the ordeal of picking up a piece of hot iron. His hand was blistered by it. The people of Pargàu were declared to have proved their claim, and papers to that effect were drawn up. Infuriated, the losers gathered to the number of thirty to forty horsemen and five hundred foot soldiers. They then attacked the worthies who had gathered for the tribunal and killed or wounded several of them. At least three, the complaint ran, were killed in cold blood while pleading for mercy.[34]

The boundary also marked the village as a living community whose membership had deep social value. This is exemplified in the long struggle of the Pendse lineage to establish that Murdi, a hamlet near the larger coastal settlement of Anjanvel, was an independent community and not just a suburb of the latter. In 1757, Balaji Krishna Pendse submitted a statement to establish his claim that it was a distinct community. The first evidence adduced was that it had its own hereditary functionaries. Beyond the Pendse lineage, which he claimed held the hereditary post of *Mahajan*, the Marathes held that of *vartak*. The priestly posts of *dharmadhikari* and *upadhye* belonged to the Vidwans lineage, and the Bhanjoshis occupied the *joshi* (astrologer) position. He then went on to list the major village temples and noted that one was to a *gramdevi*, the tutelary goddess of the village and custodian of the land. The existence of that shrine was an indication of the separate existence of a village community. Only after laying out the social geography of his claims did he describe physical boundaries by listing: to the Northeast Sukondi, the east Kongle, to the south salt marshes and an inlet of the sea, the west the roadway and the rivulet from the river Rewa that joined the salt marsh.[35]

As far as everyday life was concerned, popular geography navigated by landmarks and features known to the community. E. Valentine Daniel in an anthropological study of a Tamil village in the 1970s asked residents to draw maps of the village. Many attempted to sketch the official cadastral rendering from memory, but a folk geography also persisted alongside it. Daniel was able recover that as well and noted that it worked with landmarks of social and symbolic importance.[36]

FIELDS AND TAXES

Beyond knowing boundaries, farmers needed a close-grained understanding of the soil and climate that fed them. W. H. Sykes commanded a battalion of the Bombay Native Infantry before he was deputed to conduct a statistical survey of the recently conquered Deccan provinces in 1825–29. He was fluent in Marathi and spoke with many peasants in the course of his tours of the Deccan. His reports are therefore a way of tapping peasant views of the land they inhabited. The "people themselves," he wrote, "have a multitude of appellations for different gradations of soil." Driven by the same officious urge to simplify and systematize that had possessed earlier officials, he then declared that all of these could be reduced to the three classes: best, middling, and worst. These divisions were then applied to the three kinds of cultivable land, which (in order of quality) were the three classes each of black, red, and upland, or *māl*, thus yielding nine classes total.[37]

Here Sykes was drawing on the simplified ordering of Indian revenue officials who, required to assess on the basis of inspection and measurement, found it easiest to classify all land in a few classes and then impose a flat rate on each class. Old regime adjustments were sometimes overt—documents declare them to be the effect of *rad-badal* (negotiation). In one example, land was said to fall into three classes of regular land assessed at 5, 4, and 3 rupees per bigha respectively. Some additional types of land were assessed at lower rates.[38] Orders issued from the center might be "translated" into local measures. Thus, the regional lord titled Pant Amatya accepted a village petition asking that a land grant be made to the son of a man killed in battle. The Amatya ordered five tax-free bighas to be given him. But the document then additionally described the grant in local measures of rice. That was presumably how the villagers labeled their rice fields.[39] Adjustments were sometimes also covert, for example, by changing the size of land measures to yield a workable total assessment. In practice, an aggregate would often be demanded from the tax farmer or village or pargana chiefs. These struggles and accommodations resulted in a variety of rates and descriptions. Writing from the dependent state of Kolhapur in 1853, D. C. Graham listed the locally recognized types of soil: "'Kalee,' Black; 'Tambool,' Red; 'Mulee' or 'Malwa,' the rice and garden land; and 'Kharee' or 'Pandur,' White." But he added that each of these was divided into three classes and then further subdivided by locality and fertility, resulting in a total of 218 tax assessment classes.[40] Crop-sharing or the threat of imposing it was also a recourse; in this case, the demand was based on the visible harvest collected seasonally on the village threshing floor.[41]

In the mid-1820s, the Bombay government first attempted a survey and assessment based on the then radically new differential rent theory formulated by David Ricardo. The assessment was administered by R. K. Pringle, a newly arrived civil servant and the economist Thomas Malthus's favorite student at Haileybury College. Pringle tried to invent a new land revenue system from scratch. He therefore sent out teams of subordinates with orders to gather the enormous amount of information needed to calculate the "true" rent of each field and aggregate this up to the village level in the eastern part of the Pune district. It was an impossible task, and the result was a disaster. Entire villages left their fields and emigrated to the Nizam's adjoining dominions.

The next set of surveyors, Goldsmid, Wingate, and Davidson, formulated their working rules in 1847 on a pragmatic and empirical basis. Their object was to generate an aggregate revenue that seemed manageable based on the experience of the previous few years. Then that amount was to be distributed over each field: *this* was their innovation. After more than a decade of experience, they sorted all cultivable land into three main classes subdivided by depth and soil textures. Like local farmers, they perceived depth as key to moisture retention and consequently to potential crop yield. They observed that good black lands were rarely less than 1/4 cubit (ca. 5 in.) deep. Reddish, friable, or gravelly lands, however, tended to be very shallow, consequently, they did not consider that any patch of such land would be more that a cubit (ca. 20 in.) deep. Omitting such implausible combinations, they thus generated a table of nineteen classes, with their relative values descending from 16 to 2 annas. After that first classing by depth and type, the value was assessed through seven specific other possible defects in each field. These included a mixture of minute fragments or nodules of limestone, admixture of sand, being more or less impervious to water, and so on. Each such defect lowered the class of the field by one-sixteenth (one anna). All this minuteness still could not encompass all the distinctions known to local peasants. "There are numerous varieties of soil, known amongst cultivators by peculiar characteristics and distinguishing names; but as many of these differ little, if at all, in fertility, and our classification has reference to the latter consideration alone."[42]

This point was also confirmed by Harold Mann, a trained agronomist with many years' experience. "The water content represents, in fact, the limiting factor in the soils of the Deccan. If the water can be guaranteed, it pays to manure heavily with organic and nitrogenous manures, and also in many cases with phosphatic manures; if not, and this is frequently the case, it does not pay to manure at all. The value of any particular soil in the Deccan depends primarily (1) *on its retentiveness* and (2) *on its depth*."[43]

Fields however were not uniform, and it is unlikely a few test pits would have sufficed for actual farmers. Mann additionally observed that a few yards would sometimes separate "a piece of bare rock giving at the most a very thin grass herbage, and a rich deep black soil capable of growing the biggest and finest crops of sugarcane. We have passed along a road where there was rock on one side, and a crop of sugarcane giving a yield of thirty to forty tons per acre on the other. And such cases abound."[44]

An example of how minutely farmers had to know their land is found in a report aimed at ascertaining the yield and costs of tillage in a Konkan small-holding containing just over three acres. This farm was composed of 1.08 acres of *varkas* (rugged, often rocky upland) whose tax assessment was only a quarter rupee along with 2.28 acres of rice land assessed at almost 9 rupees. "The varkas is unfit for cultivation though it gives grazing to the cattle and some ráb materials to the rice land. The rice land is made up of small pôt numbers varying from [0.05 ac.] to [0.37 ac.]. There are no less than 18 such small plots in the holding.... One pôt number of [0.18 ac.] was selected for experiment, assessed at [4.35 rupees] per acre. It is not probable that the estimate of the holding calculated on the basis of this one plot is very accurate." Based on that sample, the yield was 1,466 pounds of grain in husk and 3,466 pounds of straw per acre.[45] The farmer had to know the peculiarities of each little patch and of each crop in order to make a living.

VILLAGE PRODUCTION AND RURAL NEEDS

We have already considered the demands made by elite consumption on the resources of the land and estimated their effects. But the demands fell directly on their subalterns and through them on the ecosystem itself. So beneath it all were peasant farmers, artisans and providers of specialized services, regular nomads, wandering mendicants, and temporary emigrants all spread across the countryside. These collectively formed the majority of the population. All dealt on a daily basis with the harsh realities of climate and periodically with the turmoil of political life. For the elites, untilled land was a source of elephants to trap, of timber for great buildings, of many kinds of animals to hunt. Peasant communities depended on tilled and untilled land for a far wider range of needs. This level of life is impossible to consider across the immense diversity of the subcontinent, so I shall focus on western Peninsular India.

Deccan farmers developed a remarkably resilient agricultural system suited to the hard circumstances in which they lived. Coats said of their farming that it might be despised at first sight by an English farmer of the time (1819). But, he added, given opportunity for closer observation, the latter would soon agree that local practice was admirably adapted to both the climate and the poverty of the people. The supposedly superior English system would (Coats thought) fail if employed under those circumstances.[46] A few years later, Sykes conversed with many farmers during his four years as statistical reporter. He also remarked that they were good observers and could explain the rationale of an agricultural process with a simplicity that he might not find in an educated English farmer.[47]

These observations were to be repeated. A parliamentary representative from Lancashire came out to Bombay in 1862–63 and wrote a survey of the possible expansion of Indian cotton exports to replace the American supply that had been cut off by the Civil War. He reported that in the mid-nineteenth century, the East India Company decided that the inferiority of Indian to American cotton was because Indian farmers did not know how to grow it. They imported six American planters who were sent to Gujarat to introduce their supposedly superior seeds and methods. American seed was also sown in "almost every part of India suited to the growth of cotton." It failed in the vast majority of cases or succeeded at too high a cost for local adoption. The American system of tillage was found unsuitable to local conditions, and the planters "were obliged to abandon it and resort to the native methods."[48]

Peasants often understood the value of processes that "scientific" agronomists initially rejected as superstition. One of these was the practice of burning small branches, cow dung, and other material on the plots destined to be seedbeds for transplant rice. A number of officials—especially Forest Department ones—argued that the neither transplantation nor the burning of organic matter on the seedbed before rice was sown there was necessary. At most, they claimed, a scientific fertilizer would suffice.

In the 1880s, the expanding Forest Department sought to prohibit both shifting agriculture and the cutting of small wood to burn when preparing seedbeds. Armed with late Victorian confidence in their own scientific understanding, they denounced these methods as primitive practices with no value. One professor, S. Cooke of the College of Science, had patented a new fertilizer rich in phosphates, lime, and potash that was supposed to provide a superior alternative to the *rāb* process. When Ozanne finally tested this scientific formula, the yield from a field so fertilized and one left entirely without manure was exactly the same—which is to say that it had been a useless expense. Several other experiments were carried with various combinations of biomass, with the result that, except in one case, yield figures were consistently in favor of what the people in each locality regarded as the best material. Ozanne also experimentally established the value of both burning and transplanting in the humid regime of coast.[49]

At the end of the century, another director of agriculture studied the methods used by specialized gardeners in the mountains of Kanara. Schooled by previous experience, he was careful to not deride local methods even if they seemed primitive. "The methods adopted are successful in practice, and although they appear at first sight extraordinarily antiquated to the casual onlooker, they may, like other time-honoured Indian practices, be found on full enquiry the most suitable for the existing natural conditions of the district."[50]

SUBSISTENCE ALONG THE FARM–FOREST ECOTONE

D. C. Graham was an army officer with many years' experience and a good eye for the relation of agrarian life and rural landscape. Writing of the relatively moist and fertile middle valley lands of the Kolhapur kingdom in 1853, he described villages as existing every few miles. Village sites were marked by trees that provided shade to work the numerous wells near them. The most intensely tilled lands were close to the villages and grew sugarcane and valuable irrigated crops. Crops decreased in value with distance until the periphery where the hardy "hill millet" called Sáwa was grown. But even hillsides might be broken up into minute fields that produced excellent rice. If a hilly ridge did not separate a village's lands from its neighbor's, a thin strip of jungle would do so.[51]

He noted that the villages in the belt extending east about thirty-five miles from the crest of the Sahyadri were generally smaller and poorer. The everyday food of the people there was a coarse millet, flavored with salt and red chilies. But it did not always suffice, and the pith of the wild date palm would be dried and powdered to supplement the grain. For three or four monsoon months, most had to supplement their cereals with a range of other wild roots, fruits, and leaves. The more affluent villages of the open country used a wider range of cultivated cereals and lentils. However, even here, wheat, rice, and gram were expensive foods eaten only on festive days by common people. Oil was commonly used among them, and ghee entered only the diets of the wealthy. *Pan* or betel was chewed only by the wealthy.

Wildland resources also provided housing to the poor. Walls were commonly made of woven reed plastered with mud, and roofs were thatch. The forests supplied poles. In the plains, sun-dried brick and tile were usually used, and the more substantial woodwork of peasant houses here included doors with frames and shutters.[52] Food, of course, is a primary need. Still, the everyday life of the villagers intimately known to Coats may serve as a basis for such study. Ordinary peasant food, he wrote, "consists of different sorts of grain, pulse, greens, pods, roots, and fruits, hot spices, and oil; all the produce of their fields; and milk, curds, and clarified butter; but they are fond of the flesh of wild hogs, and of sheep, when they can get it.... Their holiday fare is, 1st, Cakes made with wheat flour, split pulse, and coarse sugar; the latter are made by first boiling the pulse soft and mixing it with the sugar, and then kneading them with the wheat paste." Coats described a time of relative peace and prosperity. Such times were fleeting. Coats's contemporary Marshall noted that religious principles prevented three-quarters of the people in his study area of central Gujarat from eating the flesh of animals; poverty precluded nine-tenths of the rest from eating meat at all. He saw this dietary as changing the pattern of land management as land would not be set aside to raise meat for the table: "it is not anywhere an object of profit to rear animals for slaughter."[53]

There were also always many so poor that they had to supplement their consumption with foraged and wild foods. As in Kolhapur, it was the poorest communities who were most dependent on foraged foods. An inquiry in 1877 described the Katkaris, whose manufacture of catechu was at the time being curtailed by the Bombay forest regulations: "A few partly support themselves by tillage. They till upland, *warkas*, either waste or taken from Government holders, or on agreement to share the produce. They burn brushwood *ráb* on the plot of ground and use the hoe but never the plough. When their supply of grain is exhausted they gather and sell firewood and wild honey, and with their bows and arrows kill small deer, rabbits, hares and monkeys. When these fail they dig old threshing floors for rats, eating the rats and taking their stores of grain."[54]

Not only landless tribals but also many people dwelling near woodlands used wild foods. The Koli community described by Alexander Mackintosh cultivated some commonly grown crops. But they also drew extensively on the woodlands, which supplied them with many vegetables as well as fruits and berries. Jungle roots were an important source of more substantial food. Mackintosh wrote in the 1830s that "the principal jungle roots are the anway, kaudur, chaie, sardull, pundah and turpull. The anway grows in the hardest red soil among the rocks, and consequently it is a difficult and laborious task to dig it up. In appearance, and in many respects in quality, it resembles the yam. The root is found from one to two feet buried in the ground; it sends forth a shoot like a creeper, which clings to any bush or tree near it. The substance of this plant is white, and it is boiled in milk. The natives of rank prize it much." Kaudur, or wild banana root, was often eaten by the Thakoors and some Kolies during times of scarcity. They also ate other wild roots whenever grain was expensive. Some like the sardull, a large bulbous root, were eaten in severe scarcity. It was "extremely rough and unpleasant to the taste. They use it also to cure the guinea worm."[55]

Beyond food came the few luxuries that ordinary folk could afford. Little was imported from outside the region and much produced in the village itself. Salt and some spices, especially red and black pepper, were staples of even peasant cuisine. Interestingly, Coats mentions *hing* (*asafetida*) as used in everyday cookery; this is the exudate of a plant that grows only in Iran and Afghanistan and must have been imported from there.[56] Tobacco came to India around 1600 and was quickly domesticated, though it only grew in specific tracts.

EXAMPLES OF FIELDS AND CROPS

Farmers in the hot season and early rains had to decide on what they would sow and where, even though many unknowns beset the crops. Sometimes a predetermined rotation also constrained their choices. One way of coping was by planting mixtures of different crops that might compensate for one another and also draw and return different nutrients to the land. A large holding of 43.85 acres in Puntamba, Ahmednagar district was studied by the director of agriculture. A patch of two-fifths of an acre followed a regular rotation: bajri millet mixed with lentils, oilseeds, and fiber plants one year followed by wheat and kardai (an oilseed) the next. Another farm in the same area saw a general failure of the millet crop; there was barely enough grain for next year's seed and only a little fodder. But a large area had been sown to wheat, most of which yielded a good crop. All the straw, chaff, and stalks was retained to sustain the three pairs of working oxen and four milch cows. "In a year of heavy late rainfall, the rayat is able to utilize light bájri land for wheat and other crops . . . the mixed crops [sic] wheat and others with bajri and its concomitants, are wise precautions. One crop may fail and its failure is generally beneficial to the other crops sown with it, leaving them more food and sunshine."[57]

Many other considerations could enter cropping decisions. The hereditary (*watandar*) barber of Kopargaon owned a field measuring 14.75 acres. Patches of it were infested with deep-rooted weeds that would need much labor to eradicate. In the previous year (1882–83), bajri millet had been sown along with a legume mixture. The entire crop had been eaten by locusts. At sowing time, the barber had only prepared ten acres. He then decided that he could not manage the farm alongside his profession, so he sold his bullocks and agreed to sublet to a larger landowner who would keep one-third the crop. The field had not been well prepared, having been plowed only once the previous September, and the second plowing omitted. The owner and tenant then agreed to sell the standing crop in advance to a third party who would manage the watching and harvesting so that the owner did not have to supervise the tenant and prevent him from taking away more than his share. The sharecropper made no profit on the transaction after deducting his inputs. "He admits that he agreed to the sale of the crop, because the heavy crop on his other land required his whole time and labour."[58]

Another study from 1884 looked at a smaller farm. It was irrigated by water lifted from wells and located in Malsiras, Sholapur district. Its total area was 7.6 acres. In 1883–84, it grew only wheat and obtained what was described as a good crop. The ground had not been manured in the previous two years, but this year had been fertilized with goat droppings and cattle-shed refuse from the owners' four bullocks, a cow, and she-buffalo. There were five working adults in the households. No labor was hired, but a cart and two oxen were hired out for three months a year. When on the farm, the animals were fed on grass in the field and the sorghum stalks from the previous year.[59]

Sharecroppers had even more difficult conditions. Marya son of Dhumo leased 4.8 acres of land in Belgaum, of which 3.75 acres was moist enough for rice and the rest dry. He had to give the owner half the crop. The landlord loaned him a plow and oxen as well as all necessary implements. He gave some manure. Marya had to cut 20 headloads of grass for the oxen. He, his wife, and three children also collected 100 headloads of leaves for fertilizer. Once again rice paddy was only sustained by biotic resources drawn from untilled land.[60] Marya and his family somehow survived on their half share, though probably constantly indebted to their landlord.

Farmers treated different parts of the same field in different ways, as one study in the Haveli taluka of Pune found. The low land part retentive of soil and water was carefully prepared, twice plowed, and six times smoothed and leveled. A flock of sheep was folded on it for twenty-four hours before sowing, but no other manure applied. The land grew wheat and gram (a nitrogen-fixing legume) in alternate years. It still yielded only 200 pounds per acre. A poor patch of high and dry ground in a nearby field gave half that. It had never been manured. "The wheat was thin and scanty and the ears imperfectly filled."[61] But manuring unirrigable land was risky and therefore never done, as the plants would wither more quickly if there was a break in the rains.[62] Irrigable rice-growing land that fed the elite would however, absorb large amounts of time and labor.[63]

OUTSIDERS: TRAVELERS, SEASONAL NOMADS, BANDITS, AND LORDS

Before the great expansion of tillage began in the 1850s, a large proportion of the population had participated in itinerant and mobile lifeways. Many practiced essential crafts: for example, itinerant smiths and ironworkers, professional well-diggers and dam-builders, and so on. There were also large areas of uncultivated land where they could camp. The village community might feud with neighbors over boundaries, but it could not exclude powerful claimants from its lands. Thus, we find the village of Karaje in the Nira Valley complaining to the king's governor that several bands of shepherds with twenty thousand sheep had descended on their village. The animals (the plaint continued) were ravaging the crops, and if they were not restrained by a royal order, then the village would be obliterated. The shepherds had been rebuked but paid no heed; if the governor did not listen then death (*moksha*) was the villagers' lot. It is likely that these were shepherds licensed by the state or in charge of the flocks that supplied meat for the tables of the gentry. This is suggested by documents in the archives, such as this order issued in 1752–53: "Letter to Sivaji Salokhe—Baji Govere, Ravalji Manka and Yesaji Manka are in charge of the King's shepherds in Miraj province. They are permitted to graze everywhere; do not molest them. Issue stern injunctions to the Mangs and Bedars of the province to see to their safety."[64]

Thus protected, the shepherds could grab a share of the limited resources of the villages. Sheep and goats did, however, yield a return to the villagers since their urine and dung enriched the fields where they lay at night, and smaller flocks were often welcomed for this reason. (However, Coats in Loni heard grumbles that this resource was monopolized by the headmen free of charge while other farmers had to pay.) But egregious violations were known. A letter from the court of the Chhatrapati written in 1752–53 reprimanded one Yesaji of the village of Dudhi for sending his servants into the villages of Sarambe, Yeksala, and Nagdi where they cut and carried away the grass growing on the field embankments—grass presumably conserved for the village cattle.[65]

Atre's classic study of folklife reflects a time just before World War I when the colonial administration had just succeeded in mapping a demarcation of the countryside into village communities and their lands. Yet there were still many itinerants outside the walls, even at the height of imperial dominance and administrative control in 1915. Groups varied in size, but all moved with some domesticated animals. Artisans' camps contained two, five, or ten households. Some nomadic groups might be larger. One group of storytellers (*citrakathi*) described by Atre pitched thirty tents with 127 persons in them. They were accompanied by five horses, seventy buffalo, and seventeen goats, with dogs and poultry as well. Judging by the animals with the group, storytelling was supplementary to their main pursuit of transhumant buffalo herding. Others, such as snake catchers and trappers, possessed special skills at managing dangerous creatures, including snakes and crocodiles.[66]

Colonial officials generally viewed wanderers with suspicion. Atre wrote his work of rural sociology after decades of service as a junior revenue official, and it consistently emphasizes the nomads' turbulence and criminality. He claimed that many groups, while they provided a service or commodity, would also beg from door to door and pilfer unattended objects, fodder, and standing crops. He welcomed the passing of the 1911 Act that listed many of these communities as "Criminal Tribes" and gave the police extra powers of surveillance and coercion over them. He was also critical of ascetic wanderers and pilgrims, including the Warkari devotees who made the annual pilgrimage to Pandharpur. Some devotees he described as using their religious vocation as a cover for housebreaking and robbery, adding that their dress offered an excellent disguise for robbers scouting their targets.

Other wanderers, according to Atre, "practice skilled professions or provide entertainment, while others openly live by begging. But if we look behind the cloak, many will be found to live as tricksters, frauds and thieves, and some also by immoral trades." He repeatedly complained that many were accompanied by cows, goats, horses, and other animals that were encouraged to prey on unguarded crops and fodder. "Phāñsepārdhī bands are very aggressive. Up to one hundred people may gather at one encampment, with cows, buffaloes, poultry, dogs. They beg, sell herbal medicines, catch birds, and hunt deer, pigs, hares. Their women are adroit at finding opportunities. They graze their cows on the standing crops, steal stored grain, cows, goats, sheep and ripe crops. If there is a small fissure in the ground, they deepen it and hide stolen grain there." Atre saw even the transhumant cowherds who, in fact, played an essential role in the agricultural economy, as a burden upon it. Thus, he wrote of Mewati herdsmen who bought grazing licenses from the Forest Department as predators. He claimed that they came with thousands of animals and took every opportunity to feed them on peasant standing crops instead of the forest grazing to which they were entitled. Their animals were, he wrote, trained to flee at the scent of anyone other than their owners and were consequently hard to impound.[67]

This was an excessively jaundiced view. Only a few years later, the government of Bombay Province appointed an expert committee to examine the causes of the deterioration in the cattle of the province. The committee attributed it to the disappearance of the professional breeder who would move with large herds of animals, buying and selling them along the way. They would also take charge of dry cows and buffalo for a fee, relieving owners of the need to sustain them when unproductive. The herders would search for water and grazing as they became seasonally available and from long experience knew which lands to seek out and what to avoid. Diseased or weak animals that could not keep up with the herd died or were taken by wild animals. This purging served to maintain stock quality. Finally, the older system had helped perpetuate breeds adapted to subregional conditions. Thus, the Khillari breeds (named after the breeding community that raised them) were adapted to stony ground. "No other breed could survive on the small pasturage and meagre food found in their tracts." The deep black soils of the Krishna Valley had raised large, powerful animals adapted to plowing heavy lands. Each function and each region had a particular strain of ox, and the balance of these was maintained through purchase and sale by professional graziers. The extension of farming on much grassland and the closure of many woodland areas by the Forest Department had, the committee added, led to the decline of such expert traders.[68]

The importance of migrant cattlemen had been noted a century earlier. Coats observed that only one-third of the plow oxen in the Loni area were homebred; the rest were purchased from professional drovers who came from the Karnataka and Khandesh. Southern animals, he was told, were better suited for the plow and northern ones as pack animals. He also described the value of having itinerant shepherds camp in the village: "In the dry season, the shepherds drive their numerous flocks from place to place to feed; and, a permission for grazing within the limits of the township, fold their sheep at night on the arable lands in succession. But this is a precarious advantage, and only enjoyed by the Patails and inhabitants who have power, unless the others pay for it by presents of grain. A field well manured in this way is thought to yield luxuriant crops for six or seven years afterwards."[69] Atre's study of village life has become a classic. It has been reprinted several times and is, I believe, still in print. But it was only relatively recently that another rural sociologist of Maharashtra, Prabhakar Mande, published a complementary study of those outside the settled village community and its lifeways. This was allusively titled *Gāvagāḍyabāhera* (Outside the village wagon).[70] This study of communities outside the formal village order implicitly seeks to correct the prejudices against them expressed in Atre's *Gāñvagāḍa*. It is largely based on years of intermittent fieldwork among various nomadic communities of Maharashtra, several of whom had formerly been included in the "Criminal Tribes" list of the British administration. His research was conducted from the 1960s through the 1970s, during which the author traveled with and conversed with community members across central and eastern Maharashtra. Mande organized the book in successive chapters that present one community at a time. Some were craft communities such as itinerant stonemasons, woodworkers, metalworkers, rope-makers and castrators of oxen, sellers of traditional medicines, performers, and many varieties of mendicants. The latter include singers and sex workers but also groups such as those who demanded alms in an intimidating way.

Mande's study also includes communities that were accompanied by animals. Several were dependent on alms received after exhibiting animal performances. *Ḍakkalvar-s,* for example, sang while a tame peacock danced. But if some household refused them alms, then they would dress up a male and female dog and make them perform an insulting dance before the miserly house.[71] Animals were deeply symbolic in polyvalent ways and might be used by mendicants to shame villagers. Some practitioners of traditional medicine (*Vaidus*) also traveled with many kinds of animals, such as dogs, asses, fowls, and sheep. They trapped many types of wild animals, including hares, iguanas, crocodiles, and hyenas. They were especially adept in luring out and capturing snakes from houses. Traditionally they had also gathered and sold herbal and animal-derived medicines. Several communities traveled with a fortune-telling ox that also performed various tricks on command. *Tirmalis*, like *Vaidus*, also hunted many kinds of animals and bred and trained special hunting dogs.[72] Like other villagers, nomads also sought stable livelihoods through governmental recognition of their rights. In 1722, for example, letters were sent out to all the villages in six subdivisions around the city of Pune. It said that Sheikh Rustum and Sheikh Daval had complained that they possessed the exclusive right to exhibit bears and tigers in the region specified and traditionally received a little money, some bread, porters to carry their goods, and a watchman at night from each village where they halted. But other medicant showmen were encroaching on their territory, and villages were refusing them dues. The regional governor then ordered each village to maintain the traditional system and not give alms for such animal performances to others.[73]

In several cases Mande was able to attend community council or panchayat meetings. His study contains some of the usual anthropological topics—birth and death rituals, marriage patterns, the presence or absence of widow-remarriage—and he also closely observed many rituals and performances. He wrote down songs and auspicious chants used on various occasions. He also recorded the use of special languages intended to be incomprehensible to outsiders and gives examples. Finally, Mande collected *jātipurāṇa-s*, origin and charter myths of different communities, descriptions of the shrines and pilgrimages they especially frequented, feasts and fasts, and so on. His work offers a valuable corrective to the strangely circumscribed work of K. C. Malhotra, S. B. Khomne, and Madhav Gadgil, which ignored the very considerable interactions between their study communities and the larger agricultural and, indeed, industrial world of 1970s India in which they and their animal companions really lived.[74]

Hunting and trapping also provided valuable accoutrements for farmers and soldiers. A range of demands were thus made upon farmland, pastures, spontaneous vegetation, woodland, and true forest. Many crafts and professions depended on particular agrarian products from reeds and fibers for looms, to dyestuffs like indigo, to saltpeter for gunpowder manufacturers. Trappers caught animals to train as performers or process into medicines. People fed and housed themselves and their animals using a range of resources, spontaneous and cultivated. Mud, the inexhaustible soil, provided not only flooring but also walls and, on occasion, waterproofed roofing. Not all earths were equally useful; Coats remarked that a peculiar type of white soil resisted water and was therefore used to seal roofs.

Slender bamboos, tree shoots, and bundles of straw roofed many houses. The resilient thorn-brush that sprang up each year provided fencing to protect crops and threshing floors. In some regions such as Gujarat, this function was fulfilled by "live hedges" of the milk bush. Cow dung was laboriously collected, often from the fields and byways, made into cakes, dried, and used as fuel. Destitute women might collect and process it for sale.[75] Local resources gathered from all accessible sources supplied the small needs of ordinary people.

So Marshall reported from the plains region of Karnataka in 1820–21 that the buildings of the elite used teak beams imported from the coastal forests but that all the wood used in the construction of the common houses and particularly in the roofs was cut from "the innumerable strong bushes or small trees of the Mimosa and Acacia family which now cover the waste lands." These names refer to families of thorny trees that would survive the constant grazing of village animals. Woodcutters would only seek them if no other firewood was available. But their toughness meant that they were well suited for farm tools. Marshall observed that the "ordinary implements of agriculture are sought for from the same source."[76]

Harold Mann was an experienced agronomist deeply sympathetic to peasant predicaments and needs. He collaborated with Indian colleagues to publish two important studies of villages in the plateau region of Maharashtra in 1917 and 1921. He remarked on the current treelessness of the black soil region, which was characterized by bare rocky hills and undulations. Trees were found only near rivers or along seasonal watercourses. They also grew in clumps around wells: in other words, places where there was soil moisture to sustain their growth. He noted that the overwhelming majority of trees were babul or *acacia arabica*. It was thorny and hard for animals to browse, but its green twigs might be cut for fodder. Furthermore, its seed pods were eagerly eaten by cows and goats who therefore spread the seed wherever they went. Its hard and often naturally curved timber was well adapted for agricultural implements, and thorny branches made temporary fences around fields. The tree was therefore practically a human symbiont: it was spread by but resistant to domesticated animals and supplied wood for the simple implements of peasant farming.[77]

South Asia was long thought to be a land of territorially fixed, autonomous villages. This chapter has demonstrated that the village was the result of a complex historical interaction of states, communities, and ecosystems. But people and land can be recalcitrant, so governments often failed to achieve the transparency they desired. The chapter has additionally explored alternative lifeways pursued through and around the same lands as well as the importance of untilled lands, spontaneous tree growth, and wild foods in everyday life. Finally, it has included those transients and nomads who did not fit in the village frame. Their circuits, however, intersected in time and space with many villages in ways that were both symbiotic with and predatory upon peasant farming. Empires and kingdoms, domains and fiefs all ultimately depended on the extraction of many different resources from the many anthropogenic environments of Asia. It took the skill and toil of millions of peasants, herdsmen and foragers, and artisans and traders to produce those resources. Their production required all of them to each develop unconscious resource maps that told them where unused dung might be collected, where wild tubers could be found, which barks yielded dyes and which were medicinal, which trees were in fruit, and when or where to cut the long axle of a peasant cart. But production possibilities varied by time and season across the many ecological zones of the subcontinent. They also varied depending on the range of and fluctuation in political authority. Governments in South Asia have been called "soft states." But they were far from universally emollient with all; rather, they were soft with the hard and hard with the soft. These encounters were repeated through centuries. The next chapter considers the effects of conflict upon the environment at a regional and village scale.

FIVE

Lands of Resistance, Terrains of Refuge

Kings are to be reckon'd amongst ravenous Beasts.
THOMAS HOBBES | *Philosophical Rudiments* (1651)

ORGANIZED WARFARE WAS A CONSTANT FEATURE OF THE EARLY modern world. Its effects in South Asia included the large-scale resort to the building of walled cities and great forts, sometimes occupied for a few decades, or even a few years, before abandonment.[1] Tughlaq cavalry armies concentrated much of the wealth of the subcontinent in Delhi. That enabled the sultans to baffle repeated Mongol invasions. It also led them to build a succession of fortress cities around Delhi. Immense resources—including the assemblage of workers and animals for such tasks—would draw on local supplies of wood and water even if many of those buildings used locally quarried stone. Rapid construction also driven by military need changed techniques that used more energy-intensive methods. Percy Brown notes that rubble masonry cores at the short-lived fortress capital of Tughlaqabad were faced with roughly cut stone slabs. The builders could not resort to the fine molding needed for earlier, mortarless styles of construction; instead, they employed vast amounts of lime-based cement.[2] Farther south, the breakaway Bahmani Sultanate (ca. 1347–1500) also built fortress capitals in the open plains and enlarged many hilltop forts built under previous regimes. They used features such as outcrops of the original landscape to found their walls but supplemented these with local spolia and the rock hewn out to construct deep moats.[3] The production of lime mortar requires the reduction of limestone to its oxide by combustion and would have expended great amounts of firewood with consequent demands on local and regional woodlands. Brick-making is a similarly fuel-intensive process. This would denude woodlands near fortified urban centers. Furthermore, many parts of the subcontinent are perennially or seasonally short of fresh water. Growing towns, whether fortified or not, increasingly resorted to building reservoirs and aqueducts that brought water into elite residences and fed domestic wells—again changing the landscape.[4]

OFFENSIVE AND DEFENSIVE USES OF LANDSCAPE

Beyond obvious structures such as fortifications, the defensive modification of environments is known from many parts of the world and obviously varies according to local ecology. The Sahel—a long belt south of the Sahara desert in West and Central Africa—for example, was studied in a pathbreaking work of environmental history, James Fairhead and Melissa Leach's *Misreading the African Landscape*. Their study also illustrates the interaction of small-scale warfare, defensive forests, and the unwitting creation of a disease frontier. The authors were mainly concerned with the colonial and postcolonial politics of the environment, but their work has a suggestive link to the earlier history of a humanized landscape. It suggests that the interaction of longer-term swings in climate, the spread of the warhorse, and the sharp sixteenth-century increase in the slave trade toward both the Atlantic and the Mediterranean all led to the local adaptations by farmers and herdsmen alike. Each group sought to shape the Sahel zone to its own advantage. The scattered Sahelian woodlands that early colonial officials so misconstrued as remnants of vast primeval forests were the result of that contest. They served to supply needed wood products but also, more importantly, to protect farming communities against horse-riding slave raiders from the savanna beyond. Farmers on the edge of the Sahel thus sought to compensate for the inequality in military force through defensive modifications of the landscape.[5] Croplands would not long survive periods of serious political or climatic instability. They would break down into shrubland or intermittent forest, which is the landscape most suited as tsetse fly habitat. That would transform the terrain into a barrier against both pastoralists and raiding horsemen, even if at the cost of human exposure to a deadly disease.[6] The face of the land was thus shaped by inequality of power and resulting human conflicts. Whether in the imperial landscapes of Asia or the ungoverned borderlands of the Sahel, the contestation of power directly impacted the human environment. The everyday landscape was shaped by evasion and resistance, with great lords not the only ones modifying the land.

This chapter begins with a brief consideration of the perceptual ordering of a military landscape in the classic text of Indian political science, the *Arthashastra*. This great compendium of political wisdom discusses the value of different forests. It mentions that among productive forests, one watered by a river (a floodplain or riverain forest perhaps) could also be a haven for the king himself in times of adversity.[7] Offensive and defensive uses were, of course, opposite sides of the same coin. When Ibn Battuta traveled through North India in the 1330s and 1340s, he described rebellious Hindus as living in the mountains. Large organized insurgencies smoldered even in the vicinity of garrisoned towns such as Jalali, between the Ganga and Yamuna Rivers. Insurgents lived hidden behind dense forests and thick bamboo groves that served as walls and were interspersed across the land.[8] These insurgent communities were termed *mawasat* or *mawas-ha* in the thirteenth-century history titled *Tabaqat-i-Nasiri*, and they were found in the area mentioned by Ibn Battuta.[9] Francisco Pelsaert commented that the Mewat region was only about sixty miles from the imperial capital, but "owing to the hills and forests, it is mostly in rebellion against the King." Indeed, he added elsewhere that the country was intersected by many mountains, and the people there recognized "only their own Rajas, who are very numerous." The emperor Jahangir might be thought to rule only the plains and open roads.[10]

Anthropogenic woodland was not only impenetrable for cavalry; it was also opaque to the imperial gaze. Even woodlands away from static defenses such as forts were used in field campaigns. Massed cavalry lost formation and scattered if they entered forest or thick brush. François Martin witnessed an extended encounter between a Mughal detachment and the Marathas around Pondicherry. Pressed by two hundred Maratha cavalry and three hundred infantry, the Mughal forces withdrew to the woodland. The entry to the thicket was fortified, and the Mughals fired from cover, so the attacking horsemen had no advantage and retired.[11] The incapacity of cavalry to fight effectively in such lands is often mentioned in eighteenth-century campaign memoirs. Even major rulers such as Haidar Ali of Mysore sought the protection of woodlands, especially against the Marathas. In several campaigns, he sought to use such terrain to evade cavalry-heavy Maratha armies whom he could not face in the open field.[12]

Resistance from woodland bases was, of course, most utilized by small bands of insurgents, but flight into hills and woodlands was not solely a recourse of defenseless peasants. In the 1660s, the early French Company based itself at the old Portuguese settlement of São Thome (near the English Company at Madras). In the early 1670s, they faced a sizable coalition of regional powers. Martin, the governor, was advised by his ally, the warlord Sher Khan Lodi, to evacuate the settlement and defend himself from a refuge in the woods. He urged the French not to attempt a defense of the town against the many enemies who menaced it.[13] The French Company, however, carefully strengthened its defenses with walls and batteries in the approved European style of the day, as well as bastions, a curtain wall, and a glacis. But the company also added an indigenous feature, what the English termed a "bound hedge." At the time of the British siege in 1748, the "greatest part of the land lying round the town was inclosed [sic], at the distance of a mile from the walls, with a hedge of large aloes and other thorny plants peculiar to the country, intermixed with great numbers of coco-nut and palm-trees, which altogether formed a defence impenetrable to cavalry and of very difficult passage to infantry." Altogether this hedge covered five and a half miles and was traversed by five roads that entered through openings defended by redoubts mounting cannon.[14] This was not a French innovation, only a more elaborate version of a common defensive feature in South Asia.

Pennant's great compendium of early English writing about Asia in fact described the bound hedge as "the frequent concomitant of the fortresses of Hindoostan." He added that it included every thorny or caustic plant or shrub that would grow in the region. It always included the bamboo, "admirable for the purpose, since nothing equals it in resisting the edge of the ax, or the subtile [sic] fury of fire."[15] Such protective woodlands are mentioned in many parts of the subcontinent, from Assam westward across the Gangetic plain.

Mehwas as a term and a practice persisted from the thirteenth century into middle colonial times. Writing in the 1830s from today's Uttar Pradesh, the British Indian Army surgeon Donald Butter remarked that some forests were carefully protected by local gentry. These woodlands were where recalcitrant rural lords would flee to evade excessive tax demands. They had, Butter wrote, "afforded a secure asylum from the tyranny and rapacity of the Chakledārs [tax famers]."[16] The alternate view of such landholders, put forward a few years later by the British administrator William Sleeman, was that they were turbulent robber barons. But he described the woodlands in the same way. The central Gangetic valley, he wrote, was

> a level plain, intersected by rivers, which, with one exception, flow near the surface, and have either no ravines at all, or very small ones. The little river Goomtee winds exceedingly, and cuts into the soil in some places to the depth of fifty feet. In such places there are deep ravines; and the landholders along the border improve these natural difficulties by planting and preserving trees and underwood in which to hide themselves and their followers when in arms against their Government. Any man who cuts a stick in these jungles, or takes his camels or cattle into them to browse or graze without the previous sanction of the landholder, does so at the peril of his life. But landholders in the open plains and on the banks of rivers, without any ravines at all, have the same jungles.

These defensive woodlands, Sleeman continued, often contained bamboo thickets that were resistant to fire. Lodged within these were mud forts that served as an ultimate defense. If the fort's garrison was pressed hard, he added, they could often escape through secret paths into the woodland. Such woods, Sleeman estimated, covered thousands of acres of potentially productive land.[17]

Sleeman does not discuss the likelihood that the thickets also sheltered animals, such as pig, antelope, and deer, that raided peasant crops. But they must have done so. Thickets might also harbor wolves, hyenas, and tigers that preyed on domestic livestock and sometimes on humans too. Well into the 1980s, older villagers in central Rajasthan had vivid memories of how the local landlord had forbidden them to cut down the woodlands he protected because he hunted the wild pig that lived in them. The pigs came out at night and ravaged peasant crops from seedtime to harvest. Under British rule, the forest was no longer a military defense but solely a game reserve, with the animals largely fed by the peasants' crops. As a result, their crops were regularly devastated, and farmers had to spend night after night out in the fields to frighten off these animals.[18]

AGRICULTURAL RETREAT, PASTORAL OCCUPATION

Seasonal migration could also modify land use and occupation. Pastoralists traditionally migrated to the hill county in early winter as plains vegetation dried up. Large areas of the upper valleys were too rugged for tillage or abandoned for other reasons, and these were used for grazing. In Odisha, near the city of Cuttack, the English agent Thomas Motte observed large areas of grassland where a village had formerly existed. Herdsmen from the city would take large herds of dry cows and unemployed bullocks to graze there.[19] There were recognized areas termed *dhaṇgarācā kharābā* meaning "pastoralists' wasteland" in some villages in the Sahyadri mountains. If herds of cattle from elsewhere entered the grazing lands within a particular village's boundaries, they had to pay a tax. But this depended on an established balance of power. In 1776, an impostor claiming to be a slain member of the Peshwa family launched an insurrection. His forces thoroughly ravaged the several Sahyadri valleys. Accessible crossroads villages were utterly plundered and burned, but less accessible ones preserved some crops. Still, the report continues, herdsmen came in their season, and their cattle destroyed the growing crop even over the remaining fields.[20] Surviving villagers would therefore have had to emigrate—perhaps for a season or longer. The settled might wander and wanderers settle.

WOODLAND AS SHORT-TERM AND LONG-TERM REFUGE

In the 1670s, the English doctor John Fryer witnessed flight into the jungle as an escape strategy in Western India. While traveling eastward from the coastal harbor of Kalyan (near modern Mumbai), with the Mughal army campaigning nearby, he observed that the local inhabitants were "hared [*sic*] out of their Wits, mistrusting even their own Countrymen as well as Strangers, living as it were wildly, betaking themselves to the Thickets and Wildernesses among the Hills, upon the approach of any new Face; for my Horse by chance breaking loose, set a whole Gom [village] or Town upon the hoof, they thinking Auren Zeeb's Luscarry [Aurangzeb's army] at hand."[21]

Peasants hiding in the forest might still be hunted out by determined attackers setting fire to it; bamboo thickets, however, were notably resistant to fire. Nonetheless, clearing brush and trees was a common part of counterinsurgency.[22] In areas inured to repeated military campaigns, flight and return had been almost routinized. The Madras Army officer Alexander Dirom described how inhabitants of the country between Venkatagiri and Bangalore (Bengaluru) in eastern Karnataka quickly returned and resumed cultivation in late 1791, barely six months after they had fled it when the British and their allies attacked the kingdom of Mysore.[23] Nearby refuges evidently formed part of the geographical knowledge of ordinary peasants.

Such refuges were also needed for everyday resistance to extortionate taxation. We may see such resistance in the Muthekhora, a narrow valley in the mountains west of Pune in 1711–12. The hereditary officials (*deshmukhs*) of the region submitted petitions seeking reduced taxes. They reported that the area had been plundered during warfare, and peasants had taken to hiding in the hills. But the government had nonetheless sent out its tax demands: headmen and farmers who failed to meet them were being arrested and heavy summons fees exacted. Fear of arrest, the local officials wrote, was leading people in every village to descend to the Konkan country below the mountains. By implication, their lands were lying untilled, and no taxes would be forthcoming. Royal fiscal officials then sent messages reassuring them that demands would be adjusted to the actual conditions. The *deshmukhs* were encouraged to bring back emigrant peasants and repopulate the villages. The historian D. B. Parasnis, who published this document, added (presumably from other sources) that the *deshmukhs* then sought out the farmers in the various places whither they had fled. They were found in other villages, the coastal plain, the Supe and Wai districts, and elsewhere and persuaded to return.[24] It is evident, therefore, that flight was not random; there were clearly known geographic sites and social networks guiding it.

In the face of protracted turmoil, survivors might resort to a more radical alternative lifeway by retreating to less accessible areas and taking to simpler forms of subsistence. James Scott has argued that these ways of life were designed to make societies both "state resistant and appropriation resistant." Crops were grown in small, unobtrusive patches. Yams and tubers that matured at different times and were hard to locate and steal were used to supplement wild foods. Habitations were simple and scattered. "People, fields and crops were each deployed to evade capture." This would be a retreat into what has been called *Zomia*, a strategy of evasion and concealment.[25] Shifting cultivation could also defend the peoples who lived by it by rendering their territory both opaque and impenetrable.

James Forsyth wrote of the Mahadeo Hills of today's Madhya Pradesh around 1880: "The abandoned dhya [swidden] clearings are speedily covered again with jungle . . . composed of a variety of low and very densely-growing bamboo and of certain thorny bushes, which together form in a year or two a cover almost impenetrable to man or beast. I have often been obliged to turn back from such a jungle after vainly endeavouring to force through it a powerful elephant accustomed to work his way through difficult cover."[26] This secondary forest would be a greater obstacle to human movement and activity than the unaltered vegetation would have been. Even in more arid regions, thorn forest quickly overtook untilled land. Take a description of Khandesh in 1851, even after cultivation had expanded much beyond its early nineteenth-century low:

> On entering the Province from almost any quarter, the face of the country appears to be covered with low, scattered bush jungle. This jungle is composed of various kinds of thorny bushes, of which the "Bear" with its recurved thorns is the most abundant. These bushes are seldom more than 10 feet in height and usually much less. They do not generally grow very close together, but here and there dense and almost impervious thickets are met with . . . in a year or two, after a field so cultivated is relinquished, the jungle has grown as thick as ever and there is nothing to indicate that the field has ever been under tillage at all.[27]

Thus, disturbance by man or nature produced landscapes of concealment and defense. But flight did not always depend on the use of woodland refuges. Mobility would also serve as an escape. Herding communities have always been harder to find and attack than settled villages. They could migrate over considerable distances if needed and also gather for collective defense. These responses would build upon extant capacities for seasonal migration in which the herds followed the rains and new grass. Nomadic cattle keepers had been some of the earliest Iron Age occupants of the Deccan Plateau. Although still not fully explained, "ash-mounds"—sites where great accumulations of cow dung were burned during the Deccan Neolithic period, from circa 3000 to 1200 BCE—are evidence of this.[28]

Therefore, in open arid lands that afforded little concealment, semi-nomadic pastoralism could survive where tillage was impossible. Local traditions of southern Maharashtra described the region after the great famine of the 1390s. During this time, pastoral peoples rose up everywhere, as they believed that the "kingdom is without control." After thirty years of anarchy, the King of Bidar sent two officials in 1428–29 and built a fort at Paranda. Then the land was demarcated and measured, taxes were fixed, and agriculture was finally restored. Similarly, another narrative described how farther north after a great famine in 1629–30 the abandoned lands were occupied by herdsmen. The herdsmen were then summoned by royal officers and offered land rights if they took to tillage. They accepted and became founders of a new village.[29]

Mobility and militancy could also force ruling authorities into compromising with armed and mobile peoples. The Portuguese physician Garcia da Orta traveled frequently across Western India and possessed an estate on Bombay island in the 1550s. He named three communities as the former lords of the region who had been displaced by the kings of Delhi: one of these was "Venezaras"—clearly the Banjara nomadic cattle keepers of later times. These displaced lords, he wrote, could not be subdued by the northern conquerors and would plunder unless appeased by paying a tribute.[30]

MILITARIZED PASTORALISTS: THE BANJARAS

Herdsmen might also adapt to a militarized landscape and construct niches for themselves therein. Caravans of herdsmen with oxen would migrate seeking pastures and could carry large quantities of goods such as salt or grain, depending on demand. In 1795, the English officer J. T. Blunt commented that great merchants were connected with the Maratha government and worked through "Brinjarries" (Banjaras) who carried on "a constant traffic in grain and every other necessary of life." They persevered, he wrote, through difficult paths and narrow defiles, animated by an indefatigable spirit of industry.[31] Thomas Coats wrote in 1819 that a good pack-bullock would carry 180 to 200 pounds twenty miles a day for weeks on end. Cattle were from ancient times also favorite targets for raids. Migrating herdsmen would therefore be prepared for offense and defense. In North India, their camps of circled ox carts were known as *talwandi*—a term that also came to mean a "village."[32]

Other simple field fortifications were sometimes just breastworks of grain bags built each night in dangerous terrain.

By at least 1600, specialized communities of herders became professional carriers of goods. They appear frequently in British military histories of early conquests in South India. Herdsmen moved with great caravans of pack oxen under the leadership of their chiefs. By the eighteenth century, they were known as Banjaras (or Vanjari, sometimes also as Lamāṇ). Banjaras were organized into several tribes. These armed itinerants moved threateningly around the village cores and across village fields, but they generally camped in open country with grazing and water available for the thousands of oxen that formed their caravans. They were armed and far more numerous than other itinerants. At times of great demand for transport services, gatherings made up of thirty thousand oxen might be assembled. Banjara chiefs negotiated with merchants and military commanders to carry whatever commodities needed carriage across roadless terrain.

The description above is drawn from John Briggs's 1812–14 account, the first effort to write a history and ethnography of the Banjaras. A Madras Army officer, Briggs had participated in all the wars since 1801 and had been in India over a decade when he began his research. He conversed with Banjara leaders in order to collect their traditional histories. He judged their language to be identical with that spoken in southern Rajasthan (Marwadi). This may be plausibly explained by Briggs's theory that militarization as a result of long-distance military expeditions from North India began around 1300 CE. The armies, he suggested, were accompanied by a supply train drawn from nomadic herdsmen.

If detached from the armies they accompanied, Briggs plausibly suggested, the Banjaras turned into armed merchants. This whole process evidently brought a new influx of cattle keepers from Northwest India into the peninsula. Newcomers may have absorbed or displaced older migratory cattle herders of the region. Briggs also sought to set them in their geographic context. He began by remarking that any crop failure in one region of the peninsula meant that the people either migrated to more fortunate regions or that grain had to be imported for them. Since the Deccan peninsula was devoid of navigable rivers and had no long roads practicable for wheeled vehicles, all bulk commodities were carried by pack oxen. The Banjaras were their owners and managers. Briggs wrote that a "proprietor," or family head, usually owned from four or five up to two hundred cattle. Each such family head, however, claimed a share in the decisions of the encamped band, or *tanda*.

Briggs was also the first British officer to record a Banjara charter myth of their entitlements. They claimed to have received from the emperor Aurangzeb (r. 1658–1707) a grant allowing them to take "the thatch of houses, the seizure of well-drawn water, and plunder in the enemy's country." This, he added, "has furnished them with pretexts for their general predatory habits." A more florid version of the same charter myth cited "Asaf Jan" (likely intended to mean Asaf Jah, the first Nizam, 1724–48) as the grantor. He was said to have engraved some Hindustani doggerel describing this grant on a copper plate in gold letters.[33] As late as 1860, a British official reported that the Banjaras from Mahim had invaded private lands in another area, defied the government guards, and illegally felled timber trees.[34]

Grazing animals must spread out to seek fodder, and this necessarily encouraged political decentralization. Each tribe consisted of individual camps, each under its own chief, and tribes often claimed exclusive control over specific territorial ranges. This control was sometimes contested, and Briggs interviewed many Banjaras who told of bloody conflicts between them. Cases of such battles are found in the Marathi records. The autonomy of these military nomads was recognized by the Maratha government at the time (1740–41). In one case, the violence was only punished because a government clerk was accidentally killed in the affray.[35]

The Banjaras' role as transport contractors fades rapidly from records from the 1860s onward, after railways began to carry steadily increasing amounts of freight. Atre's 1915 book does not mention the presence of Banjaras and similar itinerant cattle keepers (other than the Mewatis from northern Rajasthan). They clearly had been displaced over the western and central Deccan with the construction of railroads and the spread of farming. Large areas of untilled land that could support the assembly of large *tandas* were unavailable. Many became farmers themselves, pushing especially into moist deciduous woodland that could sustain a mixed farming lifeway. A few joined the ranks of what the British police authorities classified as "Criminal Tribes."

VILLAGE DEFENSES

The peasant village was a nucleus of habitation, a center of specialization, and often also a fortified unit of defense. Lands close to its threshing floors were the most carefully tilled and intensively manured. Beyond that, cultivated lands became interspersed with rock, scrubland, and fallow or pastures. Thickets of thornbushes or clumps of larger trees became more frequent, merging, where biotic conditions allowed, into full-fledged woodland. Quite often, this woodland covered formerly tilled fields, abandoned village centers, and even sizable towns or abandoned forts. Woodlands were also part of the perceived landscape of human use, serving as bases and refuges employed by humble farmers and great kings alike. So were little forts.

W. H. Sykes, like other observers of Peninsular India, noted the strongly nucleated character of rural settlements on the plateau, or *desh*. "Most of the villages of the Desh have a Ghuree or fortlet, a small quadrangular work with very high mud walls & having narrow towers at the angles. They usually contain the habitations of the Pateel, the Deshmook or the Jagheerdar and to these persons they owe their origins . . . the villages in the Desh with rare exceptions have also their Gaokoss, which is a simple mud wall without rampart or parapet, encircling them."[36]

Lesser gentry and even humble peasants in many areas also used anthropogenic features for defense and concealment of villages. Such defensive modification of the landscape naturally varied with the historical experience and geographical constraints of each region. Traveling westward into Central India from the coast, Thomas Motte was struck by the use of bamboos for fortification. Oriya tribal warriors were armed with bows and arrows and swords. They could not, they told him, withstand Maratha cavalry in open country but declared themselves "very formidable to cavalry in the woods." The Maratha rulers did not allow larger settlements to fortify themselves—in one case, however, the inhabitants had developed a refuge atop a steep hill surrounded by dense thorny bushes.[37]

The anthropologist Barry Lewis deployed historical records alongside extensive fieldwork to study village defenses. By contrast with the open plains, in the hill forests village defense "relied on the ruggedness of the terrain; on barriers and earthworks that defended roads and trails." But there were times when even the village citadel (if it existed) was too insecure for the peasants. Then flight into the woodlands or other regions was their only recourse. They had no option but to scatter into the forest if any was to be found.[38] Like the seasons for wild fruits or spots for edible tubers, knowledge of suitable short-term refuges and the routes to them would be part of the essential geographical wisdom of ordinary villagers.

THE FORTRESS AND "HER CHILDREN"

The mountainous eastern edge of the Deccan Plateau was studded with peaks that were easily transformed into forts. These afforded strongholds for local lords and aspirant kings in the six hundred years ending 1800, an era when cavalry armies generally dominated the plains. Many of these served as bases for Maratha resistance to Mughals during the long war that ended with the latter retreating northward. Not surprisingly, the permanent garrisons of these strongholds were drawn from local populations familiar with the mountains, unafraid of the forests, and perhaps resistant to malaria. James Mackintosh, long-time commander of a local battalion, gathered local traditions about the hills. He was told of the Koli tribesmen's major role in recapturing many of the hillforts from garrisons in the Mughal service in the 1750s. He added that the fact so many of the Koli inhabitants "were either employed on the hill forts or to guard the approaches leading to them, gave the relatives of these people many opportunities of negotiating for the surrender of the forts to an enemy."[39]

D. C. Graham was the British officer assigned to manage the Kolhapur state after the suppression of a major uprising centered on the hillforts. He was a good antiquarian who was the first to publish several inscriptions found around Kolhapur. He also left a close firsthand description of the hillfort pattern of life just as the colonial government was seeking to end it. He commented that in "Native warfare"—meaning presumably that without good siege artillery and military engineers—even weak garrisons could defy powerful armies. Forts therefore could only be taken by stratagem or bribery, by subverting or starving out the defenders. In the Kolhapur hillforts he knew, Ramoshis, Mangs, and Mahars served as scouts, while Marathas formed the main garrison. Despite this evident effort to prevent their uniting against central authority, garrison militia developed a strong sense of corporate identity and entitlement. Collectively termed "Gurkurries," they held hereditary grants of land in the vicinity of the fort. Their solidarity was evident in a phrase quoted by Graham that "the fort was the mother that fed them."[40] This attitude was not confined to Kolhapur; it existed around most major hillforts. Writing of the fortress of Purandar, near Pune, Mackintosh observed that the Kolis and Mahars living around the fort had long been employed as wardens of the outposts. When the first Chatrapati Shivaji captured the fort, Ramoshis were added to the garrison.[41] The permanent garrisons were sometimes unquiet neighbors. Maratha rulers had created a game preserve near the village of Khopsi whose inhabitants managed it. However, the garrison of Kalyangad disputed their control and refused to recognize it. The court ordered the garrison to desist from interfering in the lands below the hillcrest.[42]

Graham's narrative of the great hillfort of Panhala illustrates the political importance of such fortresses. It was strengthened by the Marathas in 1677 but was taken by the Mughal armies shortly thereafter. The *gadkari*-s then recaptured it for the Marathas in 1682. In the late eighteenth century, they accepted a large sum of money to hand it over to the powerful regional warlord, Parashram Bhao Patwardhan, after he had closely besieged it for several months. But it was then retaken by the Raja of Kolhapur after ten years. Its perimeter spanned 5.5 English miles, and the permanent garrison numbered 845 men. Graham's narrative is peppered with examples of fort garrisons closing their gates and defying the king or other potentate if they felt wronged in some way. In the early 1840s, the British government imposed a new, more bureaucratic administration on the small kingdom of Kolhapur. The major hillforts of the area hitherto had their own separate administration. Its amalgamation with another office alarmed the hereditary permanent garrison. They feared the effects of the change in management on the tax exemptions of their small farms in the hills around the fort. The garrisons therefore closed their gates, manned the bastions, and defied the new administration just as they had bargained with earlier ones.

The British government, however, was consistently concerned about future insurgencies basing themselves in these fastnesses. They were confident that they would never have to use these strongholds and did not want to dissipate their field army over many small sites. They therefore began demolishing the fort defenses almost immediately after their conquest of the Peshwa's territory in 1818. Sykes remarked that this was done mainly by blowing up their gates and water reservoirs.

Kolhapur was a semi-independent state. Its forts were the last remains of the major Maratha hill defenses. The uprising occurred at a time when the Koli tribesmen of the northern part of the range were also in revolt. The Government of Bombay was determined not to negotiate. It brought in heavy siege guns from Belgaum to end the resistance. After that, they followed the policy already adopted in other parts of the Sahyadri range and demolished the defenses, blowing up gateways and breaching rain-harvesting reservoirs so as to render the forts untenable.[43] Sykes in the 1820s had remarked that "art cannot ruin their natural defences & a few stout fellows could even now maintain them against the greatest disparity of numbers."[44] But the few and unsuccessful later insurgencies in the Sahyadri mountains never used these sites. They sought to use mobility and concealment in the hills rather than rely on the ancient redoubts that had endured through the centuries. The opacity of the wooded landscape to the colonial gaze was therefore insurgents' last resort. But even that was not to endure.

ECOSYSTEMS ANCHORED BY FORTRESSES

Over the centuries until the nineteenth century, special forms of land use and resource extraction grew up around hillforts. Their difficult approaches, the surrounding woodlands populated by beasts of prey, and the hard conditions of life in the hills meant that, historically speaking, their garrisons came often from villages in their "circuit," or *ghera*, a jurisdiction that often covered many miles of upland. It also meant that far removed from specialist farmers who built terraces and managed patches of rice paddy, many militiamen lived by swidden cultivation of ragi millet and other grains. Their right to do so was based on their hereditary role in the defense of the fort. But at the same time, the great lords who built forts in the hills and palaces in the valleys also wanted forest materials, notably teak timber. Its value for architecture and ship-building had long been recognized. Many local and regional rulers sought to assert monopolies over it—efforts that became more systematic and effective under British rule. Foresters gradually began to recognize that the presence of shifting cultivators and village settlements was useful in promoting "valuable" trees. This working compromise was unavoidable for earlier regimes. They were forced to reconcile their own timber needs with their dependence on hereditary *gadkari* communities. Seemingly untouched moist deciduous forest was in fact deeply molded by human action.

Alexander Gibson, conservator of forests for the Bombay Presidency, wrote in 1851 that in some of these forests, "such as Singhur [Sinhgarh fort] the whole Ghera of the Fort containing forest is parceled out into Inams for Sunudies [*śet-sanadi-s*, or militia paid in land] and others. These parties have, however, never dreamed of making any claim to the teak growing in these grounds, but quietly cultivate their raggy on the hill sides, taking care of the trees thereon. So also in the Kuran [grazing reserve] grounds of Chas Kuman, cultivation is carried on, and the trees are lopped and attended to, nay often improved now that care is taken of their preservation."[45] In fact, lopping or cutting other trees and clearing land by burning assisted the propagation of teak by reducing competition. It was the basis of what came to be called the *taungya* system in British Burma and elsewhere. A review of teak there observed that teak was more fire resistant than competitor or associate species in moist deciduous forest. It could therefore benefit from periodic fires.[46]

Ruling authorities and their soldiers often had very specific biomass requirements. Hillfort garrisons needed palm leaf cloaks against the monsoon rain; specific villages would be required to supply them. Beyond general labor in fort maintenance, villages would have to supply thatch for roofs and firewood for everyday use. The hard wood of the thorny acacia species was needed for specialized uses such as gun carriages and farm carts. In relatively denuded areas, even this modest timber might be bought, sold, and requisitioned by the state. In 1754–55, Harji Shitole bought sixteen such trees that were then seized by an employee for use by the state artillery establishment. The Peshwa ordered an inquiry to determine if they had in fact been purchased by Shitole.[47]

The western coast of India has long known long-distance trade. Piracy and naval warfare accompanied it. Teakwood from the coastal forests was a vital resource for the construction of not only forts and palaces but also ships. Different rulers sought to control the supply of valuable timber and also to manage the supply of firewood to other jurisdictions. The British in Mumbai were well aware of the extent to which they depended on these supplies from the mainland. The Angre family that controlled much of the coast south of Mumbai imposed an effective state monopoly on teak.[48] Nor were they unique in this; it seems to have been a general policy, and the Polish scientist Hove found a similar prohibition maintained by the Raja of Ramnagar farther north.[49]

We may see the conflict with local society in the case of teak timber, where the needs of ordinary housing and of imperial authorities were radically different. In the 1860s, James Forsyth wrote of Central India:

> Forests containing any great number of tolerably large teak trees are, however, now extremely few; and, as I have said, the teak has been indiscriminately hacked down for every sort of purpose, for many generations, over nearly the whole area where it is found. Among its numerous other valuable qualities, however, it includes that of rapidly throwing up a head of tall slender poles from the stumps, if they are allowed to remain in the ground. In five years this coppice wood will attain a height of twenty-five or thirty feet, and a girth of one to two feet. Such poles are invaluable in a country where habitations are in great measure very small, and built of wood alone—far more valuable, in fact, than larger timber, which is only useful for the *exceptional class of structures* comprising the residences of wealthy persons, European houses, and public edifices.[50]

It is evident here that royal power had been deficient, and peasant needs for straight, slender poles had governed the woodlands by default. But in treeless lands, peasants were forced to adapt to very limited supplies of timber.

Thomas Marshall wrote in 1821 of the lands of the present-day Bagalkot district in Karnataka that they, like the rest of the plains, "did not produce one bit of timber of sufficient size to be employed in the building of a respectable house." So small beams less than twelve feet long and six inches square were imported from the mountain woodlands to the southwest; "four of them form a very awkward load for a Bullock."[51] Sykes was a military officer fluent in Marathi who commanded a regiment of the Bombay Native Infantry. Between 1825 and 1829, he held the temporary post of statistical reporter to the provincial government. He confirms Marshall's observation for his region. In the semi-arid eastern plains of the plateau, he wrote, "woods were so scattered, thin and low that a man on horseback is able to look over them."[52] At the end of a four-year survey, he wrote of the plateau in 1829, "Woods exist only in the ghauts, in belts on the slopes of the mountains, or in chasms or deep ravines. They are for the most part made up of medium-sized trees and tall shrubs... for extended purposes the country reported on absolutely does not produce timber."[53]

ARMIES AS MOBILE NATIONS

Forts and garrisons were generally dwarfed by the field armies they were intended to withstand. Armies were usually accompanied by vast numbers of camp followers. This feature of Mughal-period armies was often described in travel accounts. But the first complete numerical estimate was made by Dirom, an officer on the staff of the army that invaded Mysore in 1791–92. The force included two cavalry contingents from the Marathas and one from the Nizam, whose reported numbers Dirom reduced by one-third. Also present was a large part of the British Madras and Bombay armies, chiefly infantry and artillery. Along with other allies, he calculated that the combatants on March 16, 1792, amounted to nearly 84,000, including 36,000 Indian and 444 European cavalry. Dirom thought that there were at least four camp followers for every fighting man, so that there were a total of "four hundred thousand strangers in Tippoo's country." Madras Army sepoys were always accompanied by their wives and families. Desertion increased sharply if the commander insisted that they be left behind.[54]

Armies were also accompanied by tens of thousands of animals: apart from cavalry horses, there were hundreds of elephants, thousands of camels, and tens of thousands of oxen that carried everything that sustained the camp. They drew the guns and carried stores and supplies. Attendants were needed for all the animals. Every two or three bullocks had an attendant. Each horse had a "grass-cutter" devoted to securing its fodder and a groom to clean and care for it. Horses (and some other animals) were also fed peas and lentils carried by oxen. Those animals were either part of the bazaar establishment or formed special convoys guided by the militarized Banjara herdsmen who moved bulk merchandise in peacetime and military supplies during wars. The sick and wounded might be carried in simple palanquins, and officers often rode in them too. Each needed teams of porters, who might often serve in relays. Dirom, who was intimately acquainted with the logistical problems of keeping an eighteenth-century Indian army in the field, has left a vivid description of it as more resembling "the emigration of a nation guarded by its troops, than the march of an army fitted out merely with the intention to subdue an enemy!"[55]

The removal of all usable biomass that might support an enemy army heavily dependent on animal power was part of a widely used "scorched earth" strategy. Dirom observed that Tipu Sultan of Mysore had anticipated where an army advancing on Seringapatam might camp and had left the valley as bare as possible. He cleared the country of every particle of both dry and green forage that might be within reach of an expeditionary force. "The cattle and horses might be supported for a few days on the roots of grass dug up by their keepers, but there was evidently no sufficient means left for their subsistence, much less for the elephants and camels, which feed on the leaves of trees, there not being even a bush standing."[56]

Paradoxically the residual landscape of political turmoil also created barriers to kingly power. Armies withdrew, leaving denuded landscapes and smoldering villages behind them, but plants and animals recolonized the land. Even in semi-arid areas, abandoned fields and villages quickly reverted to savanna woodland of various types. In moister areas, quick-growing bamboos and thorny vegetation would be among the earliest colonizers. Such growth would then serve as an obstacle to future entry and surveillance by officials and armies.

Shankar Raman studied regenerating plots of various ages in the humid hill region of Mizoram in northeast India. Soon after a plot is abandoned, weeds, residual crop plants, and bamboo from underground rhizomes run amok, "creating a dense and vigorous tangle that at first threatened to smother forest regeneration. Bamboo then dominated regenerating fallows for at least the first 30 years. Then as the shade thickens, rainforest tree seedlings sprout and flourish; left undisturbed they take over when the bamboo flowers and dies (as it does cyclically). There is little space and sun for bamboo seed to sprout into great clumps. A century after it was cleared, the land is occupied by rainforest trees and lianas with little bamboo present."[57] The presence of humans and their swidden cultivation meant that some land was always in an intermediate stage of regrowth, with considerable bamboo always present. This has been true of all the moister parts of the subcontinent, where local societies have long adapted the bamboo to a variety of uses.

EVADING EMPIRE: ZOMIA

As noted earlier, destructive visitations of drought and war (*asmani wa sultani*) might force peasants to resort to simpler forms of subsistence for a season or perhaps permanently.[58] Such forms have been theorized by James Scott as being conscious choices by local societies seeking to evade subjection to states. Hill people of the Southeast Asian massif, he suggests, should be understood as "runaways from state-making projects in the valleys. Their agricultural practices, their social organization, their governance structures, their legends and their cultural organization in general" all reflect state-evading practices.[59] In *The Art of Not Being Governed*, Scott particularly valorized the small anarchic hill communities as examples of successful evasion of the state. He began by laying out a stylized model of the wet-rice "padi state." This needed water management, coordinated planting, and a legible landscape susceptible to, indeed requiring, control by superior authorities. It concentrated the labor force and produced large surpluses to support an overlord class. It could only exist under certain environmental conditions.

Yet there were landscapes and production methods that were resistant to monitoring and subordination. It was for these methods that Scott used Willem van Schendel's term *Zomia*. He saw the New World food crop—cassava or tapioca—as characteristically suited to such social regimes. In some areas, autonomous communities grew maize for subsistence and opium for trade. Not surprisingly, he argues, selected New World cultivars spread rapidly in the mountain massif of Southeast Asia. Tapioca did not need careful preparation or collective water management. Nor could it be located, measured, or taxed as easily as rice or wheat in the field or the granary. It was therefore well adapted to resistance and evasion. Peoples in the Zomia lands, Scott added, changed their social structures depending on their relationship to imperial powers in their vicinity.[60]

Like Scott, E. R. Leach consistently emphasizes that differences in physical environment provide only a partial explanation of differences in political or cultural organization. But he differs from Scott in that he also argues that individuals and families often made the transition between the two forms of sociocultural life. In both mythic and historical time, communities oscillated between chieftain domination and household autonomy. Colonial officials much preferred autocratic chiefs who could act as agents of colonial governance. They would be deferential to colonial authority, and so the supply of porters and food could be organized in a centralized way.[61]

Leach also offers us a glimpse of periods of political contestation in today's Myanmar between the Shan peoples of the valley bottoms ruled by princes and the Karen who were usually loosely governed by chiefs. He gives examples of the recruitment of Karen soldiers by Shan rulers and Burmese kings alike—again a widespread pattern. Most of South Asia had thinner, dryer woodland and a more densely populated agrarian order. That made the alternative of complete retreat and fully decentralized existence difficult to achieve. It was only possible in a few thinly peopled areas, such as the interior southeast of the Indian peninsula.[62]

LANDSCAPES OF CONTESTED POWER: MEHWAS

Elsewhere, the combination of defense and aggression led to the emergence of what the sultans of Delhi, the Mughals, and, after them, the British called *mehwas* lands, those inhabited by refractory peoples. This was a sociopolitical, not a geographic, designation. Any defensible region could become a *mawas* or *mehwas*; Sleeman observed that such areas existed across the densely inhabited Gangetic plains well into the nineteenth century. Intermediate lands and contested frontier zones were especially prone to becoming *mehwas*. Disturbed conditions would, as I have argued, spontaneously generate thorny forest or bamboo thicket that served for concealment and defense.

One of the best documented of *mehwas* was in the western sector of the Vindhya forests, a region extending from today's southern Rajasthan to north Gujarat and northeast Maharashtra. Mountstuart Elphinstone's Indian career culminated as governor of Bombay. He had by that time developed a conscious model of what we call political ecology seen from an imperial point of view. He recognized that contestation was a feature, not of peoples as such, but of their political relations with central power. Elphinstone thus says of the Surat district in south Gujarat that previous regimes had granted much land on a tax-reduced or exempt basis in order to pacify chiefs whom they could not subdue. Village communities also often paid such lords additional customary dues known as *giras*. Both types of grant were held by proprietors whom Elphinstone describes as men whose "outrages and exactions at one time greatly disturbed the district."[63] They had evidently been pacified by the grants they now held.

From a non-imperial point of view, these chiefs were sub-imperial claimants to the agrarian surplus. Indeed, this was how Garcia da Orta perceived analogous communities in the mid-sixteenth century. He wrote that the lands of Gujarat ("Cambaya") and the Deccan had been conquered by the kings of Delhi some three hundred years before his time. But the former Hindu ("gentio") rulers—Rajputs, Kolis, and Vanjaras—were not entirely subdued but continued to rob and plunder. This prevented the new rulers from controlling their conquests. The displaced chiefs were therefore paid a tribute from their old lands to purchase their forbearance from plunder.[64]

Elphinstone also understood how some terrain was better adapted to such contestations because it was less accessible to surveillance and control. He generally explained the extent of government authority by the physiographic possibilities of defiance. The mountain ranges that bounded central Gujarat (the Mahi Kantha) to the north and northeast, he wrote, sent out many spurs. The lands between these hill spurs were generally covered with jungle. Eastward the land was less mountainous, but there were many rivers. Their banks abounded "in long, deep, and intricate ravines, overgrown with thick jungle." Gradually, however, the rivers merged into two large ones, and the terrain became level and open. This last area was largely settled in sizable villages. Geography in his view thus explained "the degrees of subjugation" across the province. Villages in the fertile plain had long been fully subjected to the ruling authority—here the Maratha kings of Baroda. But even in the level plains, wooded valleys sheltered "independent villages," meaning thereby villages and clusters of villages that only paid tribute under threat of, or under actual, attack. Independent villages were often governed by tributary chiefs or headmen. In the Mahi River watershed, most such chiefs belonged to a widespread peasant-warrior community, the Kolis. Some others were classed as Rajputs. Both these names occur in slightly different form in Garcia da Orta's work as those of the former rulers of these territories.

Koli and Rajput modes of warfare varied with their social aspirations and physical capacities. Rajputs aimed at a lordly style in war and consumption. They used horses and matchlock muskets, very rarely the bow. It was ignoble to flee, so they generally resorted to a static defense of their fortified villages. But they were quite incapable of the mobile guerrilla tactics used by the

Kolis, whose plainer dress, physical hardiness, and simply contrived weapons allowed for swift flight and sudden attack. "They wear small turbans and few clothes, and are seldom seen without a quiver of arrows and a long bamboo bow, which is instantly bent on any alarm, or on the sudden approach of a stranger.... The natives describe them as wonderfully swift, active and hardy; incredibly patient of hunger, thirst, fatigue, and want of sleep; vigilant, enterprising, secret, fertile in expedients, and admirably calculated for night attacks, surprises and ambuscades." Elphinstone's officials told him of several Koli villages that had open fields in one direction and were sited with access to the thicket-filled ravines in case of need. They would defend their villages, but if that failed, they retreated to the jungles and relied on night attacks and ambushes. If their external food supplies were cut off, they could subsist for a long time on the flowers of the wild mahua tree and other foraged foods. Not surprisingly, their greater adaptability enhanced their independence. Kolis and the socially similar Makwanas predominated among the tributary chiefs recognized by the early British in 1813. Out of 121 chiefs, 79 were Koli, 31 Makwana, and only 11 Rajput.[65]

Elphinstone had long remarked on the cultural continuity between communities that called themselves Bhil with those termed Koli. In an overview of the British conquests in Western India written in 1821, he described the ethnic geography of the region in relation to its physiography, just as he did for Gujarat. He noted the similarities of Kolis, Bhils, and Ramoshis, as well as the distinct territorial distribution of each community.[66] Their upper strata in some areas acculturated toward a "Rajput" model of lordship. That, however, risked alienating the peasant warriors on whom defense of their lordship depended. Effective power was founded not on imperial grant, but on a capacity for continuous resistance. Acceptance of a pattern of punctuated resistance by a ruling power that was prepared for compromise after spells of hostilities would then produce the pattern that Elphinstone described of the "independent villages" of *mehwas* Gujarat. The "Mehwas" lands were subject to *mulk-giri*—military expeditions to exact tribute by an aspirant ruling power. For central Gujarat, it was the Maratha dynasty based at Baroda (Vadodara). This was an unstable equilibrium, however.

Bhil settlements were politically constituted by adherence to a headman but not physically clustered. The tactical advantages of this structure were noted by a colonial officer tasked with repressing them. Their scattered habitations made "it difficult if not impossible" to surprise and surround them in their own hills. The best season for military operations against them, wrote William Hunter, the commander of the Mewar Bhil Corps, was early summer. Water was scarce in the uplands, and Bhils were vulnerable only when they and their cattle congregated in the few valleys that were perennial water sources.

In uplands occupied by the Bhil community, the abundance of land allowed many small clusters of farmhouses to form, with adult sons building huts near their fathers. Not surprisingly, huts usually lay in the midst of the best land. Only this land was continuously cultivated. The millets were cultivated only with seasonal fallows. Boggy lands in lower valleys were used to grow rice. Maize, an American crop, was swiftly adopted in areas remote from the coasts where the Portuguese had first introduced it. It fitted well into the political ecology of hill communities. It needed more moisture than the arid zone millets but, unlike wheat or barley, tolerated heat. It yielded well and grew in the rainy season when attack and plunder was nearly impossible. Maize benefited from fertile soils such as grew up around homesteads where dung and domestic refuse continuously enriched the soil. Such locations were easier to guard against wild birds and animals as maize stalks and cobs were devoured by pigs, monkeys, jackals, rats, and parrots. It was therefore cultivated in patches near the homestead where it was easily watched.[67] Maize soon became a staple in the Mehwas lands of Central India. Hunter noted that the dread that their maize crop would be destroyed "has often induced the rebellious Bheels to surrender and to give hostages and security for future good conduct." Yet agreements on the payment of compensatory dues to Bhils were sometimes evaded, resulting in new raids by them.[68]

Agreements broke down in the Tapi River Valley or Khandesh during the later eighteenth century.[69] There had been a modus vivendi between different royal powers that shared the region and the Bhils in the hills and plains for some decades before 1800. Many Bhils were settled as watchmen with hereditary perquisites from each harvest they guarded. But major marauding expeditions combined with severe famine in 1802–3 caused a breakdown. Dues could not be paid from shrunken harvests. Surviving Bhils gathered to subsist by robbery and braved brutal reprisal. Violence escalated, settled agriculture retreated, and thorn forest spread. The Bhil communities that survived lived in an uninterruptedly refractory or mehwasi condition. But the experienced British officer John Malcolm remarked on these hill communities' dependence on grain supplies as well as tobacco from the plains villages. He also noted that there was a "natural spirit of independence" among what he calls the hill Bhils. This meant that chiefs who aspired to power greater than that of village chiefs had to recruit mercenaries from outside the community to enforce their authority. They also had to establish wider authority over plains villages. But the weapons and tactics of the Bhils were not suited to fighting in the plains, being best adapted to woods and ravines. Military movements in open country required new weapons and tactics. These often came with an importation of mercenaries. Dependence on and indebtedness to them often hollowed out the authority of the chief.[70]

After 1810, the Maratha regime in Pune had deployed the time-tested processes of coercion and negotiation to secure a renewal of peace. The region was in this uncertain equilibrium when the British annexed the area in 1818. Meanwhile, political authority in the Mehwas lands began to be broken down by targeting the foreign mercenaries who bolstered the authority and military power of local chieftains. Such men were important targets of the colonial government. It began to systematically flush out the non-tribal soldiers of fortune who had stiffened the incipient states of the forest fringe. This tended to "devolve" tribal political structures into simpler forms of ethnic dominance rather than chiefly power.

The British had a more pervasive view of the landscape and a stronger desire to impose their hierarchical authority. One of the first measures was to remove—and in some instances deport—the mercenaries who had cemented chiefly authority.[71] The partitioning of agricultural surpluses with various claimants and its renegotiation by violence was intolerable for them. They systematically assembled an apparatus designed to suppress such phenomena. Ajay Skaria's important work on the oral histories of the mountain (Dangi) Bhils reflects the effects of this strategy. He analyzes how the most fundamental transformations that followed British takeover were the remaking of payments such as *giras* (for protection) and stern repression of raids to secure additional payments or collect extant claims. This radical transition was described in Bhil memory as one between *moglai* and *mandini*. The first word literally means "of the Mughals"—it referred to precolonial rule generally. "Mandini" is derived from a verb meaning to organize, lay out, or regulate and referred to the British era. A key step in this was that formerly self-enforced tributes collected by the Bhils and distributed through their chiefs were now collected as a part of British taxation. They were then apportioned by special officers appointed to control and "settle" the Bhils. Lesser chiefs who had been paid by their overlord now got direct access. This meant the Bhil capacity for collective action was being fragmented. Additionally, special paramilitary battalions were raised from the forest communities around the region. The Khandesh Bhil Corps was the earliest but was followed by others in analogous areas, as Skaria observed. Importantly, these men did not come under their own leaders but were commanded by Indian and one or two British officers appointed by the East India Company. The British apportionment of "pensions" to the chiefs was recollected in Dangi historical memory as the establishment of the *gadis*, or thrones. But as the more astute chiefs said at the time, the real throne was Bombay, Calcutta (where the Government of India's headquarters were located), or even London.[72] Once authority had been established, the survey systems, landmarks, and boundary marks and maps that signaled the physical installation of the colonial knowledge apparatus could begin. Empire and information, the encompassing gaze and overpowering hand were to arrive together.

LANDS OF SHARED SOVEREIGNTY: GARHJAT COUNTRY

In parts of the Bhil lands and eastward into the large tract known from at least Mughal times as Gondwana, politics and geography had led to the creation of tributary lordships among a peasant-warrior population. But they retained the capacity to reclaim their autonomy. Bhil chiefs in the southern territories claimed by the Rajput Rana of Mewar told a British officer that as the Rana had taken back some villages granted to the chiefs, they had repudiated any dependence on that Raj. Autonomy extended down the social hierarchy. Ordinary Bhil peasants made some semi-voluntary gifts to their rulers. They also shared in the protection money collected from traders and travelers and in the plunder of hostile country. Nonetheless, there were large areas of cereal cultivation in their lands, and they grew tradable commodities such as ginger and sugarcane. Additionally, many valuable drugs used in Indian medicine were collected from their hills. But Hunter also remarked on the centrality of the maize crop to their subsistence.[73] Their defensively dispersed habitus avoided the need for permanent fortresses that might turn into traps. It also bypassed the authoritarian hierarchies of kingship needed to manage and maintain such defenses. But such phenomena were historically contingent. If absent from Bhil lands, they were found farther east in Central India.

In moister areas with a more secure power structure, little states emerged around key fortresses with a production base in reservoir-irrigated rice fields. One major region was named Chattisgarh, meaning "the Thirty-Six Forts," a name that reflected the older political structure of the region.[74] But states could collapse. There were major ruined religious and political sites around the periphery of much of the Central Indian forest region. The ruins probably represented the collapse of a complex political society under political and climatic stress in the century ending around 1400 CE. They were then followed by simpler "tribal" polities that renewed the process of state formation in Mughal times. Especially to the south, they were associated with the builders of a large number of reservoirs. These irrigation works, early British officials noted, were located in the skirts of the hills wherever suitable terrain was to be found. These reservoirs then irrigated rice lands on the pattern found across the Deccan peninsula and supported the reemergence of small kingdoms.[75] When, in 1821, Richard Jenkins's emissary Vinayakrao asked the local gentry of Umrad about the history of their town, he was told that there were initially only fifty or one hundred houses ruled by Dilip, a Gond Raja. At that time, the land "was covered with trees and bushes, and *there were the ruined walls of an old mud fort.*"[76] A little state had risen and fallen and been forgotten.

State failures would lead to a reversion to swidden farming and a simpler political structure. Across east Central India, peasants cultivating by swidden tended to be labeled Gond and especially identified with hill regions. It was their farming that also kept the hill forests clear and created meadows for seasonal grazing. The colonial official, Richard Temple, termed their hills "the great pasturage whither the cattle from the plain districts resort." He added that if "they were not in the country, the last state of the forests would be worse than the first. For then the traces of human habitation, settlement, and clearance, would disappear. The foresters and the woodmen could no longer live in, or even enter into, the wilderness, rank and malarious with uncleared jungle, and overrun with wild beasts. These animals are already so destructive as to constitute a real difficulty. The only check upon their becoming masters of the forests is the presence of the hill tribes."[77]

Not surprisingly, early British officials viewed the forests in exactly the same way as their Maratha predecessors had done. In 1824, Assistant Collector H. F. Dent proposed various measures to relieve the impact of a severe crop failure. Among other steps, he recommended that villagers "might perhaps be advantageously employed in clearing the thickest and worst jungles on their lands, at present a harbour for Bheels and tigers."[78] Gradually, however, the forests receded, as trees went to feed the demand for beams and rafters, for railroad sleepers and firewood, and shrubs and brushwood were thinned out to fence fields and fuel hearths.

This chapter has shown that intra-human conflict plays a key role in shaping ecosystems. The building and destruction of kingdoms and empires in South Asia drew on many biotic resources—from water to stone, from captured elephants to forced laborers. Most of all, it drew on horses and oxen. But these species made their own demands on the ecosystem, on forests and plains. Human beings changed their behavior, their farming systems, and their subsistence strategies in anticipation of future warfare. Entire provinces were depopulated by military operations. Military logistics, defensive and offensive, thus inadvertently shaped the ecosystem. Even the roots of grasses were laboriously excavated to feed horses and oxen; even thorny brushwood would still be eaten by camels. New niches appeared for other species. Kingdoms built great fortresses to secure their power. These were constructed through the anonymous toil of thousands. But an ecosystem of tenacious communities took shape around them, and, on occasion, these were prepared to defy kings and emperors. It was many decades before British imperial power fully mastered the landscape, until its surveyors and forest wardens could travel unchecked through the densest woodland, unresisted save by mosquitoes. Farms and forests were opened to a closer gaze and a tighter grasp than ever before. This was a phase change in the political ecology of South Asia and forms the subject of the next chapter.

SIX

Colonialism, Disarmament, and the Closing of the Forest Frontier

> The disciplining of the landscape took place within the scope of the map, within the archive and panopticon.
> MATTHEW EDNEY | *Mapping an Empire*

THE IRISH SOLDIER OF FORTUNE W. H. TONE COMMANDED AN infantry battalion in the Maratha service in the 1790s. He wrote a careful assessment of the Marathas' collective strength and emphasized the vast numbers of homebred horses that they could muster. Of the 274,000 soldiers that he mentions as being the aggregate strength of the five Maratha states in 1796, 210,000 were horsemen.[1] They clearly maintained hundreds of thousands of horses.

It is possible that Tone saw the Maratha light cavalry complex at an unsustainable height at the end of the eighteenth century. Light horses were still numerous until 1818: William Chaplin, who had participated in the war of 1817–18 that overthrew the Peshwa, vividly recollected "the swarms of horse that covered the plains of the Deckan in 1817 and 1818." That war was followed by a sudden and dramatic collapse in the horse population, concomitant with a general collapse of the old military economy. The Peshwa's territories were annexed in 1817–18. The new administration, fearing a Maratha resurgence, was anxious to learn what cavalry potential the region still retained. Chaplin reported with some surprise that the whole number of horses from the Tapti to the Tungabhadra Rivers was not more than 20,000 (excluding only the newly established Satara kingdom). Few even of these would serve for the East India Company cavalry; indeed, only half might be thought of as horses. Regarding the Patwardhan princes' joint contingent, he wrote that of the 1,300 horsemen turned out at muster, one-third rode mere ponies, and another third rode horses worn out with age or strenuous service. Only the balance were efficient soldiers. Within the Company's directly administered territory, barely 6,000 horses remained. No one (Chaplin judged) would venture the expense of maintaining the Arab stallions the government was trying to introduce.[2] The old peasant militia/Dakhani horse complex had lost its raison d'être and was disappearing before his eyes. Through the next half century, that was to transform the political ecology of Peninsular India.

DISARMAMENT, CONTROL, AND TRANSPARENCY

In Western India, the British defeat of their only serious rivals, the Marathas, in the early years of the century had led to a massive change in the livestock economy and consequently on the landscape. The successful suppression of the uprising of 1857–58 led the new imperial government to use its awe-inspiring coercive power to force through a widespread disarmament of rural India. This was formalized by the passing of the Arms Act in 1878 but had been policy for the preceding twenty years. The former resources of the old militarized countryside may be estimated from the brutally thorough disarmament of the kingdom of Oudh, or Awadh, in 1858–59. It had a population of approximately eleven million.[3] By August 1859, the British had compelled the surrender of 684 cannon, 186,177 firearms, 565,321 swords, 50,311 spears, and 636,683 weapons of miscellaneous character. "The number of forts destroyed and under course of demolition up to the same date was 1,569."[4]

The disarmament effort was especially focused on refractory communities in difficult terrain, such as the ravines and thorn jungle of Western India, even if in the territory of subordinate and tributary rulers. The basis for a rigorous, territorially based control of woodlands came after the successful suppression of the great uprising of 1857–58. Some small insurgencies had broken out in the rugged woodlands of eastern Gujarat. They were followed by the extension of the rigorous disarmament that occurred all across British India to the princely states of the area as well. Villages that had any history of resistance were destroyed. For example, a punitive expedition attacked the Kolis of a Baroda village and defeated them. After they fled, the entire village of eight hundred houses was burned to the ground. The military officer in charge wrote that the "town is totally destroyed and never ought to be allowed to raise its head again." The British political agent stationed in Baroda was alert to the military ecology of the old location, He recommended to the Baroda government that a "fresh site should be chosen for the creation of a new village, at least a mile further from the Taringha Hills, and the jungle which intervened between them and the very entrance to the houses."[5]

DEMILITARIZATION ENABLED MAPPING AND DEMARCATION

Unprecedented change came to South Asia after the consolidation of the British Empire in the nineteenth century. Some changes were a result of the spread of the Industrial Revolution and its technologies, especially railroads.[6] But others were the result of changes in power relations across the face of the land. It became possible for the imperial government to transfer mapping techniques from sea to land and therefore "know" it in an unprecedented way (see map 4). The new imperial state was costlier than that of the East India Company. Like the Mughals and previous rulers, early colonial rule had sought revenue through the expansion of tax-paying agriculture. In colonial administrative parlance, "waste" often simply referred to untilled land of any description. But from the later nineteenth century, a new official agency, the Forest Department, began to aggressively classify and demarcate lands as forest and then exclude not just tillage but also woodcutting and grazing. As a result, there was a continual tussle between wildland users of all types and the parvenu department.

The ragged margin between forest and field had shifted back and forth across the Deccan landscape for centuries. It began a steady retreat after 1800. But well before this necessarily slow process began, the new colonial regime was faced with the need to manage the forest folk and to assert a level of control over them to which the ancient régime may have aspired but never actually attained. We may see this process most clearly in the western part of the Central Indian forest, the Bhil lands between the upper Chambal and Godavari Rivers. This was not a region where horsemen had ever been militarily dominant. Jagged terrain covered with obscuring woodland made it terra incognita for the kingly gaze. But the indirect effects of colonial demilitarization extended here too.

Following the defeat of the Holkars of Indore, the Bhosles of Nagpur, and

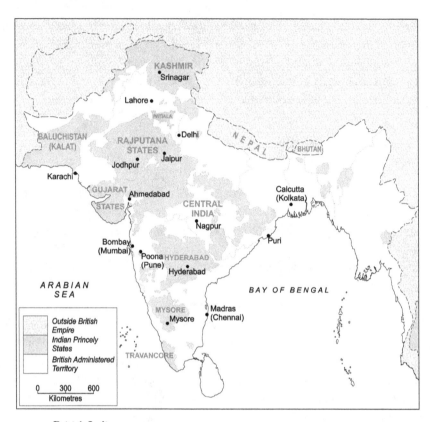

MAP 4. British India, ca. 1900.

the annexation of the Peshwa's territory in 1818, the colonial regime was able to institute policies of subjugation and settlement along the entire periphery of the great Central Indian forest, as well as its extensions into the Deccan. An important first step had already been taken in 1816–17 in the campaigns that destroyed the Pindaris as an organized mobile military formation and either killed their leaders or confined them to petty territorial lordships. Subsequent years (1818–20) also saw the seizure and deportation of the Arab mercenaries who had abounded in Central India.[7] At the same time as thickets were cleared, the mercenaries who provided military strength to the small chieftaincies of the Mehwas began to be expelled. No previous regime could have achieved this: all had depended heavily on contractor-supplied mercenary military units whose freedom of action they could not infringe.

The East India Company began with that model but gradually dissolved it. It stopped hiring Indian soldiers for "the season," replacing them with permanent units recruited and trained individually. It then refused to allow them to seek new employers at will; when one contingent attempted this, many were executed for mutiny. It also actively sought to enhance the loyalty of its key expatriate personnel to their country of origin.[8]

Thus, the mobile and mobilizable military resources of the chiefs and princes of the region were significantly reduced, and they were thrown back on local followings. With those who remained refractory, Elphinstone wrote in 1822, "The plan adopted . . . was to stop the supplies of the Beels, which are all drawn from the plain; to cut off any parties that attempted to issue to plunder, and to make vigorous attacks on the points in the hills, to which the principal Beel Chiefs had retired. These measures soon reduced the Beels to accept the very favorable terms held out to them; which were to forbear their depredations, the Chiefs receiving pensions, and allowances for a certain number of men, and binding themselves to restrain the excesses of their people."[9]

In Malwa, John Malcolm initially made similar arrangements for the hill peoples in the 1820s. He wrote that he was "giving them their ancient dues, encouraging cultivation in their Hills, instituting markets for their wood." He also raised a Bhil militia, commanded by their own chiefs.[10] Since the chiefs had often taken to the hills precisely in order to secure allowances, fees, and positions, it is scarcely surprising that many of them accepted such arrangements. However, disputes over demands soon tested the arrangements. Furthermore, regional and local potentates had found it useful to occasionally use bandit networks to promote their claims against a colonial government that they could not openly resist. F. J. Marriott, the British officer in charge of the northern Konkan, found that the bandit Khandoji Naik had been instigated by Deoba Rao Mukney, a courtier of Jawar state whose goal was the creation of a post of "Superintendent of the Police of the Jungle Districts" and the grant of a tax-free village for himself. Various parties to an intricate succession dispute in that state were also connected with the dacoit gangs. Such maneuvers became more difficult.

The greater striking power of the new regime, however, allowed more sweeping actions than had been open to officers of previous governments, though the tactics would have been familiar to them. Thus, James Outram, on investigating a series of armed robberies in the eastern part of Khandesh, "had no doubt that all the Turvee [Bhil] clans were more or less implicated." He then sought to preclude mass flight to the hills by sowing dissension among the hill chiefs. Having thus prepared the ground, he rounded up 469 men, 94 women, and 54 boys, the latter being the wives and children of those who evaded arrest. They were held as hostages to prevent the absconders from retaliating. With one exception, the pensioned chiefs were found to have been either "guilty or remiss" with regard to the robberies, a complaint also being made in the Sahyadri ranges in the same period. Both Outram's raids and Marriott's intelligence reports show us how the colonial government was increasingly able to penetrate and surveil woodlands in a way none of their predecessors had done.

Woodlands also began to be cleared for peasant farming, leaving little concealment for insurgents. Previous governments had hired local chieftains with extant followings as wardens of the passes. That was the post to which Mukney had aspired. Gradually, such contingents were replaced by local corps under British officers. Such was the Khandesh Bhil Corps, the Mairwara battalion, and the Mewar Bhil Corps, all of which were created in the first half of the nineteenth century. These battalions were placed under "outsiders," Indian non-commissioned officers from regular regiments, with English officers in overall charge. Chiefs were pensioned off, mercenaries expelled, and older patterns of authority dissolved.[11] Bhil oral traditions collected by Ajay Skaria remembered a great change in the regime of the forests in the Age of Regulation (*mandini*), a time when regulations were few but rigorously applied. But the very possibility of *mandini* was the consequence of two uniquely intense processes under colonial rule: military disarmament and geographic demarcation. The two went together. Exact surveys would conceptually mark out the limits of villages and states; the installation of durable boundary markers would manifest them. Neither was possible without sustained military control over villages and forests. The early colonial regime began serious military operations in the 1820s and had the political solidity and financial capacity to sustain them through the next century.

IDEOLOGICAL AND INSTITUTIONAL ROOTS OF THE FOREST DEPARTMENT

Nineteenth-century political economy desired a minimalist state: intervention was only permissible if the market could not work. Interestingly, this idea of market failure needing state remediation arose in the same period when free-market theory was ascendant in the West and being applied to Britain's Indian Empire. The struggle between these opposed ideological impulses played out in colonial policy in the half century before 1900. It produced several paternalist measures intended to protect favored, but commercially naive, landed classes from market forces.[12] The colonial government in India was torn between immediate tax revenue, social conservatism, and desiccationist alarm for the future of the agrarian empire. If the government budget was a "gamble on the monsoon," then anything that increased the risk of future losses was a source of present concern. Even in 1848, some still saw privatization rather than state control as the answer to territorial management. The influential Revenue Survey officer George Wingate was interested in expanding tillage and thereby increasing tax revenue. He advocated secure property rights as the best way to ensure the most productive use of land. He argued on impeccable Ricardian principles that the "natives" could be trusted to put their land to its best use and would preserve trees if it was profitable to do so. He added the argument that no landholder would plant trees if he feared that the government would then claim them as state property.

Still, the Bombay forest officer Alexander Gibson was in 1848 already warning that Indians could not be trusted to own trees: "the natives cannot, in the present state of their habits, be safely trusted with a property in nearly all the trees in the open country; for, in the parts of the country hitherto surveyed, there may be said to be few or no trees, excepting in land which is arable."[13] Since the "country hitherto surveyed" was all in the semi-arid to arid plateau zone, Gibson had entirely inverted the causal relationship between aridity and tree growth. Trees, as W. H. Sykes had observed twenty years earlier, largely existed near villages or in moister locations. Their presence was often the result of conscious human action.[14]

But how important was the scientific argument being developed by early foresters and naval strategists for the eventual launch of the imperial forestry project? Richard Grove certainly gave it pride of place.[15] But, as Mariadas

Ruthnaswamy pointed out in 1939, early British administration was shaped essentially by the interlocking imperatives of sustained military power and stable tax collections.[16] The military ensured its dominance, but the revenue paid for it. This meant that rural India post conquest was shaped by the needs of the Revenue Department. This apparatus assessed and collected the taxes that sustained the military-bureaucratic colossus of the empire. The Forest Department was an interloper. In British Asia, fiscal success, which paid the high salaries and considerable perquisites of European officers, was the paramount priority (for them, at any rate). Other expenditures were secondary. That meant that even a small expenditure on early teak plantations in Bengal was sanctioned only because timber imports from "Malabar" (Southwest India) had been disrupted in the 1790s.[17] After all, as Mahesh Rangarajan has pointed out, once the naval timber shortages of the Napoleonic Wars were over, early efforts at creating a sustainably managed Indian teak supply also lapsed.[18]

Ramachandra Guha has thus rightly criticized Grove for exaggerating the importance of early environmental thinkers for colonial forest policy, as well as exaggerating its continuity with pre-British regimes. Forest conservancy began with the needs of the British Royal Navy during the Napoleonic Wars but lapsed for several decades after their end. It was revived with new force when railways began to be laid across the Indian subcontinent.[19] Furthermore, many civil and military officers firmly believed that malaria originated in dense woodland and clear-cutting made it less prevalent. This was such a truism that malaria or similar illnesses were often referred to simply as "jungle fever." After serious droughts in the 1830s, the Bombay government asked its administrators submit their opinion on the value of protecting woodland. Responses were summarized by the divisional commissioners. R. K. Pringle wrote that "destruction of the Jungle, so far from being looked on as an evil, has in that Province rather been considered as a benefit and measures have been proposed with a view to accelerate it.... Mr. Pringle gives it as his opinion that, admitting the growth of wood to have a tendency to attract moisture, the advantage would be dearly purchased at the expense of the salubrity of the climate." Pringle added that there were well-watered woodlands in the region that for more than half the year were "deadly to Europeans and noxious to natives, and are therefore thinly, if at all, inhabited." He was strongly convinced that timber reserves, if needed, should not be created in "inhabited parts of the country."[20] A few years later, the influential Wingate suggested that the "redundant" population of the western coast should be encouraged to migrate to the Tapti valley in order to cut down forests for cultivation and thereby make the region healthier.[21] Desiccationism was therefore far from intellectually dominant. The value of clearing woodland for cultivation was also axiomatic for many in India. Indeed, before 1850, "the Company Raj chiefly viewed forests as limiting agriculture."[22]

This changed after mid-century as desiccationism reemerged as the dominant environmental discourse in nineteenth-century Europe. It was quickly turned to use by Forest Department officials fighting to hack out a domain in the bureaucratic jungle of British India. As Sivaramakrishnan has percipiently observed, the colonial state, or any state, was not a single entity: "class forces and interests do not exhaust the range of forces and interests involved in the state . . . the state system itself engenders political interests."[23] Desiccation was usually seen as a consequence of human action, especially via deforestation.[24]

The observed relationship between aridity and the absence of dense woody vegetation is usually a consequence of long-term climatic patterns in which high temperatures, periodic fires, and high evapotranspiration preclude the existence of water-hungry trees. This is often misinterpreted as a causal relation created by imprudent, but reversible by prudent, humans.[25] For the purposes of this agenda in an imperial setting, that desirable prudence was lodged in the imperial administration, mainly in the Forest Department. In British India, "far-sighted management," therefore, became the rallying cry of a fledgling Forest Department that had to struggle for a place in the sun within the colonial bureaucracy. Later historians have tended to accept the desiccationism as "received doctrine" arising solely from "western science, or from the imperial, exploitative project of colonialism." But desiccationist orthodoxy had more complex roots in the forms of government themselves.[26] As the sharp-tongued John Beames of the Indian Civil Service (ICS) described it in his plainspoken memoirs, a "department of any kind in India always assumes that the world exists solely for the use of itself, and considers that anything that interferes with the working of the department ought to be removed." In the Arakan hill country, for instance, the newly empowered Dr. Schlich in his position as conservator of forests "calmly proposed that the whole Mugh and Chakma population should be removed from their native hills." In retort, the commissioner (who was answerable for law and order and tax collection) declared that "he thought it would do less harm if the trees were removed."[27]

Agricultural expansion unfailingly brought additional tax revenue to the British Empire; forest managers had to develop a narrative that denudation-induced drought would erode that tax base. Rural taxation was managed by the long-established Revenue Department, which hitherto had unchecked control over much of colonial India. That department was also headed by members of the "Heaven-born," the elite ICS, whereas the Forest Department was led by men of less elevated position, further handicapped by often being of foreign—usually German—origin. Still, a Forest Department was gradually constructed by the shrewd bureaucratic infighting of provincial conservators of forests armed with the spreading desiccationist orthodoxy.[28] The late nineteenth century also saw a wave of legislation aimed at restricting the working of markets in British India on the assumption that many Indians were incapable of rational behavior. Forest protection thus fitted into the emerging regulatory frame.[29]

Forest protection won crucial victories by convincing senior members of the old Civil Service, such as Richard Temple, a Civil Service appointee of 1844. Temple was also an experienced land settlement officer. He was at various times chief commissioner of the Central Provinces, finance member of the Governor-General's Council (meaning finance minister), lieutenant-governor of Bengal, and governor of Bombay.[30] When governing the Central Provinces, he was still skeptical of the foresters' agenda there and suggested that it would generate rebellion.[31] In the later decades of his career, however, he was entirely dazzled by the "science" of the Forest Department. In the 1870s, he became a convert to the model of rainfall being dependent on the preservation of tree cover and consequently on the pressing need for unlimited authority being conferred on the Forest Department. Early nineteenth-century felling and clearance was "a proof that formerly neither the Government nor its officers adequately appreciated the value of scientific forestry." His opinions were confirmed when he was assigned to oversee relief operations during the great South Indian famine of 1877. Coming from Eastern India, he was struck by the treelessness of the great "black soil" plains of the peninsula. He cited that observation in support of state forest control in Bombay when he became governor there. Yet the phenomenon was not new: the same observation had been made by Thomas Munro, governor of Madras, sixty years earlier. Efforts at afforestation were made after that. But as the junior officer who wrote the *Manual of the Bellary District* in 1872 observed, "large sums of money have been spent in planting topes [mango groves] and trees and some success has been attained. It has however been found almost impossible to get trees to grow in this [black] soil, and those that do take root are stunted miserable-looking objects. Water is very scarce, and what there is, is brackish and highly impregnated with lime."[32]

Common sense and local observation were of no avail against the rise of desiccationist orthodoxy, even if the scientific credentials of several early officials were less than resplendent. A. T. Shuttleworth was one of the more striking examples of the adroit assumption of special expertise. Shuttleworth came out to India in 1856 with a junior appointment in the Marine branch of the Bombay government.[33] That naval establishment was wound up as part of the reorganization of government under the Queen after 1858. Stranded ashore, Shuttleworth managed to find an appointment in the office of the conservator of forests under Alexander Gibson. Gibson was a medical officer turned botanist who had been given charge of the entire Bombay Presidency, from present-day west Karnataka north to central Gujarat, in 1847.[34] Shuttleworth rose to be conservator of forests, Northern Circle, with jurisdiction over thousands of square miles. His importance can be understood through considering his compensation. Shuttleworth's salary in 1877 was 1,200 rupees per month with a 200 rupee traveling allowance, larger than that of middle-ranking ICS officers or judges.[35]

Shuttleworth often figures as an empire-building tyrant even in the writings of brother Englishmen, especially officers in the Revenue Department. But as governor, Temple saw the existence of woodlands in the Bombay Presidency as proof of the value of Shuttleworth's ministrations. In general, he wrote approvingly of the practices extant in 1882: "The State forester is always cutting wood, large or small, and sending it to market, whereby the public really draws interest from the store of forest wealth. But he is careful to leave enough for reproduction, the decrement from felling is replaced by a corresponding increment from fresh growth, and the corpus of the forest, as representing principal, is preserved. The public, however, if left to itself would carve and hack the woods and forests without any care for reproduction or any regret for wastage, in the end destroying uselessly as well as consuming."[36]

Thus, the weight of Western science overbore local officials' resistance to the pretensions of the Forest Department. The latter grew steadily. In 1869, when the first graded list of (European) forest officers was published, there were only 57 of them, with aggregate salaries of 95,000 rupees a year. By the early twentieth century, when the *Imperial Gazetteer* was compiled, there were 175 officers in the imperial and 134 in the provincial services. The supporting staff numbered 14,824, and the aggregate annual salary bill was almost 4.5 million rupees. At one point, approximately one-fifth of the surface area of British India was partly or wholly within their domain.

But the political protest they had stirred up resulted in checks upon Forest Department officers. They were placed under the control of the local executive officers (collectors, magistrates, or deputy commissioners) in matters directly affecting the "welfare of the people." These included the reservation of grazing, grazing fees, minor forest produce, and the like.[37] Such supervision was bitterly resented by the anonymous forest officer who wrote to the *Times of India* that the rules were "most iniquitous," as they were directed solely "to the maintenance of the absolutism of the C[ivil] S[ervice]." The worst of it in his view was that district collectors might prefer the evidence of an (Indian) *mamlatdar* for the sole purpose of insulting the forest officer concerned.[38]

The challenge of the Revenue Department was met at one level by arguing that agriculture depended indirectly on the preservation or creation of woodlands and a regulated supply of forest materials. But the pressure to generate its own revenue was always present. The commercial orientation that Benjamin Weil observed in the official journal *The Indian Forester* only became, I would argue, more overt in the twentieth century.[39] But the seizure of large areas of open savanna or marginal woodland that began in the 1880s was, in effect, already a revenue-oriented measure. Forest closure also extended simultaneously over large regions, while land revenue settlements were done subdivision by subdivision and did not usually arouse large numbers to protest them. As forest closure was a more potent issue than any other, the Government of Bombay often had to reconsider the effects of the sweeping early closures.

The governor and his council debated the matter in 1897–98. One member of the Governor's Council declared that Richard Temple's main error had been "putting into the Forest Department's hands large areas of waste [i.e., uncultivated land] that they could not enclose, plant or utilise, but which they could get grazing fees off. . . . the department's fault is land-grabbing and making themselves needlessly unpopular."[40] In the east Khandesh (now Jalgaon) district, two-thirds of the Forest Department's revenue came from grazing fees, not from forest production proper. J. Monteith, the chief secretary, also wrote a memorandum in this debate, declaring roundly that the Forest Department "has been weighed in the balance and found wanting. It has not created forests where there were none: it has barely maintained in their original condition those which did exist: over vast areas of so-called forest lands it has not succeeded in producing a tree, barely a bush . . . by its futile attempts to protect what really are grass lands and slopes, often without even grass to cover them, and its wholesale impoundings of cattle wandering mainly on such lands, it has, without benefiting the progress of afforestation, created gross discontent and widespread exasperation."[41]

The debate on both sides invoked emergent forms of statistical knowledge. Statistics, Arun Agrawal writes, "allowed forests to be apprehended summarily and unambiguously."[42] But different participants in argument could produce different numbers. Responding to the claim that so-called forest was in fact just pasture, the divisional forest officer claimed that a sample of plots showed that there were more than twenty "useful trees" per acre in most villages. A senior revenue officer (assistant collector) and the divisional forest officer were ordered to conduct a joint survey and decide on the classification of the land in each case.[43] The implication is obviously that departmental reports were not objective. Equally, "facts on the ground" were not as firm as in imperial statistics. One Bachu Patil testified in 1886 that he knew of 3,000 *khair* trees being cut in his village by traders in collusion with forest guards for a period of three months. When this was reported, the guards employed workers to dig out and burn the stumps to erase all evidence of where the wood had been cut. It was then reported as cut on privately owned lands.[44]

What the Forest Department initially achieved, in conjunction with the new continent-wide surveys instituted by the British government, was to demarcate and control about one-fifth of British India. It took some eighty years, but by the 1930s a large section of the historically most ungoverned region of the Indian subcontinent was ring-fenced against the demands of both local villagers and seasonal itinerants. Forest villages were increasingly labor camps for the Forest Department, as the Forest Grievances Enquiry Committee revealed.[45] The activist anthropologist Verrier Elwin wrote, "I cannot think of anything more shameful, anything meaner, anything more disgraceful to an administration that claims to be enlightened than the way subordinates openly rob these poor people, some of the poorest in the world, of the few goods they have and of many hours of [forced] labour."[46] Protection against "other Indians" did not protect against the minions of the state, then or after the formation of the Republic of India in 1950. Forested lands were now opened to supra-local knowledge and management in an utterly unprecedented way. Struggles against the intrusive presence of the new government department began almost immediately. They grew into major conflicts that fed into nationalist agitations to the end of colonial rule.

NATIONALIST RESPONSES TO INTENSIFIED COLONIAL PRESENCE

Several different responses to this unprecedented display of power emerged from the nascent nationalist intelligentsia in British India. In the hinterland of Bombay city, many of the new intellectuals educated in British colonial law were drawn from the landowning and trading classes of the Konkan and coastal Gujarat. The Forest Department's unprecedented claims of control over land and trees were a direct threat to their economic interests, whether by an inquisitorial attention to trees on their village lands or interference in the firewood and timber trade. Not surprisingly, many therefore saw the Forest Department as merely a redundant and oppressive bureaucracy. *Kesari*, an important Marathi newspaper, declared in 1885 that ordinary people perceived the Forest Department as a useless drag on rural life. They judged it essentially driven by the desire for revenue. The newspaper indeed suggested that the department had no visible function other than to collect taxes and fees.[47] Many ordinary peasants were similarly aggrieved as old practices were interdicted or now cost money. Bachu, son of Ram Patil, headman of Khadki, spoke to the Forest Commission on February 8–9, 1886: "We obtain our fuel and wood for agricultural implements from our forest notwithstanding the prohibition because we cannot help doing so. . . . the guards cannot be everywhere. The guards seldom visit the forests, they go from village to village receiving food from the *pátils*. None of the other department subordinates receive their rations from the *pátils*."[48]

He added that, in any case, there were many paths known to villagers, and the forest guard could not watch them all. Aggrieved forest users now united under gentry leadership to assert traditional or customary practices and challenge the authority of the colonial state, initially by petitioning higher authorities. Used to being unquestioningly obeyed, local officials were infuriated by even peaceful protests and even more by lawsuits. They were inevitably attributed to the machinations of selfish "native" elites who were duping those whom imperial rule was working to help. Many decades later, Gibson, the first conservator of forests, still fumed about a long-past protest in 1851, when (he claimed) timber merchants had brought three hundred Varli tribespeople to Bombay to protest the introduction of a fee on forest produce.[49]

Intelligentsia organizations such as the Poona Sarvajanik Sabha (PSS) and Thane Sabha, however, steadily pursued these methods, much to the fury of many officials in India. They also began to cultivate sympathetic MPs in Britain. Before the British election of 1880, the British India Association in Calcutta and the PSS appealed to British voters to elect Liberals. In May 1880, after the Liberals came back to office after a six-year Conservative administration, the president of the PSS explained that alliances and petitions were the only way to secure the help of the British Parliament: "You must throw in your lot with one or the other of the two great political parties at home [Britain] and make fast friends with them."[50] Additionally, both officials and members of the educated public periodically invoked the specter of tribal rebellion or banditry to warn against interference with local custom.[51] *Kesari* consistently opposed bureaucratic control of the forests and suggested that each district's elected local board should have charge of them.[52]

The early nationalists nonetheless espoused the developmental agenda of the colonial government and argued for its more energetic implementation, freed from the fiscal priorities of the British government. This was especially the case in irrigation. All across arid India, farmers generally approved state provision of water. Dams, reservoirs, and canals had widespread support among the intelligentsia and peasant communities. Occasionally, these agendas diverged when, as in the Mulshi dam project, the costs were seen as inflicted upon hill peasant communities for the benefit of corporate electricity supply. There was strong—if ultimately unsuccessful—opposition from both the population to be displaced and Maharashtrian nationalists.[53]

The most radical critique offered by a significant political leader came, of course, from Mahatma Gandhi in the famous tract *Hind Swaraj* (1909). He challenged the very premise of bureaucratic, large-scale management as such and instead emphasized limiting consumption accompanied by village-level self-government. The separation of human life and "nature" implicit in much environmentalism would have been alien to Gandhi. His advocacy of vegetarianism and non-violence generally would limit violence against animals too. The agricultural system he and his followers envisaged was a low-impact one, where a renewable fraction of primary production was diverted to crops needed for human consumption. Gandhian thought therefore combined an opposition to markets with the exaltation of a reformed village community, one purged of caste discrimination and unhygienic customs.

Gandhi's many preoccupations prevented him from developing his ideas in detail. J. C. Kumarappa was lead organizer of the All India Village Industries Association, one of the key elements of the Gandhian "constructive" programs. These were activities that sought to bypass the colonial state to shape ethically sound social organizations that did not need state support. Kumarappa was periodically imprisoned by the administration, but his focus on societal programs left him more time to flesh out detailed plans both inspired and endorsed by Gandhi.[54] These emphasized especially the idea of limited consumption, village self-sufficiency, and common management of collective property, such as grazing, woodland, and water sources.[55] In 1946, Kumarappa analyzed the then acute food crisis in India and prescribed a remedy: "The basic cause of food shortage is departure from the village economy of self-sufficiency. Our custom has been to grow in every village material to meet all its needs, and to afford a reserve for a year or two in cereals. The advent of money economy broke through this rampart of safety."[56]

Evidently, despite the recent experience of the Bengal famine of 1943, Kumarappa did not consider the possibility that there might be deficit villages, or indeed regions, where mass starvation was avoided only by imports. For him, it was the intrusion of the market under colonial rule that marked the collapse of an imagined self-sufficient and self-contained village. Gross inequalities of power were always assumed to be limited to the colonial present. Paradoxically, Kumarappa's vision slipped easily into a top-down authoritarian statist model. The temptation to use the power of the newly independent state caused him to suggest clearly implicitly coercive and un-Gandhian methods, such as licensing to ensure a specific crop mix. "Every village should determine what food materials, fodder and other necessaries like cotton and oil seeds it requires and concentrate its production on these, not for the exchange market, but for its own use. Every plot of ground must be earmarked for growing a particular crop, not according to the whims of the farmer but according to the dictates of the needs of the village, as determined by its council or Government, which will authorize such use of the land by a system of careful licensing."[57] One wonders how this would have been enforced in earlier times, without the coercive capacity of the colonial state behind it. Furthermore, profound inequalities between propertied and landless, between high and low castes, existed within the real villages that dotted the Indian subcontinent. The great power over individual farmers granted to the "council" would easily have perpetuated inequality and tyranny.

Two ideological oppositions therefore operated in Kumarappa's thought: one between the mutualism of the community and the individualism of the market, and the other of the break between a long era of harmony and its interruption by colonial rule that forcibly introduced the market. In modern pop environmentalism, these stereotypes have grown into the binary opposition of traditional conserving cultures with rapacious modern ones. Finally, elements of colonial depiction of indigenous institutions are redeployed in nativist idealization of a far from ideal past. This despite the presence of a growing body of scholarship has sought to analyze the diverse ways in which societies have, in fact, spared and conserved resources for long-term use and the conditions under which this has been achieved.[58]

We may also notice that neither the pre-British nor the British city were considered in either Gandhi's or Kumarappa's schemes. Nor, it must be confessed, has urbanism, as distinct from mobile camp and fortress life, received a full-scale analysis in this book. In part, this is because other than colonial Bombay, cities were relatively small in the region and period on which I have focused. As centers of rule, they were obviously more closely watched and monitored than any other part of the precolonial kingdom. They drew on resources from afield. Their ecosystem effects may be approximated by those of military camps and itinerant courts that I have considered. The impermanence of the latter likely meant that their long-term impact was smaller than that of permanent cities. Impacts intensified during the British era and reached out into areas where they had never previously existed.

COLONIAL PARADISES AND IMPERIAL ARCADIAS: CANTONMENTS AND HILL STATIONS

As British power expanded across South Asia, so too did the colonial elite, both civil and military. Its numbers grew steadily through the nineteenth century. The number of European soldiers in permanent garrisons also increased, and niche habitats began to be carved out for them at considerable expense. Military units were placed in tightly managed and carefully sanitized "cantonments" strategically spread across the empire. Special care was taken to preserve the health of white soldiers, who after 1857 were considered the linchpin of the imperial apparatus worldwide. Between 1860 and 1877, 110 million rupees were spent on barracks for the 70,000 or so European soldiers who garrisoned India.[59]

The upper tiers of the bureaucracy—initially British and later increasingly elite Indian—were housed in "civil lines," designed to be spacious islands of well-serviced sanitation in what was perceived as the pathogen-laden environment of Asia. Significant parts of the new colonial cities were taken up by these elite spaces that consumed the lion's share of municipal budgets. This maldistribution was to be a chronic source of Indian political protest, but it still exists.[60] The term *paradise* originally referred to the walled pleasure parks of the Persian kings and became models for Christian and Islamic visions of heaven. The gardens of the civil and military elite were not so elaborate but again strove to create English landscapes to which their residents ultimately hoped to return. These were certainly important in introducing new vegetables and flowers that were added to the market gardens of South Asia. Specialized firms such as Pestonjee Pocha grew up to dispense seeds by mail order. A range of ornamental plants and trees from all over the world were tested and acclimatized in both the experimental gardens of the agri-horticultural societies and then around the bungalows of scores of civil lines and cantonments across the British Empire.[61] The provincial agriculture departments that came into being as a consequence of the 1880 Famine Commission set up experimental farms and tried to introduce new crops and methods. In its last decades, the empire looked back to its Mughal predecessor. Viceroy from 1899 to 1905, Lord Curzon identified himself as a worthy successor to the Mughal emperors. When the new imperial capital in Delhi was built, major streets were named for British founders but also for eminent men from the Mughal era. But the new Mughals did not want their grand vistas to become like the old Mughal legacy of Chandni Chowk, described as "a narrow crowded street confined by slums."[62]

The fact that malarial mosquitoes could not survive above a few thousand feet from sea level together with the resemblance of the mountains and their flora to imagined landscapes of northern Europe meant that garrison and civilian summer resorts were established at all sites accessible from the major centers in the plains. Railroads aided travel to and from them. Expensive hill railways came to link viceregal hill resorts and major capitals.[63] Thus, "hills" higher than any mountain in the British Isles were added to the list of colonial omnivore travel and recreation destinations. Forced labor was the dark underside of colonial travel all across the subcontinent. Denser populations and more efficient road and rail networks of the plains minimized it by the early twentieth century. The burden of forced labor was, however, maintained and even increased in the lower Himalaya at that time.[64] Initial protests were scattered episodes of passive resistance. In 1903, one of these cases was appealed to the provincial high court in faraway Allahabad, and forced labor was declared to have no legal basis. But the practice continued even as opposition to it grew.[65]

In the early twentieth century, the Edwardian high period of the British Empire in Asia saw a culmination of two key processes that I have tracked throughout this book. The first was the cumulative transformation of the earth resulting from the vastly unequal effects of human actions, those of the subordinated many *and* the powerful few. They did not all perceive the same world or desire the same outcome. The disparity of power has only increased through recent centuries. The second change has been immense growth in the apparatus of knowledge that has paralleled the rise of empires and was initially driven by their needs for frequent navigation across great oceans. It moved onto terrestrial domains when that became possible and adapted for the purposes of demarcation and taxation. In South Asia, thousands then toiled on surveys that mapped the land in unprecedented, three-dimensional detail. Then a whole secondary establishment was created for the Sisyphean maintenance of those records.

The Forest Department then presented not just a knowledge of terrain, but an active dissection of it by tree and plant species—often in response to popular and official challenges to its views. The dissection was preliminary to projects that went beyond enumeration to active modification. In ambition, at any rate, the woodland was to be weeded and planted like a garden, establishing an imagined "dominion over palm and pine." Neither of these two processes, the survey and demarcation of the most arable land and the ring-fencing of woodland, had been within the capacities of the Mughal or previous empires. Britain's was a transoceanic empire founded by a country at the cutting edge of the military, industrial, and scientific revolutions. Its gaze was wider, its reach deeper, and its grasp more tenacious than any previous regime. Clock time and standard measurement were now ubiquitous. Some minion of the state became a permanent presence in everyday life in every locality under direct rule. Such an intense colonial presence in and knowledge of the locality produced reactions that reached up to the metropole.

This examination exposes the improvisational working of empires, whether Mughal or British. Such entities are too often reified into omnipotent monoliths: in fact, they were assembled out of corporate groups, family lineages, and individual freelancers with varying degrees of understanding of and commitment to the imperial project. Constructing commitment, securing compliance, and projecting power were constant efforts that occasionally failed. The British Empire certainly built a more lasting apparatus of control and knowledge than its Mughal or Maratha predecessors had been able to do. As Parliament and the press in Britain demanded more and more information, anyone who reads archival records can see how a standard government of India narrative solidified under this external pressure. Internal fissures were confined to confidential records and personal letters. This occasionally bubbled up in public print through anonymous letters in the Bombay press.[66] But facts on the ground and on official record might still diverge.

Finally, in the twentieth century, military interests in aerial surveys followed by the Cold War desire for orbital surveillance led to new mapping of our biosphere. Nowadays, thanks to centuries of state-building and the wonders of satellite technology, the Indian subcontinent has come closer to being what generations of empire builders dreamed of making it. It can be viewed as subdivided and measured down to cells of a few meters square and seemingly transparent at a glance to an imperial gaze. The Forest Survey of India, for instance, has used a satellite that had a ground coverage of 23.5 meters per pixel.[67] The village as such is therefore an anachronism in the information space. Politicians, officials, NGOs, and villagers all know one another in the intersection of various grids. The state is haphazardly and imperfectly seeking to locate the individual at a unique intersection of set, identifiable by ineradicable biometric features. The village, as Dipankar Gupta writes, has been hollowed out. It "is shrinking as a sociological reality, though it still exists as a space."[68] This is an unprecedented change: it is a culmination of efforts begun in the high imperial period and renewed into the present. But the gaze from above is met by active responses from below. Finally, the rift between official classification and empirical reality still exists, as the reduction of Sariska sanctuary to a paper tiger reserve more recently demonstrated.[69]

Conclusion

HOMO SAPIENS IS MERELY ONE OF MANY ANIMAL SPECIES AND ONE of the newest among them. But in the past few thousand years, our species has modified the world with unprecedented speed. Human activity has changed major chemical cycles, notably those of carbon and nitrogen. It has laid and is laying down a layer of fossil plastic detritus that will endure through geological time on land and sea. Human decisions have marked the entire crust with a layer of radioactive material that will be traceable through immense spans of time. Its expansion across the earth has been accompanied by dramatic changes in terrestrial flora and fauna. Humanity has sought to extirpate its competitors and transform its commensals through selection and domestication. When human societies developed stable patterns of inequality, some animals also became more equal than others. Humans have preyed on one another and deployed animals in that process. They were enlisted to sustain diverse forms of display, livelihood, and predation.

Many disciplines have deepened our understanding of the earth's past. The political ecosystem that emerged out of repeated struggles between humans created a new class of apex predators. Gadgil and Guha have called them the "omnivores": the people who control and consume vast portions of the world's resources, whose reach extends deep into the earth's mantle and across its oceans. Their capacities are generated by profoundly hierarchical structures of power over our environment, indeed over our knowledge of the environment.[1]

This book opened by considering the idea that "environment" is an entity that can only be grasped through complex technologies designed to apprehend it. The environment is, in this view, not something shaped by our unaided senses. It is constructed through a web of devices and processors that already embody their makers' targets of perception.[2] The environment is apprehended, indeed conceived, only through the mediation of this apparatus. And the apparatus, I argue, is the result of centuries of state effort to surveil and control—it has a history. This book has laid bare that history by using two successive empires in Asia: the Mughal and British. One came over land and the other over seas. But they are exemplars of a wider process that unfolded at a global scale.

My introduction invoked the ancient and evolving hominid capacity for "niche construction"—a concept that I took from Nicole Boivin. But I have linked it to another idea: the "habitus" as a collective anthropogenic environment that I derive from the sociologist Pierre Bourdieu.[3] These niches were shaped by humans' interaction with inanimate materials and all sorts of living beings, including other humans. Other species and even members of our own species have been treated as building blocks of our own niche. They have been enslaved, domesticated, or exterminated in the interest of those with power over them. Their labor has been deployed to change the world—sometimes with unintended consequences.

Viewed as historically extant—meaning embodied and not abstract—the "humanity" or *Homo sapiens* of my first paragraph is, and has been, deeply riven by geographical distance and social inequality for at least five thousand years. That has meant that the need and ability to possess a cosmological vision was itself limited for centuries. Closer mapping, deeper knowledge has been cumulatively achieved through time in part as an effort at imperial niche building on a grander and grander scale. The institutional setting of this arrangement, in turn, has resulted in an unequal capacity to recognize and modify the physical environment.

As elites developed complex networks of observation and record, differential access to these apparatuses of knowledge left those outside the imperial centers with fractional but often deeper perceptions of the pragmatic world. Intensifying the opacity of their small habitus was often the response to a totalizing imperial gaze that sought to grasp and exploit. We have seen how strategies of opacity at various levels of the landscape worked through Mughal and Maratha regimes up through the first century of British rule. This was especially true of unequal political systems, of the empires that dominated the world after 1500 and into the twentieth century.

But access to what were once state secrets held in dark sites is now vastly wider due to the unanticipated explosion of corporate information processes fueled by the mass consumption of pragmatic knowledge. This extends to observation from space. What was once a closely guarded imperial apparatus of observation has now laid empires themselves open to the gaze of many. Privately owned satellites have improved their imaging capacities, and vendors of their information multiplied. A combination of high-resolution images and social media posts betrayed the Russian military buildup weeks before the Russian invasion of Ukraine in 2022.[4]

Opacity is still, however, understood and deployed. It operates alongside lawsuits and political lobbying to baffle satellite observation and resist the top-down apparatus of the environmental agencies of the state in India. Farmers around the national capital, Delhi, understand the harmful effects of smoke pollution resulting from the burning of agricultural stubble. But they evaluate that cost as acceptable against other expensive choices, regardless of what the National Green Tribunal may decree. They seek state investment to solve the problem in a way that more fairly allocates burdens and benefits between town and country.[5]

If we are to understand the Anthropocene fully, we need to engage the human record of inequality. It was in that setting that the deployment of and resistance to power created the information and cosmological ecosystems of today. Global domains of action open to emerging imperial elites demanded and created global but unequal information systems. This book has developed its exposition on the basis of the history of South Asia through recent historic time. But I hope that reading it has also left the reader with the conceptual tools needed to think through global patterns of change and conflict that continually shape our larger world. We have not reached the end of history. The age of deepening inequality is still with us and the age of empires not yet behind us. Capacities for surveillance and control are continually enhanced and still meet resistance and evasion.[6] There is no sign that these processes will end. I hope this book has left the reader with a deeper sense of the historical underpinnings of phenomena that still operate around us and will do so into the foreseeable future.

Notes

INTRODUCTION

1. Brondízio and Chowdhury, "Spatiotemporal Methodologies."
2. S. Guha, *Environment and Ethnicity*.
3. Latour, *Facing Gaia*, 78–79.
4. "The scenario is based on a non-linear empirical relationship between forest cover on land suitable for crop or pasture and country-level population density observed in Europe over the past 2 millennia on the basis of demographer estimates of population density and reconstructions of forest cover." They claim that this relationship is best represented by the "logistic function" in which the middle of the range, population densities 50–100 persons per km^2, sees the most rapid deforestation. Klein Goldewijk et al., "Anthropogenic Land Use Estimates," 929.
5. The definitions adopted by the FAO statistical office are found in Food and Agriculture Organization, *FAO Statistical Yearbook 2014*, appendix, "Metadata."
6. S. Guha, *Health and Population*.
7. Alter, "Evolution of Models."
8. Klein Goldewijk et al., "Anthropogenic Land Use Estimates."
9. Ruddiman, *Plows, Plagues, and Petroleum*.
10. Ruddiman, *Plows, Plagues, and Petroleum*, 137–38.
11. Pritchard, "Trouble with Darkness," 312.
12. Dorling and Fairbairn, *Mapping*, 103–11; see also Warde, Robin, and Sörlin, *Environment*.
13. "The GPS system deploys a constellation of 31 satellites, each beaming a one-way radio signal towards Earth. 'Those signals are being broadcast continuously,' said Gen. Burt. 'And when you're in view of that satellite, your receiver will pick the four best satellites in view. You want one directly overhead and three on the horizon—that gives you the best position.'" CBS, "Preparing the New Generation of GPS," *CBS News*, December 1, 2019, www.cbsnews.com/news/global-positioning-system-preparing-the-next-generation-of-gps/.
14. Sörlin and Wormbs, "Environing Technologies," 103. Or, as they formulate it elsewhere, "envisioned and imagined through the activities and outputs that these

networks produced—imagined as a kind of networked planet." Warde, Robin, and Sörlin, *Environment*, 143–44.

15. Marsh, *Man and Nature*, 39–43. The debate around the environmental history of the Mediterranean world is too large for me to address here.

16. Thomas, *Man's Role*.

17. United Nations, *Framework Convention*.

18. For example, Ruttan, "Induced Innovation."

19. Kingsland, *Modeling Nature*, 8.

20. Quote and paraphrase from P. Taylor, "Conceptualizing the Heterogeneity," 90.

21. Hettinger et al., "Extending the Vision"; and Kingsland, "Importance of History."

22. Sivaramakrishnan, *Modern Forests*, 14–15.

23. McNeill and Engelke, *Great Acceleration*, 209–10.

24. Scoones, "New Ecology."

25. Sörlin, "Environment."

26. Ehrlich, *Population Bomb*. For an overview of the debate over culpability after the World Resources Institute's report, see Dove, "North-South Differences."

27. For the intellectual and institutional background to one of the foundational speeches on the global environment, see Ramesh, *Indira Gandhi*, 151–54, 164–65.

28. Sengupta, "Defending 'Differentiation.'"

29. An engaged participant's overview from the 1990s to 2017 is found in Narain, *Conflicts of Interest*, 85–120.

30. *State of India's Environment, 1982*.

31. Narain, *Conflicts of Interest*, 88–95.

32. Hayes and Smith, *Global Greenhouse Regime*.

33. Raikes, "Mohenjo-daro Floods." As I am only concerned with the idea of environmental effects on early states, I do not discuss the subsequent controversy around Raikes's theory.

34. Trautmann, "Elephants and the Mauryas." Trautmann recently followed up his early article with a full-length monograph that traces the environmental history of early Old World empires in relation to their deployment of war elephants: Trautmann, *Elephants and Kings*.

35. Habib, *Atlas*.

36. Richards and Flint, "Century of Land-Use Change."

37. Gadgil and R. Guha, *This Fissured Land*.

38. Gadgil and R. Guha, *Ecology and Equity*, 1–6.

39. Sörlin and Wormbs, "Environing Technologies," 117.

40. Birkenholtz, "Contesting Expertise."

41. Warde, Robin, and Sörlin, *Environment*, 138.

42. For a subtle analysis of all these, see Hughes, *Animal Kingdoms*; for an extensively documented survey of hunting that includes earlier empires, see Mitra, *History and Heritage*.

43. The description is taken from Barker et al., "'Cultured Rainforests.'"

44. This paragraph and the two following draw heavily from the lucid analytic summary of an early version of my book by the same anonymous reader quoted earlier. There are several phrases where I could simply not improve on the reviewer's prose.

45. By remote "wilderness" I refer to woodlands beyond the village woods which were clumps of trees and bushes that thickened away from the village site. These were familiar. Remote wilderness refers to denser forest where even the sites of abandoned hamlets might be forgotten. In Western India, this mirrors the distinction between *śivār* (fields and trees) and *rāṇ* (wilderness).

46. Jared Diamond, Paul R. Ehrlich, and William F. Ruddiman, respectively.

One | INEQUALITY, COMPLEXITY, AND ECOLOGY

1. Diamond, *Guns, Germs, and Steel*; and Ruddiman, *Ploughs, Plagues, and Petroleum*.
2. Boivin et al., "Ecological Consequences," 6388.
3. Surveyed in Pyne, *Fire*.
4. Barker, *Agricultural Revolution*; and Barker et al., "'Cultured' Rainforests."
5. For a fine-grained anthropological study of wild, tame, and feral species in a complex human society, see Govindrajan, *Animal Intimacies*.
6. Bourdieu, *Outline*, 72–87, 122–32.
7. Read and van der Leeuw, "Extension of Social Relations," 45; Ullah, "Water, Dust and Agro-pastoralism."
8. Grove and Dunbar, "Local Objects, Distant Symbols," 18. I regret that I lack the space to more fully explore the truly enlightening book in which Grove and Dunbar's chapter appears.
9. Cited in Hay-Edie, "Cultural Values," 93.
10. Schama, *Landscape and Memory*, 6–7.
11. DeBuys, *A Great Aridness*, 75–85
12. Iggers and Wang, *Global History*, 46
13. An overview of the whole theme is found in Eck, *India*, 40.
14. Tucker and Williams, *Buddhism and Ecology*, xvi.
15. Eck, *India*, 39.
16. Gole, *Indian Maps*, 20–21.
17. Apart from Eck, *India*, see the excellent overview of shrines dedicated to Shiva and the variously named great goddess in Fleming, "Mapping Sacred Geographies."

18. Eck, *India*; and Lahiri, Singh, and Oberoi, "Preliminary Field Report."

19. Netton, *Golden Roads*; and Campo, "Visualizing the Hajj."

20. An early and famous example is the shrine of Salar Masud in submontane North India that attracted large numbers of villagers in the early summer. It is discussed in S. Guha, *History and Collective Memory*, 58–61.

21. Bayly, *Rulers, Townsmen and Bazaars*, 171.

22. Gole, *Indian Maps*.

23. S. Guha, *Tribe and State*, 46.

24. Gibson, "Violation of Fallow"; and Adams, "Historic Patterns."

25. The preceding two paragraphs are drawn from Adams, *Heartland of Cities*, 249–52 passim. A combination of field archaeology and textual research enables him to trace a deep history of the Diyala plain and of irrigated farming in Mesopotamia generally.

26. Shiba, "Environment versus Water Control."

27. Elvin and Su, "Action at a Distance."

28. Elvin, *Retreat of the Elephants*, 130–31.

29. Lander, *King's Harvest*, 34–36.

30. Elvin, *Retreat of the Elephants*, 130–33.

31. Wittfogel, *Oriental Despotism*, 11–12.

32. Bauer, "Questioning the Anthropocene."

33. Sinopoli, Johansen, and Morrison, "Changing Cultural Landscapes."

34. Morrison, *Daroji Valley*.

35. Seefeldt, "Upwelling of Stone."

36. Seefeldt, "Upwelling of Stone," 26–27.

37. This paragraph is based on Lattimore, *Inner Asian Frontiers*, xl–xlviii, 24–25, 38–39.

38. This paragraph is based on Di Cosmo, *Ancient China*, 58–70. I have discussed the "steppe frontier pattern" more extensively in S. Guha, *Tribe and State*, 48–57.

39. Rackham, *History*, 176–203

40. Antonio Barbosa offers an extensive review of how Mediterranean navigational and cartographic techniques changed with the requirements of navigation far from land. For the Papal Bull embodied in the Treaty of Tordesillas of 1494, see Barbosa, *Novos subsídios*, 189–90.

41. Thomaz, *De Ceuta a Timor*.

42. Richards, *Unending Frontier*; and Divyabhanusinh, *End of a Trail*.

43. Foreword to Taylor, *Haven-Finding Art*, x, 3–20.

44. Campbell, "Portolan Charts," 371–74.

45. Taylor, *Haven-Finding Art*; and Dorling and Fairbairn, *Mapping*, 16–17.

46. Campbell, "Portolan Charts," 437–45.

47. Law, "On the Social Explanation."

48. An early Indian Ocean example of such study is cited in Amrith, *Unruly Waters*, 59–62.

49. Dorling and Fairbairn, *Mapping*, 4, 30–31.

50. Introduction to Linschoten, *Voyage*, 1:xxiii–xlii.

51. Taylor, *Haven-Finding Art*, 252–63.

52. Lander, *King's Harvest*.

53. Needham, *Mathematics and the Sciences*, 514–20, 535, 544–56.

54. McNeill, *Mosquito Empires*, 15–60, 234–303.

55. Glacken, *Traces*. For a contemporary assessment of its lasting value, see S. Ravi Rajan's introduction to Glacken, *Genealogies of Environmentalism*, xx.

56. The grafting of Middle Eastern lore onto Greco-Roman cosmology led to the abandonment of the older Indo-European idea of a perpetual cycle of four ages, with the current one always being the fourth and worst. That idea, however, survived in Indic thought as the concept of four successive *yugas* with the fourth being followed by *pralaya*, universal dissolution.

57. Glacken, *Traces*, 5.

58. Marsh, *Earth*, 43.

59. Buffon, *De l'homme*. For differences arising from climate, diet, and environment more generally, see pages 264–67. Rostand's introduction to this volume considers the eighteenth-century milieu in which his work appeared.

60. Sepkoski and Tamborini, "Image of Science."

61. Boyns and Edwards, *History of Management Accounting*, chap. 3.

62. *Oxford Dictionary of National Biography*, s.v. "Edward Long, 1734–1813," https://www.oxforddnb.com.

63. Long, *History of Jamaica*, 3:351–53. He evaded the problem of biblical monogenesis implied in the descent from Adam and Eve. See 353n.

64. Glacken, *Traces*, 540–41.

65. S. Guha, "Lower Strata, Older Races."

66. Rainger, "Race, Politics, and Science" gives a complete account of John Hunt and his efforts.

67. An early example was Knox, *Races of Men*, 2: "Men are of various Races; call them Species if you will; call them permanent Varieties, it matters not."

68. Grove, *Green Imperialism*, 95–308.

69. Grove, *Green Imperialism*, 286–90.

70. Stebbing, *Forests of India*, 1:351–52, 356–57.

71. Yet it has now been amply demonstrated that regional conditions in South Asia barely affected the monsoon. Sarkar et al., "Monsoon Source Shifts."

72. Fairhead and Leach, *Misreading*.
73. Jacoby, *Crimes against Nature*, 14, 200 passim.
74. McCann, *Green Land*.
75. Smil, "Nitrogen in Crop Production."

Two | SOUTH ASIA IN THE IMPERIAL GAZE

1. Scott, *Seeing Like a State*, 1–52; quotations are from pages 36 and 45.
2. Wikipedia, s.v. "Köppen Climate Classification," accessed April 20, 2022, https://en.wikipedia.org/wiki/K%C3%B6ppen_climate_classification.
3. Peel, Finlayson, and McMahon, "Updated World Map."
4. Spate and Learmonth, *India and Pakistan*; and Pai et al., "District-Wide Drought Climatology."
5. See the introduction in S. Guha, *Health and Population*, 1–23.
6. Olivelle, *King, Governance, and Law*, 152–53.
7. Abu al-Fazl ibn Mubarak, *Āʾīn*, 2:72–74.
8. Seppel, "Cameralist Population Policy," 92.
9. Elvin, *Retreat of the Elephants*.
10. Trautmann, *Elephants and Kings*, 14–15; and Prasad et al., "Prolonged Monsoon Droughts."
11. Trautmann, "Elephants and the Mauryas."
12. Roe, *Embassy*, 2:368.
13. Dirom, *Narrative of the Campaign*, 25–26, 119–21.
14. Trautmann, *Elephants and Kings*, 46–47.
15. Trautmann, "Elephants and the Mauryas."
16. Caudharī, *Jātakamālā*, 333–45.
17. Cited in Ballhatchet, *Social Policy*, 124.
18. Forsyth, *Highlands*, 302.
19. Forsyth, *Highlands*, 219–20.
20. Koirala et al., "Feeding Preferences."
21. See the chapter "Forests, Fires, and Grasslands" in Sukumar, *Living Elephants*.
22. An officer reported from the Pune area that his elephants had been newly imported from Ceylon and would not eat enough of the stockpiled dry millet stalk available as fodder to sustain them. He therefore had to buy sugarcane for them until the rains produced green fodder in the hills that grass-cutters could bring in. Wellington, *Supplementary Despatches*, 4:42. Sukumar, *Asian Elephant*, reports that in Sri Lanka grass predominated in elephant diets, while in South India browse predominated in the dry season, and grass increased in the first wet season (69–75).

23. Sukumar, *Living Elephants*, 151–239, 252–53.

24. Rangarajan, *India's Wildlife History*; and Shahabuddin and Rangarajan, *Making Conservation Work*.

25. Webber et al., "Elephant Crop-Raiding."

26. Pokharel et al., "Lower Levels of Glucocorticoids."

27. Trautmann, "Towards a Deep History," 47–74.

28. Jothish, "Frugivory and Seed Dispersal."

29. For wild pigs, see Gold and Gujar, *Time of Trees*, 241–50; and Mitra, *Indian Game Hunting*, for a longer history.

30. Babur, *Baburnama*, 330–57

31. Pelsaert, *Jahangir's India*, 4–5, 7–9.

32. Roe, *Embassy*, 1: 88.

33. Raychaudhuri and Habib, *Cambridge Economic History of India*, 1:360–81.

34. Babur, *Baburnama*.

35. Roe, *Embassy*, 2:363.

36. Foster, *Early Travels*, 146–47.

37. Foster, *Early Travels*, 278–79.

38. The preceding two paragraphs are entirely based on Habib, "Cartography in Mughal India."

39. Stoneman, "How Many Miles to Babylon?"

40. Ibn Batoutah [Battuta], *Voyages*, 3:95–97.

41. Preceding sentences are based on Nayeem, *Evolution*, 2–3.

42. This measure varied. Some estimates of it are given by Edward Moor in *Narrative*, 505–6.

43. Deloche, *Transport and Communications*, 167.

44. Nayeem, *Evolution of Postal Communications*, 1–4.

45. Roe, *Embassy*, 1:99.

46. McCrindle, *Ancient India*, 184–85.

47. Rood, "Xenophon's Parasangs."

48. Deloche, *Transport and Communications*, 149–59.

49. Roe, *Embassy*, 2:368.

50. Moor, *Narrative*, 505–6.

51. Moor, *Narrative*, 302.

52. Hodivala, *Studies in Indo-Muslim History*, 1:34–70.

53. Gole, *Indian Maps*, 26–39; Taylor, *Haven-Finding Art*, 120–31; Harley and Woodward, *History of Cartography*, vol. 2, bk. 1, chaps. 17, 18; and Sheikh, "Gujarati Map."

54. S. Guha, "Rethinking," 559.

55. Dorling and Fairbairn, *Mapping*, 44–45.

56. Habib, *Atlas*, 43.
57. Cited in Gole, *Indian Maps*, 90.
58. Gole, 88–93; one was also printed in Gommans, *Mughal Warfare*, facing page 7.
59. Fukazawa, "Local Administration," 7–11.
60. Verified in Steingass, *Comprehensive Persian-English Dictionary*.
61. See S. Guha, *Beyond Caste*, 85–86, for an affray and a death that resulted from such a visit.
62. Gole, *Indian Maps*, 144–48, see also n. 160.
63. In fact, both the names evidently refer to the Malayalam-speaking region of Kerala.
64. MSS Mar G.28. I, BL. It is further discussed in S. Guha, "Conviviality and Cosmopolitanism," 275–92.
65. See the military records cited in the next paragraph.
66. *Early European Travellers*, 51.
67. This quote and the whole paragraph are from Scott, *Routes*, ii–iv.
68. Shuldham, *Table of Routes*, 1, 35, 84–85, 96–97, 111–12, 132, 477–79.
69. For a discussion of how the economics of information has resulted in a paradigm shift in modern economics by an economist who pioneered it, see Stiglitz, "Information."
70. Tanzi, "Uses and Abuses."
71. I develop this argument in S. Guha, "Rethinking."
72. Guha, "Rethinking," 547–48.
73. Nayeem, *Evolution*.
74. S. Guha, "Rethinking," 559.
75. Qaisar, *Indian Response*, appendix E, 148–49. Qaisar perhaps over-generalizes in assuming that maps *not* drawn to the graticular frame were of no practical value. From trekking experience, in the Himalaya, I can say that strict adherence to scale might have little practical value and could even seriously mislead someone planning a route over variedly rugged, wooded, or arid terrain.
76. Gole, *Indian Maps*.
77. A. R. Khan's *Chieftains* gives a detailed account of such men and their territories.
78. I cannot here explore the 1980s debate on the reality of "Indian feudalism." It is judiciously reviewed by Hermann Kulke in his introduction to an edited volume on the state in India. Kulke, *State in India, 1000–1700*, 1–47.
79. Leonard, *Social History*; Gupta, *Kāyasthas*; and S. Guha, "Serving the Barbarian," 497–525.
80. Ibn Batoutah [Battuta], *Voyages*, 3:388.
81. Documents translated in Zilli, "Two Administrative Documents," 367–72.

82. Cited, along with other evidence, in S. Guha, "Rethinking," 548–49.

83. Elliott, *Oonao*, 112.

84. Hasan, "Zamindars," 18–19.

85. Khan, *Chieftains*, 206–19.

86. Babur, *Baburnama*, 330–57.

87. Moreland, "Pargana Headman."

88. Pelsaert, *Jahangir's India*, 58.

89. Hasan, "Zamindars," 24–25.

90. Rana, *Rebels to Rulers*, 107–18.

91. For the development of one such script, see S. Guha, "Serving the Barbarian"; for a detailed and careful study, Prachi Deshpande, *Scripts of Power*, 29–111.

92. Elliott, *Oonao*, 112–13.

93. These paragraphs draw heavily from S. Guha, "Rethinking"; see also Habib, *Agrarian System*, 323–25.

94. Coupland, *Final Report*, 89–93.

95. Gold and Gujar, *Time of Trees*.

96. Abu al-Fazl ibn Mubarak, *A'in*, 2:72.

97. Marshall, "Pergunna of Jumboosur," 375.

98. Elliott, *Oonao*, 108–9n.

99. This was the observed situation in 1915. A. C. Guha, *Brief Sketch*, 120–21. Atul Chandra Guha, however, accepted the myth of Mughal omniscience and thought that the *patwari* had been a "public servant" during their time.

100. Stevenson-Moore, *Final Report*, 26.

101. Ramsbotham, *Studies*, 4–5.

102. Edney, *Mapping an Empire*. Edney brings out the improvised way in which regional and village maps were fitted into a graticular frame created by the Trigonometric Survey. The creation of British India on the map allowed its imagining, for the first time, as a spatially bounded entity (and future nation-state).

103. Ramsbotham, *Studies*, 16–17 (for Chittagong), cites the collector's letter, July 10, 1773.

104. Government of Bengal, *Agricultural Statistics*.

Three | IMPERIAL GAZE, LORDLY GRASP

1. Pelsaert, *Jahangir's India*, 58.

2. Shaha, "Khāndeś."

3. MSS Eur D.148, fos. 43–47, 204–5, BL.

4. Cited in S. Guha, *Environment and Ethnicity*, 126.

5. One of the best short English descriptions of their ubiquity and role is Hasan, "Zamindars."

6. This paragraph is based on an important article by S. N. Vatsa Joshi. He demonstrated the title's functional connection with earlier inscriptional records. He noted that *deshmukh* (he wrote *deśmūkh*) only begins to appear after the fall of the Yadava dynasty (ca. 1300 CE). Joshi, "Desmukhi watan."

7. For the denunciations, see Ali, "Image of the Scribe."

8. Abu al-Fazl ibn Mubarak, *A'īn*, 2:45–47.

9. *Paḍ zamīn* (fallen or dead land) was land that had gone out of tillage. Persian has a similar metaphor: "A ناتوم *mautān*, Uncultivated land; —*mawatān*, Inanimate, lifeless; dead stock." Steingass, *Comprehensive Persian-English Dictionary*.

10. Purandare, *Śivacaritrasāhitya*, 1:67. The *deshmukh* was also accused of appropriating the taxes on tobacco instead of giving them to the tax farmer appointed for that commodity.

11. Marshall, "Pergunna of Jumboosur," 375.

12. S. Guha, "Serving the Barbarian"; and Joshi, "Desmukhi watan."

13. Graham, *Statistical Report*, 69n.

14. Avaḷaskar, *Aitihasik Sadhane*, 60–61.

15. Quoted in Ballhatchet, *Social Policy*, 122.

16. Quoted in Ballhatchet, *Social Policy*, 116.

17. Letter of H. E. Goldsmid, *SRGB*, n.s., no. 531, 2:151.

18. *MIS*, o.s., vol. 12, comp. and ed. V. K. Rajwade, 171–73.

19. Purandare, *Purandare Daphtar*, part 1, 104. The next document in the collection discusses a conflict between Nadir Shah and the Ottomans and its reported effect on the affairs of North India.

20. Candy, *Selections with Notes*, 13–14.

21. Dhume, *Śrī Mangeś Devasthān*; see pages 60–71 for Portuguese text with Marathi summary.

22. Cunha Rivara, *Archivo Portuguez*, vol. 5, part 1, 35–36, 50–51.

23. Forrest, *Selections from the Letters*, 2:44–45.

24. Forrest, *Selections from the Letters*, 2:383–87.

25. Pendse, *Penṇḍse Kulavṛttānta*, 33.

26. *SSRPD*, I, 200.

27. Sykes, "Land Tenures," 368–69.

28. This important and neglected point is the focus of Tirthankar Roy's important new book, *Monsoon Economies*.

29. Olivelle, *King, Governance, and Law*, 351–52.

30. The richest study of this overlap is M. Kumar, *Monsoon Ecologies*, 73–75, 270–75.

31. The state also includes Khandesh, the valley of the Tapi on the north and Vidarbha to the east. For a full regional geography, see Diddee et al., *Geography of Maharashtra*.

32. As in Jaswantrao Holkar to Pant Pratinidhi, ca. 1803. Khare and Joshi, *Aitihasik Marāthī Sādhane*, 56.

33. Mann et al., *Land and Labour*, 1:1.

34. Elphinstone, *Report*, 5.

35. *Gazetteer of the Bombay Presidency*, vol. 19, Satara, 4–5.

36. *SRGB*, n.s., no. 634, 7–8.

37. MSS Eur D.141, fo. 4, BL.

38. Manwaring, *Marathi Proverbs*, 3, 191, 201.

39. Sykes, "Special Report," 220.

40. *Gazetteer of the Bombay Presidency*, vol. 11, Kolaba and Janjira, 95–96 (in text and hereafter cited as *Kolaba Gazetteer*).

41. Morrison, Reddy, and Kashyap, "Agrarian Transitions."

42. T.-T. Kumar, *History of Rice*, 12–15, 56–95.

43. Rajan and Yatheeskumar, "New Evidences."

44. Fuller and Qin, "Water Management."

45. Morrison, *Daroji Valley*; and Morrison, *Human Face*, 12–15.

46. Morrison, *Daroji Valley*, 2–5, 38–42.

47. *SSRPD*, IX, part 1, 117–18. This is one of several orders regarding his food allowance.

48. Manwaring, *Marathi Proverbs*, 202–3.

49. Graham et al., *Statistical Report*, 32–33.

50. Morrison, "Pepper in the Hills."

51. The right to maintain this practice despite English dislike of it was carefully stipulated in the agreement of 1675 between the East India Company and the landlords of the island of Bombay. Forrest, *Selections*, 2:385.

52. *Kolaba Gazetteer*, 2.

53. E. C. Ozanne in BFC, 236.

54. *Kolaba Gazetteer*, 52.

55. Bhattacharyya, *Empire and Ecology*, 1–41.

56. See Avāḷaskar, *Konkancyā Itihāsācī Sādhane*, for the family.

57. *SCS 9*, "Chaul Adhikari Daftar," 11–12.

58. Avāḷaskar, *Konkancyā Itihāsācī Sādhane*, 9–13.

59. *Kolaba Gazetteer*, 90–91.

60. Mollison, *Text-Book*, 3:35.

61. Morrison, *Daroji Valley*, 2–5, 38–42; and Morrison, *Human Face*, 12–15.

62. *RCE*, 1885–86.
63. Candy, *Selections with Notes*, 19.
64. Candy, *Selections with Notes*, 28–29.
65. *SRGB*, n.s., no. 539, 11.
66. *SRGB*, n.s., no. 402, 5–6.
67. *RCE*, 1885–86, 66–70.
68. In order of citation in the text, these are from the annual *Report on Crop Experiments* (*RCE*) in the Bombay Presidency printed by the Agriculture Department for the years 1883–84, 32–33; 1885–86, 20; 1884–85, 66–70. Orthography as in original.
69. Mollison, *Text-Book*, 3:35–36.
70. Mollison, 3:257–72, quotation is on page 270.
71. S. Guha, "Serving the Barbarian," 504.
72. Evidence in S. Guha, "Theatre State."
73. Mollison, *Text-Book*, 3:57–60.
74. *SRGB*, n.s., no. 402, 6.
75. Coats, "Lony," 211–12.
76. Atre, *Gāñv-Gāḍa*, 171–72.
77. Jagalpure and Kale, *Sarola Kasar*, 68.
78. Oturkar, *Pesvekālīn*, 7.
79. *SSRPD*, I, 182–83.
80. S. Guha, "Claims on the Commons," 190.
81. Coats, "Lony," 237–40; and Gibson, "Notes," 101–2.
82. *Karvir Sardarācya Kaifiyati*, 84, 96–97.
83. Paraphrasing S. Guha, "Claims on the Commons," 193.
84. Wellington, *Supplementary Despatches*, 4:56–57, 63–67.
85. Chitnisi Daftar, Rumal 4, Pudka 1, no. 1768, PA.
86. Tone, *Letter to an Officer*, 24–25.
87. Cited in S. Guha, "Kings, Commoners," 24–25.
88. S. Guha, "Claims on the Commons," 195.
89. S. Guha, "Claims on the Commons," 196.

Four | THE VILLAGE AND ITS INHABITANTS

1. Marriott, "Caste Ranking," 26–36.
2. Leach, *Political Systems*, 237–45.
3. *Early European Travellers*, 19, 21.
4. Babur, *Baburnama*, 268.
5. See Cadell quoted in the source in note 6.

6. Bombay Government Records, A Proceedings, April 1905. Revenue Department (Confl.), "Papers relating to Village Police," 2–3, 10–11, BL.

7. Colebrooke, *Remarks* paraphrased in S. Guha, *Beyond Caste*, 89–90.

8. Carstairs, "Bhil Villages," 68–69.

9. Marshall, *Statistical Reports*.

10. Olivelle, *King, Governance, and Law*, 99–101.

11. Marshall, "Pergunna of Jumboosur," 362–68.

12. Scott, *Seeing Like a State*, 81–82.

13. *Imperial Gazetteer of India*, 1:455.

14. I have elsewhere argued that the pargana is the functional descendant of the older *janapada*. S. Guha, *Beyond Caste*, 45–82.

15. Coats, "Lony," 172.

16. Oturkar, *Pesvekālīn*, preface, 6–8.

17. Compiled from MSS Eur D. 148, BL.

18. Oturkar, *Pesvekālīn*, 5 (text).

19. Elphinstone, *Report*, 15–16, 35–37.

20. Olivelle, *King, Governance, and Law*, 99.

21. Olivelle, *King, Governance, and Law*, 197.

22. Gole, *Indian Maps*, 18; and Gole, "Iṭṭagi Plates," 62–69.

23. Vad, Mawjee, and Parasnis, *Sanadāpatreñ*, no. 39.

24. Examples of all these are in Oturkar, *Pesvekālīn*.

25. *IS* 7, nos. 1–3 (1915–16): 243–44.

26. This heading is my translation of the polysemic Marathi terms *gāṇvṭhān* and *pāṇḍhrī*.

27. Atre, *Gāṇv-Gāḍa*, 1–6; Coats, "Lony"; and Marshall, "Statistical Account."

28. Cited in S. Guha, "Kings, Commoners," 25.

29. One litigant declared "I will prove the truth of this by the testimony of the village communities (*pāṇḍhrī*) of the three villages." *SSRPD*, II, part 2, 157.

30. Mande, *Gāvagāḍyabāhera*, preface.

31. Goldsmid, Wingate, and Davidson, "Joint Report," 9–12.

32. Purandare, *Purandare Daphtar*, 8–9.

33. Purandare, *Purandare Daphtar*, 12–13.

34. Potdar and Mujumdar, *Sivacaritra Sāhitya*—2, 115–18.

35. Pendse, *Pēṇḍse Kulavṛttānta*, 33.

36. Daniel, *Fluid Signs*, 74–78.

37. MSS D.141, fo. 16, BL.

38. *SSRPD*, 7, 2, 5–12, for examples.

39. Khobrekar and Shinde, *Konkancyā Itihāsācī Sādhane*, 34–35.

40. Graham et al., *Statistical Report*, 9.
41. Marshall, "Pergunna of Jumboosur."
42. Goldsmid, Wingate, and Davidson, "Report," 15–17.
43. Mann et al., *Land and Labour*, 6–17 (emphasis added).
44. Mann et al., *Land and Labour*, 6.
45. *RCE*, 1883–84, 32–33.
46. Coats, "Lony," 233. It is not clear what English system Coats is referring to here. It may have been the alternation of clover or turnips for beef animals with grain farming, which he saw as impossible owing to lack of demand for meat. Or perhaps it was the then much praised moldboard plow.
47. Sykes, "Special Report," 271.
48. Smith, *Cotton Trade of India*, 32–33.
49. BFC, 1:221–35.
50. Mollison, *Text-Book*, 3:256.
51. Graham et al., *Statistical Report*, 8–9; and Mollison, *Text-Book*, 3:62–64.
52. Graham et al., *Statistical Report*, 109–11 for houses, 161–64 for food.
53. Coats, "Lony," 194–96; and Marshall, "Pergunna of Jumboosar," 339–40.
54. BFC, 1:115.
55. Mackintosh, "Mhadeo Kolies," 99.
56. Watt, s.v. *"ferula," Dictionary of the Economic Products*.
57. *RCE*, 1883–84, 58–60. The same point was made by Jagalpure, *Sarola Kasar*, 65–66.
58. *RCE*, 1883–84, 62–65.
59. *RCE*, 1883–84, 65–67.
60. *RCE*, 1883–84, 93–94.
61. *RCE*, 1879–80, 1880–81, 19–20.
62. Jagalpure, *Sarola Kasar*, 42.
63. *RCE*, 1884–85, 66–70; fully described on p. 99 .
64. Cited in S. Guha, "Claims on the Commons," 195.
65. S. Guha, "Claims on the Commons," 195–96.
66. Mande, *Gāvagāḍyabāhera*, 137.
67. Atre, *Gāṇv-Gāḍa*. All references to Atre in this section are taken from the chapter titled "Phiraste" (nomads), 115–41.
68. *Report of the Committee*, 1–6.
69. Coats, "Lony," 235–38.
70. Mande, *Gāvagāḍyabāhera*, preface.
71. Mande, *Gāvagāḍyabāhera*, 36–38.
72. Mande, *Gāvagāḍyabāhera*, 137–38, 205–8.
73. Oturkar, *Pesvekālīn*, 24–25.

74. Malhotra, Khomne, and Gadgil, "Hunting Strategies," 21–39. This article is part of a larger body of work unsuccessfully attempting a sociobiological explanation of the caste system.

75. Marshall, "Jumboosur," 335; Manwaring, *Marathi Proverbs*, 136.

76. Marshall, *Statistical Reports*, 181–82.

77. Based on Mann et al., *Land and Labour*, I, 55–59; *Land and Labour*, II, 52–55.

Five | LANDS OF RESISTANCE, TERRAINS OF REFUGE

1. The great fortress city of Tughlakabad near Delhi (1320–25) and Fatehpur Sikri (1571–75), each occupied five years, are striking examples. Brown, *Indian Architecture*, especially chaps. 5, 13, 17, 18.

2. Brown, *Indian Architecture*, 20–24.

3. Brown, *Indian Architecture*, 62–72.

4. Mate, *History of Water Management*, 123–43.

5. Fairhead and Leach, *Misreading the African Landscape*.

6. However, forest clearing and suppression by seasonal burning, a standard pastoral custom, would sharply reduce the suitability of the land for the different species of tsetse fly that attack humans and domestic livestock. A recent continental level survey of tsetse suitability has demonstrated the major effect of vegetational modification on tsetse habitat. Some species of the fly were well adapted to mosaic forest and savanna, others to closed and riverine forest areas. Fully cleared cropland came lowest on the scale, as did grassland with sparse shrubs. Seasonal burning, however, cleared land of tsetse and also of young trees and brushwood. The resulting open grassland was healthier for cattle and horses and also therefore for mounted slave-raiding. "Mosaic" forest was better suited to tsetse transmission. Land with more than 50 percent under crops was among the least suitable. Cecchi et al., "Land Cover," 364–73; and Magez and Radwanska, *Trypanosomes and Trypanosomiasis*.

7. Olivelle, *King, Governance, and Law*, 310.

8. Ibn Battuta, *Voyages*, 3:133, 389–90, 4:8–13.

9. Hodivala, *Studies in Indo-Muslim History*, 1:286–88.

10. *Jahangir's India*, 15, 58–59.

11. Martin, *Mémoires*, 3:192, 196–97, also 262–63.

12. For examples, see Banerjee, *Peshwa Madhav Rao I*, 47, 198–99.

13. Martin, *Mémoires*, 1:604–5.

14. Orme, *History*, 1:102.

15. Pennant, *View of Hindoostan*, 2:85–87, 360.

16. Butter, *Topography and Statistics*, 4–6.

17. Sleeman, *Journey*, 1: 230, 2:235–36, 2:279–86.
18. Gold and Gujar, *Time of Trees*, 261–76.
19. *Early European Travellers*, 14.
20. *IS* 2, no. 6, "Aitihāsik Tipneñ," item no. 25 (1909–10): 39–42.
21. Fryer, *New Account of East India*, 141, 124–25 (all orthography original).
22. Detailed information is in S. Guha, *Environment and Ethnicity*, 49–52.
23. Dirom, *Narrative*, 86.
24. *IS*, vol. 2, no. 6, "Aitihāsik Tipneñ," item no. 24 (1909–10): 37–39.
25. Scott, *Art of Not Being Governed*, 178–80.
26. Forsyth, *Highlands of Central India*, 98.
27. Wingate, *Report by Captain Wingate*, 1, 2.
28. Johansen, "Landscape, Monumental Architecture."
29. S. Guha, *Environment and Ethnicity*, 48–49.
30. Orta, *Coloquios dos Simples*, 119.
31. *Early European Travellers*, 128–29.
32. Hodivala, *Studies in Indo-Muslim History*, 1:410–11.
33. This and the preceding two paragraphs are based on Briggs, "Account," 170–96. The later quote is "ranjar ká pání, chappar ká ghás/aur din ká tín khún máf. Aur jahán Ásaf Ján ke ghore/wahán Jhangi Bhangi ke báil" (you may seize water (even) from (the peasants') pitchers, fodder (even) from their roof thatch and be pardoned up to three murders a day. But where go Asaf Jan's horses, there must go Jhangi and Bhangi's oxen). Lyall, *Gazetteer*, 196 (orthography original, my translation).
34. S. Guha, "Kings, Commoners," 31.
35. *SSRPD*, I, 183–84.
36. MSS Eur D.148 fo. 40, BL.
37. *Early European Travellers*, 21, 24–28, 61–62.
38. Lewis, "Village Defenses," 92–93.
39. Mackintosh, "Mhadeo Kolies," 258–59.
40. Graham et al., *Statistical Report*, 494–504.
41. Mackintosh, "History of the Ramoosies," 201.
42. S. Guha, "Claims on the Commons," 195.
43. Graham et al., *Statistical Report*, 124–25, 521–25.
44. MSS D.148, fos. 39–40, BL.
45. Government of Bombay, *Survey and Settlement Manual*, 113.
46. Ryan, "Burmese Teak Forests," 117, 115–20. James Forsyth, a forest officer in Central India, wrote a century earlier that "teak seeds will germinate and produce seedlings where the grass has been fired better than where it has not; and it is not well established that much permanent injury is afterwards done to the seedlings." Forsyth, *Highlands*, 224n.

47. *SSRPD*, II, part 2, 82.

48. Avāḷaskar, *Nāgāv*, 90, 141; see S. Guha, "Kings, Commoners," 18–21, for additional information on state management of teak forest along the Arabian Sea.

49. Cited in S. Guha, "Kings, Commoners," 17–18.

50. Forsyth, *Highlands*, 214 (emphasis added).

51. Marshall, *Statistical Reports*, 180–81.

52. S. Guha, "Kings, Commoners," 21.

53. MSS Eur D. 148, fo. 19, BL.

54. Dirom, *Narrative*, 242–43.

55. Dirom, *Narrative*, 242–43.

56. Dirom, *Narrative*, 129.

57. Raman, *Wild Heart of India*, 66–70.

58. This phrase literally means "from the heavens and from the kings": it meant that calamities could come from either source.

59. Scott, *Art of Not Being Governed*, 127–28.

60. Scott, *Art of Not Being Governed*, x, 127–28, 207–8. These paragraphs also draw from S. Guha, *Tribe and State*, 63–65.

61. Leach, *Political Systems*, 198–99, 231–45.

62. For a careful study of socioeconomic life in three regions from the early 1960s, see Bose, *Carrying Capacity of Land*.

63. Elphinstone, *Selections*, 447–550.

64. Orta, *Coloquios dos Simples*, 119–20.

65. This paragraph is based on Elphinstone, *Selections*, 535–40.

66. Elphinstone, *Report on the Territories*, 2–3.

67. *SRGB*, no. 644, 1–3; and Mollison, *Text-Book*, 3:54.

68. The preceding two paragraphs are mainly based on *Papers Relative to the Meywar Bheel Corps;* and Hunter, "Hill Population in Meywar," 176–90.

69. S. Guha, *Environment and Ethnicity*, 105–21.

70. Malcolm, "Essay on the Bhills," 65–91. I have previously developed some of these ideas in S. Guha, *Environment and Ethnicity*, 81–85, 138–40.

71. S. Guha, *Environment and Ethnicity*, 130–38.

72. Skaria, "Hybrid Histories," 83–87.

73. Hunter, "Hill Population in Meywar," 180.

74. Berkemer and Frenz, *Sharing Sovereignty*. See especially Gutschow, "Ranpur," 137–51.

75. S. Guha, *Environment and Ethnicity*, 122–26; and S. Sinha, "State Formation," 304–42.

76. Cited in S. Guha, *Environment and Ethnicity*, 126 (emphasis added).

77. Richard Temple, preface to Hislop, *Aboriginal Tribes*, vi.

78. H. F. Dent to Collector, Khandesh, 11 November 1824, Revenue Department, vol. 11/95 of 1824, fo. 358, MSA Bombay.

Six | COLONIALISM, DISARMAMENT, FOREST FRONTIER

1. Tone, *Letter to an Officer*, 23–24, 45–46. For Chaplin, see note 442.

2. Chaplin, *Report*, 168–69.

3. Estimated from *Report on the Census of Oudh*, 1:27. This would be about one-twenty-fifth of the total population of the British Empire in South Asia in 1870, but Awadh was, by all accounts, an exceptionally militarized region.

4. Prichard, *Administration of India*, 1:35.

5. Government of Bombay, *Source Material*, 1:214–16.

6. Amrith, *Unruly Waters*, 51–56.

7. A good contemporary account is Malcolm, *Memoir of Central India*, esp. 1:426–62.

8. S. Guha, "Meritocratic Empires?," 125–35.

9. Elphinstone, *Territories Conquered*, 3–4.

10. Malcolm, "Minute," in Bombay Judicial Proceedings, 20 February 1828, P/400/15 no. 6, BL.

11. Dixon, *Sketch of Mairwara*, 40–44; Simcox, *Memoir*; and *Papers Relative to the Meywar Bheel Corps*. I have published a longer analysis of the subjugation of the Bhil communities in S. Guha, *Environment and Ethnicity*, 108–21, 138–53.

12. The ideology of infantilization as basis for denying the efficacy of laissez-faire market processes is discussed in S. Guha, *Environment and Ethnicity*, 182–84.

13. Alexander Gibson, 29 September 1848, and George Wingate, 26 October 1848, both printed in Government of Bombay, *Survey and Settlement Manual*, 92–93, 95–97.

14. W. H. Sykes, unpublished papers, cited in S. Guha, "Kings, Commoners," 20–21, 33.

15. R. H. Grove, *Green Imperialism*, 390–418.

16. Ruthnaswamy, *Some Influences*.

17. Sivaramakrishnan, *Modern Forests*, 108–9.

18. Rangarajan, *Fencing the Forest*, 22–23.

19. R. Guha, *Omnibus*, 216–18; and Gadgil and R. Guha, *This Fissured Land*, 118–23.

20. J. Vibart, Commissioner, N.D. to Secretary to Government, 23 March 1841, Mumbai Revenue Department, vol. 63 of 1844, fos. 117–18, MSA.

21. Wingate, *Report by Captain Wingate*, 4–6; and S. Guha, *Agrarian Economy*, 6–7.

22. Quote from Sivaramakrishnan, *Modern Forests*, 108; official report on forest clearance, cited in Sivaramakrishnan, 46–47.

23. Sivaramakrishnan, *Modern Forests*, 8.

24. Amrith, *Unruly Waters*, 74–76.

25. The fact that the extensive denudation of the Indian subcontinent that has occurred over the past one hundred years (if not longer) has not produced any visible countrywide trend in recorded rainfall does not seem to have weakened this factoid (or fictoid) in public discourse. Over 1951–2010, the Intergovernmental Panel on Climate Change (IPCC) declares with "high confidence" that rainfall *increased* in nearly the whole subcontinent. Intergovernmental Panel on Climate Change, *Climate Change 2014*, figure 1.1(e), p. 41.

26. For this argument, see Sivaramakrishnan, *Modern Forests*, 23.

27. Beames, *Memoirs*, 282.

28. S. Guha, *Environment and Ethnicity*, 164–68.

29. S. Guha, *Beyond Caste*, 190–95.

30. For his career, see *Oxford Dictionary of National Biography*, s.v. "Temple, Sir Richard, first baronet (1826–1902)," accessed August 6, 2017, https://www.oxforddnb.com.

31. Rangarajan, *Fencing the Forest*, 60–61.

32. Kelsall, *Bellary District*, 4.

33. *Allen's Indian Mail* [1856], 330; and Temple, *Men and Affairs*, 444–49, 471–73.

34. *Oxford Dictionary of National Biography*, s.v. "Gibson, Alexander (1800–1867), botanist," accessed August 6, 2017, https://www.oxforddnb.com.

35. Details in *Bombay Civil List* for other salaries.

36. Temple, *Men and Events*, 472–73.

37. *Imperial Gazetteer of India*, 3:108.

38. *Times of India*, May 23, 1894, ProQuest.

39. Weil, "Conservation, Exploitation," 322.

40. Minutes only bore initials. This member's initials are illegible; cited in S. Guha, *Environment and Ethnicity*, 166.

41. Bombay Revenue Department Compilations 89 of 1898, fo. 369, MSA.

42. Agrawal, *Environmentality*, 28–30.

43. Dogdson, Divisional Forest Officer, East Khandesh, 23 May 1899, Revenue Department, vol. 115, fos. 93–98, MSA.

44. BFC, vol. 2, Witness no. 24.

45. Conservator of Forests A. G. Edie admitted the practice of forced labor in a letter to Minister for Excise and Forests G. B. Pradhan, 10 March 1927, Revenue Department, File 7324/24 pt. 2, MSA. His having to answer to an Indian minister was itself a consequence of power-sharing arrangements resulting from nationalist agitations across India.

46. Inquiry Committee and Elwin both cited in S. Guha, *Environment and Ethnicity*, 169–72.

47. "[T]he forest officials have become so anxious to show increasing revenue figures that they have started harassing the people increasingly." *Kesari* cited in Rao, *Forest Ecology in India*, 112n7.

48. BFC, vol. 2, Witness no. 24 (orthography original). The Forest Commission was appointed to inquire into alleged abuses by the Forest Department. The commission was dissolved after it had submitted its report.

49. Alexander Gibson cited in Rao, *Forest Ecology*, 58.

50. *Quarterly Journal of the Poona Sarvajanik Sabha* 3, no. 1 (May 1880): 12–13.

51. Rao, *Forest Ecology*, 175.

52. Rao, *Forest Ecology*, 177–78.

53. Vora, *First Anti-Dam Movement*.

54. The third edition of Kumarappa's *Why the Village Movement?* appeared in early 1939, with a preface by M. K. Gandhi, which stated, inter alia, that Kumarappa "answers almost all the doubts that have been expressed about the necessity and feasibility of the movement. . . . No doubter can fail to have his doubts dispelled."

55. This long-neglected thinker was brought back to public attention by Ramachandra Guha. See R. Guha, *Environmentalism*, 22–24; and "The Green Gandhian," in R. Guha, *An Anthropologist*, 81–86.

56. Kumarappa, *Gandhian Economy*, 69.

57. Kumarappa, 69–72. Even a backyard gardener knows how difficult it is to predict what will succeed on a given plot from year to year and how unrealistic Kumarappa's prescription is.

58. Ostrom, *Governing the Commons*, was foundational to such analysis. More recently, a symposium gathered scholars from many regions to present a review of such work. Dolšak and Ostrom, *Commons*.

59. S. Guha, *Health and Population*, 111–16.

60. Two books by Mariam Dossal—*Imperial Designs and Indian Realities* and *Mumbai*—jointly offer a rich history of the transformation of an old port city.

61. Eugenia W. Herbert's *Flora's Empire* offers a wonderfully rich study of the phenomenon and its place in the society and ideology of the Victorian empire.

62. Herbert, *Flora's Empire*, 216 (for Curzon), 277 (for denigration of Chandni Chowk).

63. Pradhan, *Empire in the Hills*.

64. R. Guha, *Unquiet Woods*, 99–104. Shekhar Pathak has written an entire monograph on the exaction of forced labor. Pathak, *Uttarākhand*.

65. Pathak, *Uttarakhānd*, 126–30.

66. A vituperative series of letters between Forest Officer "Yardrod Pickling" and "Revenue Officer" appeared in 1893–94. The Revenue Department was accused (among many offenses) of soliciting false evidence and stirring up the people against the Forest Department. *Times of India*, May 23, 1894, ProQuest.

67. Forest Survey of India, *ISFR 2021*, table 1.1, https://fsi.nic.in/isfr-2021/chapter-1.pdf.

68. D. Gupta, *Caged Phoenix*, 104–16.

69. A 2005 probe into the tiger population at the Sariska Tiger Reserve revealed that all its tigers had disappeared. Pinglay, "Missing Tigers."

CONCLUSION

1. Gadgil and Guha, *Ecology and Equity*, 1–6.

2. Sörlin and Wormbs, "Environing Technologies." Bruno Latour's sociological study of the workings of laboratory science afforded me this crucial insight. Latour, *Science in Action*.

3. Boivin et al., "Ecological Consequences"; and Bourdieu, *Outline*.

4. "Open-Source Intelligence."

5. An *Indian Express* reporter interviewed farmers west of Delhi who were preparing to burn the stubble left from their rice crops but knew how to evade satellite surveillance. "'There is enough fog now. Satellite mein nahin dikhega (It won't be caught by satellite trackers),' smiles Pradeep. He has a B.Tech degree, but, as he says, 'There are no jobs for us, we all have to eventually rely on farming.'" "Farmers admit they burn stubble at night or in the early hours of the morning to get around the N[ational] G[reen] T[ribunal] order." Goyal and Johri, "Smoke and Mirrors."

6. See, for example, Stephen Castle, "EU Plans to Require Biometrics of All Non-European Visitors," *New York Times*, February 10, 2008; and Goel, "India's Top Court Limits Sweep of Biometric ID Program," *New York Times*, September 26, 2018.

Bibliography

ABBREVIATIONS

BFC Bombay Forest Commission, *Report of the Bombay Forest Commission*
BISM Bharata Itihas Samshodhak Mandal, Pune (historical institute)
BISMT *Bharata Itihas Samshodhak Mandal Traimasik* (quarterly journal of the BISM)
BL British Library, London
IS *Itihāsa Saṁgraha* (journal)
MIS *Marathyancya Itihasaci Sadhane*
MA Mumbai Archives (branch of MSA)
MSA Maharashtra State Archives
PA Pune Archives (branch of MSA)
RCE *Report on Crop Experiments in the Bombay Presidency* (issued annually by the Department of Agriculture)
SCS *Śiva Caritra Sāhitya*
SRGB *Selections from the Records of the Government of Bombay*
SSRPD *Selections from the Satara Raja's and Peshwa Diaries*

ARCHIVAL COLLECTIONS

British Library, London, Oriental and India Office Collections
Deccan College Postgraduate Research Institute Archive, Pune
Maharashtra State Archives, Mumbai
Maharashtra State Archives, Pune

PUBLISHED WORKS

Abu al-Fazl ibn Mubarak. *The A'īn-i Akbari*. Vol. 1, translated by H. Blochmann, edited by D. C. Phillott. Vol. 2, translated by H. S. Jarrett, corrected by Jadunath Sarkar. Vol. 3, translated by H. S. Jarrett, revised by Jadunath Sarkar. Calcutta: Asiatic Society of Bengal, 1927–49.

Adams, Robert McC. *Heartland of Cities: Surveys of Ancient Settlement and Land Use on the Central Floodplain of the Euphrates.* Chicago: University of Chicago Press, 1981.

———. "Historic Patterns of Mesopotamian Irrigation Agriculture." In *Irrigation's Impact on Society,* edited by Theodore E. Downing and McGuire Gibson, 1–6. Tucson: University of Arizona Press, 1974.

Agrawal, Arun. *Environmentality: Technologies of Government and the Making of Subjects.* Durham, NC: Duke University Press, 2005.

Ali, Daud. "The Image of the Scribe in Early Medieval Sources." In *Irreverent History: Essays for M. G. S. Narayanan,* edited by Kesavan Veluthat and Donald R. Davis Jr., 167–87. Delhi: Primus Books, 2013.

Allen's Indian Mail, and Register of Intelligence for British and Foreign India, China, and All Parts of the East (newspaper). London: William H. Allen, 1845–1857.

Alter, George C. "The Evolution of Models in Historical Demography." *Journal of Interdisciplinary History* 50, no. 3 (Winter 2020): 325–62.

Ambre Rao, Neena. *Forest Ecology in India: Colonial Maharashtra, 1850–1950.* Delhi: Foundation Books, 2008.

Amrith, Sunil. *Unruly Waters: How Mountain Rivers and Monsoons Have Shaped South Asia's History.* London: Penguin Books, 2020. First published 2018 by Basic Books.

Atre, Trimbak Narayana. *Gāṇv-Gāḍa.* Pune: Varda Books, 1989.

Avaḷaskar, Shantārām. *Aitihāsik Sādhane (1588–1821 CE).* Mumbai: Government Central Press, 1963.

———, ed. *Konkancyā Itihāsāci Sādhane: Āṅgrekālīna Astagār.* Pune: BISM, 1947.

———. *Nāgāv: Ārthik va Sāmājik Jīvan, 1760–1840.* Pune: Gokhale Institute of Politics and Economics, 1962.

Babur. *Baburnama: Memoirs of Babur, Prince and Emperor.* Translated and edited by W. M. Thackston. New York: Modern Library, 2002.

Ballhatchet, Kenneth. *Social Policy and Social Change in Western India, 1817–1830.* London: Oxford University Press, 1957.

Banerjee, Anil Chandra. *Peshwa Madhav Rao I.* Calcutta: A. Banerjee and Bros., 1943.

Barbosa, Antonio. *Novos subsídios para a história da ciência náutica portuguesa da época dos descobrimentos.* Porto: Imprensa Portuguesa, 1948.

Barker, Graeme. *The Agricultural Revolution in Prehistory: Why Did Foragers Become Farmers?* Oxford: Oxford University Press, 2006.

Barker, Graeme, Chris Hunt, Huw Barton, Chris Gosden, Same Jones, Lindsay Lloyd-Smith, Lucy Farr, Borbala Nyirí, and Shawn O'Donnell. "The 'Cultured Rainforests' of Borneo." *Quaternary International* 448 (2017): 44–61.

Bauer, Andrew M. "Questioning the Anthropocene and Its Silences:

Socioenvironmental History and the Climate Crisis." *Resilience: A Journal of the Environmental Humanities* 3 (2015–2016): 403–26.

Bayly, C. A. *Rulers, Townsmen and Bazaars: North Indian Society in the Age of British Expansion, 1770–1870*. Delhi: Oxford University Press, 1993. First published 1983 by Cambridge University Press.

Beames, John A. *Memoirs of a Bengal Civilian*. London: Chatto and Windus, 1961.

Berkemer, Georg, and Margret Frenz, eds. *Sharing Sovereignty: The Little Kingdom in South Asia*. Berlin: Klaus Schwarz, 2003.

Bhattacharyya, Debjani. *Empire and Ecology in the Bengal Delta: The Making of Calcutta*. Cambridge: Cambridge University Press, 2018.

Birkenholtz, Trevor. "Contesting Expertise: The Politics of Environmental Knowledge in Northern Indian Groundwater Practices." *Geoforum* 39, no. 1 (2008): 466–82.

Boivin, Nicole L., Melinda A. Zeder, Dorian Q. Fuller, Alison Crowther, Greger Larson, Jon M. Erlandson, Tim Denham, and Michael D. Petraglia. "Ecological Consequences of Human Niche Construction: Examining Long-Term Anthropogenic Shaping of Global Species Distributions." *Proceedings of the National Academy of Sciences* 113, no. 23 (2016): 6388–96.

Bombay Civil List Corrected to 1st January 1877. Bombay: Government Central Press, 1877.

Bombay Forest Commission. *Report of the Bombay Forest Commission*. 4 vols. Bombay: Government of Bombay, 1887.

Bose, Saradindu. *Carrying Capacity of Land under Shifting Cultivation*. Asiatic Society Monograph Series, vol. 12. Calcutta: Asiatic Society, 1967.

Bourdieu, Pierre. *Outline of a Theory of Practice*. Translated by Richard Nice. Cambridge: Cambridge University Press, 1977.

Boyns, Trevor, and John Richard Edwards. *A History of Management Accounting: The British Experience*. New York: Routledge, 2013.

Briggs, John. "Account of the Origin, History, and Manners of the Race of Men Called Bunjaras." In *Transactions of the Literary Society of Bombay*, vol. 1, 170–96. Bombay: Bombay Education Society, 1877. First published 1819.

Brondízio, Eduardo S., and Rinku Roy Chowdhury. "Spatiotemporal Methodologies in Environmental Anthropology." In *Environmental Social Sciences: Methods and Research Design*, edited by Ismael Vaccaro, Eric Alden Smith, and Shankar Aswani, 266–98. Cambridge: Cambridge University Press, 2010.

Brown, Percy. *Indian Architecture (Islamic Period)*. 4th ed. Bombay: Taraporewala, 1964.

Buffon, Georges-Louis Leclerc. *De l'homme: Histoire naturelle*. Introduction by Jean Rostand. Paris: Académie Française, 1971.

Bulliet, Richard W. *Cotton, Climate, and Camels in Early Islamic Iran: A Moment in World History*. New York: Columbia University Press, 2009.

Butter, Donald. *Topography and Statistics of Southern Districts of Awadh.* Delhi: Idarah-i Arabiyat-i Dilli, 2009. First published 1839.

Campbell, Tony. "Portolan Charts from the Late Thirteenth Century to 1500." In *Cartography in Prehistoric, Ancient, and Medieval Europe and the Mediterranean,* edited by J. B. Harley and David Woodward, 371–463. Vol. 1 of *The History of Cartography.* Chicago: University of Chicago Press, 1987.

Campo, Juan E. "Visualizing the Hajj: Representations of a Changing Sacred Landscape Past and Present." In *The Hajj: Pilgrimage in Islam,* edited by Eric Tagliacozzo and Shawkat M. Toorawa, 269–87. Cambridge: Cambridge University Press, 2015.

Candy, E. T. *Selections with Notes, from the Records of Government, Regarding the Khoti Tenure.* Bombay: Reprinted at the Government Central Press, 1895. First published 1873.

Carstairs, G. Morris. "Bhil Villages of Western Udaipur: A Study in Resistance to Social Change." In *India's Villages,* 2nd ed., edited by Mysore N. Srinivas, 68–76. London: Asia Publishing House, 1960.

Caudharī, Sūryanārāyāṇa, ed. *Jātakamālā. Āryaśūra-kṛta. Mūla Saṃskṛta aura Hindī anuvāda.* Delhi: Motilal Banrasidass, 1971.

Cecchi, G., R. C. Mattioli, J. Slingenbergh, and S. de la Rocque. "Land Cover and Tsetse Fly Distributions in Sub-Saharan Africa." *Medical and Veterinary Entomology* 22, no. 4 (2008): 364–73.

Chaplin, William. *A Report Exhibiting a View of the Fiscal and Judicial System of Administration Introduced into the Conquered Territory above the Ghauts.* Bombay: Government of Bombay at the Courier Press, 1824.

Coats, Thomas. "Account of the Present State of the Township of Lony: In Illustration of the Institutions, Resources, &c. of the Marratta Cultivators." In *Transactions of the Literary Society of Bombay,* vol. 3, 172–264. London: Printed for Longman, Hurst, Rees, Orme, Brown, and Murray, 1823.

Colebrooke, Henry T. *Remarks on the Husbandry and Internal Commerce of Bengal.* 1804. Reprint, Calcutta: "Statesman" Steam Printing Works, 1884.

Coupland, Henry. *Final Report on the Survey and Settlement Operations in the District of Monghyr (North), 1905–1907.* Calcutta: Bengal Secretariat Book Depot, 1908.

Coward, Fiona, Robert Hosfield, Matt Pope, and Francis Wenban-Smith, eds. *Settlement, Society and Cognition in Human Evolution: Landscapes in Mind.* New York: Cambridge University Press, 2015.

Crosby, Alfred W. *Ecological Imperialism: The Biological Expansion of Europe, 900–1900.* 2nd ed. Cambridge: Cambridge University Press, 2004.

Crossley, Pamela Kyle. *A Translucent Mirror: History and Identity in Qing Imperial Ideology*. Berkeley: University of California Press, 1999.

Cunha Rivara, J. H. de. *Archivo Portuguez Oriental*. Vol. 5. Delhi: Asian Educational Services, 1992. First published 1865.

Daniel, E. Valentine. *Fluid Signs: Being a Person the Tamil Way*. Berkeley: University of California Press, 1984.

DeBuys, William. *A Great Aridness: Climate Change and the Future of the American Southwest*. New York: Oxford University Press, 2011.

Deloche, Jean. *Transport and Communications in India Prior to Steam Locomotion*. 2 vols. Translated by James Walker. Delhi: Oxford University Press, 1993–1994.

Deshpande, Prachi. *Scripts of Power: Writing, Language Practices and Cultural History in Western India*. Ranikhet: Permanent Black, 2023.

Dhavalikar, Madhukar K. *The First Farmers of the Deccan*. Pune: Ravish Publishers, 1988.

Dhume, Vinayak N. S. *Śrī Mangeś Devasthān: Samagra Itihāsa*. Fatorda, Goa: T. S. Kakodkar, 1971.

Diamond, Jared. *Guns, Germs, and Steel: The Fates of Human Societies*. New York: Norton, 1997.

Di Cosmo, Nicola. *Ancient China and Its Enemies: The Rise of Nomadic Power in East Asian History*. Cambridge: Cambridge University Press, 2002.

Diddee, Jaymala, S. R. Jog, V. S. Kale, and V. S. Datye, eds. *Geography of Maharashtra*. Jaipur: Rawat Publications, 2002.

Dirom, Alexander. *A Narrative of the Campaign in India, which Terminated the War with Tippoo Sultan in 1792*. New Delhi: Asian Educational Services, 1985. First published 1793.

Divyabhanusinh. *The End of a Trail: The Cheetah in India*. New Delhi: Banyan Books, 1995.

Dixon, C. J. *Sketch of Mairwara*. London: Smith, Elder, 1850.

Dolšak, Nives, and Elinor Ostrom, eds. *The Commons in the New Millennium: Challenges and Adaptation*. Cambridge, MA: MIT Press, 2003.

Dorling, Daniel, and David Fairbairn. *Mapping: Ways of Representing the World*. London: Longman, 1997.

Dossal, Mariam. *Imperial Designs and Indian Realities: The Planning of Bombay City, 1845–1975*. Bombay: Oxford University Press, 1991.

———. *Mumbai: Theatre of Conflict, City of Hope*. Mumbai: Oxford University Press, 2010.

Dove, Michael R. "North-South Differences, Global Warming, and the Global System." *Chemosphere* 29, no. 5 (1994): 1063–77.

DeBuys, William. *A Great Aridness: Climate Change and the Future of the American Southwest*. New York: Oxford University Press, 2011.

Deshpande, Prachi. *Scripts of Power: Writing, Language Practices and Cultural History in Western India*. Ranikhet: Permanent Black, 2023.

Duff, James Grant. *A History of the Mahrattas*. 3 vols. London: Longmans, Rees, Orme, Brown, and Green, 1826.

Early European Travellers in the Nagpur Territories: Reprinted from Old Records. Nagpur: Printed at the Government Press, 1930.

Eck, Diana L. *India: A Sacred Geography*. New York: Harmony Books, 2012.

Edney, Matthew H. *Mapping an Empire: The Geographical Construction of British India, 1765–1843*. Chicago: University of Chicago Press, 1997.

Ehrlich, Paul R. *The Population Bomb*. New York: Ballantine Books, 1968.

Elliott, Charles Alfred. *The Chronicles of Oonao: A District in Oudh*. Allahabad: Allahabad Mission Press, 1862.

Elphinstone, Mountstuart. *Report on the Territories Conquered from the Paishwa*. 2nd ed. Bombay: Government Press, 1838.

——— . *Selections from the Minutes and Other Official Writings of the Honourable Mountstuart Elphinstone, Governor of Bombay*. Edited by George W. Forrest. London: Richard Bentley and Son, 1884.

Elvin, Mark. *The Retreat of the Elephants: An Environmental History of China*. New Haven, CT: Yale University Press, 2004.

Elvin, Mark, and Su Ninghu. "Action at a Distance: The Influence of the Yellow River on Hangzhou Bay since A.D. 1000." In *Sediments of Time: Environment and Society in Chinese History*, edited by Mark Elvin and Liu Ts'ui-jung, 344–407. Cambridge: Cambridge University Press, 1998.

Fairhead, James, and Melissa Leach. *Misreading the African Landscape: Society and Ecology in a Forest-Savanna Mosaic*. With the research collaboration of Dominique Millimouno and Marie Kamano. Cambridge: Cambridge University Press, 1996.

Fleming, Benjamin J. "Mapping Sacred Geography in Medieval India: The Case of the Twelve *Jyotirlingas*." *International Journal of Hindu Studies* 13, no. 1 (2009): 51–81.

Food and Agriculture Organization. *FAO Statistical Yearbook 2014: Asia and the Pacific Food and Agriculture*. Bangkok: FAO Regional Office, 2014.

Forest Survey of India. *ISFR 2021*. Uttarakand: Forest Survey of India, 2021.

Forrest, George W., ed. *Selections from the Letters, Despatches, and Other State Papers. Home Series*. Vol. 2. Bombay: Government Central Press, 1887.

Forsyth, James. *The Highlands of Central India: Notes on Their Forests and Wild Tribes, Natural History and Sports*. London: Chapman and Hall, 1889.

Foster, William, ed. *Early Travels in India, 1583–1619*. London: Oxford University Press, 1921.

Fryer, John. *A New Account of East India and Persia in Eight Letters Being Nine Years Travels. Begun 1672. And Finished 1681*. London: Printed for Ri. Chiswell, 1698.

Fukazawa, Hiroshi K. "The Local Administration of the Adilshahi Sultanate (1489–1686)." In *The Medieval Deccan: Peasants, Social Systems and States: Sixteenth to Eighteenth Centuries*, edited by Hiroshi K. Fukazawa, 1–48. Delhi: Oxford University Press, 1991.

Fuller, Dorian Q., and Ling Qin. "Water Management and Labour in the Origins and Dispersal of Asian Rice." *World Archaeology* 41, no. 1 (2009): 89–111.

Gadgil, Madhav, and Ramachandra Guha. *Ecology and Equity: The Use and Abuse of Nature in Contemporary India*. London: Routledge, 1995.

———. *This Fissured Land: An Ecological History of India*. Delhi: Oxford University Press, 1992.

Gazetteer of the Bombay Presidency. Bombay: Government Central Press, 1877–1904.

Gazetteer of the Bombay Presidency. Vol. 11, *Kolaba and Janjira*. Bombay: Government Central Press, 1883.

Gazetteer of the Bombay Presidency. Vol. 19, *Satara*. Bombay: Government Central Press, 1885.

Gibson, Alexander. "Notes on Indian Agriculture, as Practised in the Western or Bombay Provinces of India." *Journal of the Royal Asiatic Society of Great Britain and Ireland* 8 (1846): 93–103.

Gibson, McGuire. "Violation of Fallow and Engineered Disaster in Mesopotamian Civilization." In *Irrigation's Impact on Society*, edited by Theodore E. Downing and McGuire Gibson, 7–19. Tucson: University of Arizona Press, 1974.

Glacken, Clarence J. *Genealogies of Environmentalism: The Lost Works of Clarence Glacken*. Edited by S. Ravi Rajan. Charlottesville: University of Virginia Press, 2017.

———. *Traces on the Rhodian Shore: Nature and Culture in Western Thought from Ancient Times to the End of the Eighteenth Century*. Berkeley: University of California Press, 1967.

Gold, Ann Grodzins, and Bhoju Ram Gujar. *In the Time of Trees and Sorrows: Nature, Power, and Memory in Rajasthan*. Durham, NC: Duke University Press, 2002.

Goldewijk, Kees K., Arthur Beusen, Jonathan Doelman, and Elke Stehfest. "Anthropogenic Land Use Estimates for the Holocene—HYDE 3.2." *Earth System Science Data Discussions* 9, no. 2 (2017): 927–53.

Goldsmid, H. E., G. Wingate, and D. Davidson. "A Report Made to the Revenue Commissioner . . ." [1847]. In *The Survey and Settlement Manual*, 1–46. Bombay: Government Central Press, 1882.

Gole, Susan. *Indian Maps and Plans: From Earliest Times to the Advent of European Surveys.* New Delhi: Manohar, 1989.

———. "The Ittagi Plates of Kadamba Jayakeśī I." In *Copper Plate Inscriptions from Karnataka—Recent Discoveries,* edited by M. S. Nagaraja Rao and K. V. Ramesh, 62–69. Mysore: Government of Karnataka, 1985.

Gommans, Jos. *Mughal Warfare: Indian Frontiers and High Roads to Empire, 1500–1700.* London: Routledge, 2002.

———. "The Silent Frontier of South Asia, c. AD 1100–1800." In *The Indian Frontier: Horse and Warband in the Making of Empires,* 51–77. Delhi: Manohar, 2018.

Government of Bengal. *Agricultural Statistics by Plot to Plot Enumeration in Bengal, 1944–45.* 3 parts. Calcutta: Government of Bengal, 1946.

Government of Bombay. *Source Material for a History of the Freedom Movement in India.* Vol. 1, *1818–1885.* Bombay: Government Central Press, 1957.

———. *The Survey and Settlement Manual.* Bombay: Government Central Press, 1882.

Govindrajan, Radhika. *Animal Intimacies: Interspecies Relatedness in India's Central Himalayas.* Chicago: University of Chicago Press, 2018.

Goyal, Divya, and Ankita Dwivedi Johri. "Smoke and Mirrors: Punjab, Haryana Farmers Say Why They Burn Stubble." *Indian Express,* November 14, 2017. https://indianexpress.com/article/india/smoke-and-mirrors-delhi-air-pollution-smog-stubble-crop-burning-farmers-4933291/.

Graham, D. *Statistical Report on the Principality of Kolhapoor.* Bombay: Government of Bombay, 1854.

Grove, Matt, and Robin Dunbar. "Local Objects, Distant Symbols: Fission-Fusion Social Systems and the Evolution of Human Cognition." In *Settlement, Society and Cognition in Human Evolution: Landscapes in Mind,* edited by Fiona Coward, Robert Hosfield, Matt Pope, and Francis Wenban-Smith, 15–30. New York: Cambridge University Press, 2015.

Grove, Richard H. *Green Imperialism: Colonial Expansion, Tropical Island Edens and the Origins of Environmentalism, 1600–1860.* Cambridge: Cambridge University Press, Indian edition, 1995.

Guha, Atul Chandra. *A Brief Sketch of the Land Systems of Bengal and Behar.* Calcutta: Thacker, Spink, 1915.

Guha, Ramachandra. *An Anthropologist among the Marxists and Other Essays.* New Delhi: Permanent Black, 2001.

———. *Environmentalism: A Global History.* New York: Longman, 2000.

———. *The Ramachandra Guha Omnibus.* New Delhi: Oxford University Press, 2005.

———. *The Unquiet Woods: Ecological Change and Peasant Resistance in the Himalaya.* Exp. ed. Berkeley: University of California Press, 2000.

Guha, Sumit. *The Agrarian Economy of the Bombay Deccan, 1818–1941*. Delhi: Oxford University Press, 1985.

———. *Beyond Caste: Identity and Power in South Asia, Past and Present*. Leiden: Brill, 2013.

———. "Claims on the Commons: Political Power and Natural Resources in Pre-colonial India." *Indian Economic and Social History Review* 39, no. 2–3 (2002): 181–96.

———. "Conviviality and Cosmopolitanism: Recognition and Representation of 'East' and 'West' in Peninsular India c. 1600–1800." In *Cosmopolitismes en Asie du Sud: Sources, itinéraires, langues (XVIe–XVIIIe siècle)*, edited by Corinne Lefèvre, Ines G. Županov, and Jorge Flores, 275–92. Paris: Éditions de l'École des hautes études en sciences sociales, 2015.

———. *Environment and Ethnicity in India, c. 1200–1991*. Cambridge: Cambridge University Press, 1999.

———. "Forest Polities and Agrarian Empires: The Khandesh Bhils, c. 1700–1850." *Indian Economic and Social History Review* 33, no. 2 (1996): 133–53.

———. *Health and Population in South Asia: From Earliest Times to the Present*. New Delhi: Permanent Black, 2001.

———. *History and Collective Memory in South Asia, 1200–2000*. Seattle: University of Washington Press, 2019.

———. "Kings, Commoners, and the Commons: People and Environments in Western India, 1600–1900." NMML Working Paper 3rd Series, no. 11, 1996.

———. "Lower Strata, Older Races, and Aboriginal Peoples: Racial Anthropology and Mythical History Past and Present." *Journal of Asian Studies* 57, no. 2 (1998): 423–41.

———. "Meritocratic Empires? South Asia ca. 1600–1947." In *Making Meritocracy: Lessons from China and India from Antiquity to the Present*, edited by Tarun Khanna and Michael Szonyi, 118–36. New York: Oxford University Press, 2022.

———. "Rethinking the Economy of Mughal India: Lateral Perspectives." *Journal of the Economic and Social History of the Orient* 58, no. 4 (2015): 532–75.

———. "Serving the Barbarian to Preserve the *dharma*: The Ideology and Training of a Clerical Elite in Peninsular India c. 1300–1800." *Indian Economic and Social History Review* 47, no. 4 (2010): 497–525.

———. "Theatre State or Box Office State? A Note on the Political Economy of Eighteenth Century India." *Indian Economic and Social History Review* 31, no. 4 (1994): 519–24.

———. *Tribe and State in Asia through Twenty-Five Centuries*. New York: Columbia University Press for the Association of Asian Studies, 2021.

Gupta, Chitrarekha. *The Kāyasthas: A Study in the Formation and Early History of a Caste*. Calcutta: K. P. Bagchi, 1996.

Gupta, Dipankar. *The Caged Phoenix: Can India Fly?* Stanford, CA: Stanford University Press, 2010.

Gutschow, Niels. "Ranpur—the Centre of a Little Kingdom." In *Sharing Sovereignty: The Little Kingdom in South Asia*, edited by Georg Berkemer and Margret Frenz, 137–51. Berlin: Klaus Schwarz, 2003.

Habib, Irfan. *The Agrarian System of Mughal India, 1556–1707*. 2nd ed. New Delhi: Oxford University Press, 1999.

———. *An Atlas of the Mughal Empire: Political and Economic Maps with Detailed Notes, Bibliography and Index*. Delhi: Oxford University Press, 1982.

———. "Cartography in Mughal India." *Proceedings of the Indian History Congress* 35 (1974): 150–62.

Hämäläinen, Pekka. *The Comanche Empire*. New Haven, CT: Yale University Press, 2008.

Harari, Yuval Noah. *Homo Deus: A Brief History of Tomorrow*. New York: Harper, 2017.

Harley, J. B., and David Woodward, eds. *The History of Cartography*. Vol. 2, bk. 1, *Cartography in the Traditional Islamic and South Asian Societies*. Chicago: University of Chicago Press, 1992.

Hasan, S. Nurul. "Zamindars under the Mughals." In *Land Control and Social Structure in Indian History*, edited by Robert Eric Frykenberg, 17–31. 1st rev. Indian ed. Delhi: Manohar, 1979.

Hashim. *The Emperor Shah Jahan Standing on a Globe*. Mid-seventeenth century. Opaque watercolor, ink, and gold on paper. https://upload.wikimedia.org/wikipedia/commons/f/ff/Shahjahan_on_globe%2C_mid_17th_century.jpg.

Hay-Edie, Terence. "The Cultural Values of Protected Areas." In *The Full Value of Parks: From Economics to the Intangible*, edited by David Harmon and Allen D. Putney, 91–102. Lanham, MD: Rowman and Littlefield, 2003.

Hayes, Peter, and Kirk R. Smith, eds. *The Global Greenhouse Regime: Who Pays? Science, Economics and North-South Politics in the Climate Change Convention*. London: Earthscan Publications, 1993.

Herbert, Eugenia W. *Flora's Empire: British Gardens in India*. Philadelphia: University of Pennsylvania Press, 2011.

Hettinger, Annaliese, Anjali Kumar, Tatiana Eaves, Sarah Anderson, Bethann Garramon Merkle, and Skylar Bayer. "Extending the Vision: Highlighting the Human Dimensions of the Ecological Society of America." *Bulletin of the Ecological Society of America* 100, no. 4 (2019): 1–5.

Hislop, Stephen. *Papers Relating to the Aboriginal Tribes of the Central Provinces*. Edited, with notes and preface by Richard Temple. N.p.: n.p., 1866.

Hodivala, S. H. *Studies in Indo-Muslim History by S. H. Hodivala*. Edited by Sanjay

Garg. Vol. 1, *A Critical Commentary on Elliot and Dowson's History of India as Told by Its Own Historians*. New Delhi: Manohar, 2019.

Hughes, Julie R. *Animal Kingdoms: Hunting, the Environment, and Power in the Indian Princely States*. Cambridge, MA: Harvard University Press, 2013.

Hunter, William. "Report on Some of the Rights, Privileges, and Usages of the Hill Population in Meywar." *Journal of the Royal Asiatic Society of Great Britain and Ireland* 8 (1846): 176–92.

Ibn Batoutah. *Voyages d'Ibn Batoutah*. Vols. 3, 4. Translated and edited by C. Defremery and B. R. Sanguinetti. Paris: Imprimerie Nationale, 1878, 1879.

Iggers, Georg G., and Q. Edward Wang. *A Global History of Modern Historiography*. 2nd ed. New York: Routledge, 2013.

Imperial Gazetteer of India . . . Published under the Authority of His Majesty's Secretary of State for India in Council. Vols. 1, 3. Oxford: Clarendon Press, 1909, 1908.

Intergovernmental Panel on Climate Change. *Climate Change 2014: Synthesis Report*. Geneva: IPCC, 2014. www.ipcc.ch/site/assets/uploads/2018/05/SYR_AR5_FINAL _full_wcover.pdf.

Itihāsa Sāṃgraha. Irregularly published by D. B. Parasnis, the editor, between 1908 and 1916.

Jacoby, Karl. *Crimes against Nature: Squatters, Poachers, Thieves, and the Hidden History of American Conservation*. Berkeley: University of California Press, 2014.

Jagalpure, L. B., and K. D. Kale. *Sarola Kasar: Study of a Deccan Village in the Famine Zone*. Ahmednagar: L. B. Jagalpure, 1938.

Johansen, Peter G. "Landscape, Monumental Architecture, and Ritual: A Reconsideration of the South Indian Ashmounds." *Journal of Anthropological Archaeology* 23, no. 3 (2004): 309–30.

Joshi, S. N. Vatsa. "Desmukhi watan." In "Aitihasika Samkirna nibandha," *BISMT*, 24, no. 2 (1943): 59–74.

Jothish, P. S. "Frugivory and Seed Dispersal of Woody Species by the Asian Elephant (*Elephas maximus*) in a Mid-elevation Tropical Evergreen Forest in India." *Journal of Tropical Ecology* 29, no. 2 (2013): 181–85.

Karvir Sardarācya Kaifiyati. Edited and published by Khanderav Gaikwad. Kolhapur, 1971.

Kelsall, John. *Manual of the Bellary District*. Madras: Lawrence Asylum Press, 1872.

Khan, Ahsan Raza. *Chieftains in the Mughal Empire during the Reign of Akbar*. Simla: Indian Institute of Advanced Study, 1977.

Khare, G. H., and K. N. Joshi, eds. *Aitihāsik Marāṭhī Sādhane*. Pune: BISM, 1983.

Khobrekar, V. G., and S. S. Shinde, eds. *Kokancyā Itihāsācī Sādhane*. Bombay: Government Central Press, 1971.

Kingsland, Sharon E. "The Importance of History and Historical Records for Understanding the Anthropocene." *Bulletin of the Ecological Society of America* 98, no. 1 (2017): 64–71.

———. *Modeling Nature: Episodes in the History of Population Ecology*. 2nd ed. Chicago: University of Chicago Press, 1995.

Knox, Robert. *The Races of Men*. London: Henry Renshaw, 1862.

Koirala, Raj Kumar, David Raubenheimer, Achyut Aryal, Mitra Lal Pathak, and Weihong Ji. "Feeding Preferences of the Asian Elephant (*Elephas maximus*) in Nepal." *BMC Ecology* 16, no. 54 (2016): 1–9. https://doi.org/10.1186/s12898-016-0105-9.

Kulkarni, Bhimrao, ed. *Sabhāsad Bakhar*. Reprint, Pune: Anmol Prakashan, 1987.

Kulke, Hermann, ed. *The State in India, 1000–1700*. Delhi: Oxford University Press, 1995.

Kumar, Mayank. *Monsoon Ecologies: Irrigation, Agriculture and Settlement Patterns in Rajasthan during the Pre-colonial Period*. New Delhi: Manohar, 2013.

Kumar, Tuk-Tuk. *History of Rice in India: Mythology, Culture and Agriculture*. Delhi: Gian Publishing House, 1988.

Kumarappa, Joseph C. *The Gandhian Economy and Other Essays*. Wardha: All-India Village Industries Association, 1948.

———. *Why the Village Movement? A Plea for a Village-Centered Economic Order in India*. 3rd ed. Foreword by M. K. Gandhi. Rajahmundry: Hindustan Pub., 1939.

Lahiri, Nayanjot, Upinder Singh, and Tarika Oberoi. "Preliminary Field Report on the Archaeology of Faridabad—the Ballabgarh *Tehsil*." *Man and Environment* 21, no. 1 (1996): 32–57.

Lander, Brian. "Environmental Change and the Rise of the Qin Empire: A Political Ecology of Ancient North China." PhD diss., Columbia University, 2015.

———. *The King's Harvest: A Political Ecology of China from the First Farmers to the First Empire*. New Haven, CT: Yale University Press, 2021.

Latour, Bruno. *Facing Gaia: Eight Lectures on the New Climatic Regime*. Translated by Catherine Porter. Cambridge: Polity Press, 2017.

———. *Science in Action: How to Follow Scientists and Engineers through Society*. Milton Keynes: Open University Press, 1987.

Latour, Bruno, and Steve Woolgar. *Laboratory Life: The Construction of Scientific Facts*. Princeton, NJ: Princeton University Press, 1986.

Lattimore, Owen. *Inner Asian Frontiers of China*. Boston: Beacon Books, 1967.

Law, John. "On the Social Explanation of Technical Change: The Case of the Portuguese Maritime Expansion." *Technology and Culture* 28, no. 2 (1987): 227–52.

Leach, E. R. *Political Systems of Highland Burma: A Study of Kachin Social Structure*. Boston: Beacon Press, 1965.

Leonard, Karen Isaksen. *Social History of an Indian Caste: The Kayasths of Hyderabad.* Berkeley: University of California Press, 1978.

Lewis, Barry. "Village Defenses of the Karnataka Maidan, AD 1600–1800." *South Asian Studies* 25, no. 1 (2009): 91–111.

Linschoten, Jan Huygen van. *The Voyage of John Huyghen van Linschoten to the East Indies: From the Old English Translation of 1598: The First Book Containing His Description of the East.* 2 vols. Edited by P. A. Tiele. 1885. Reprint, New Delhi: Munshiram Manoharlal, 1997.

Long, Edward. *The History of Jamaica, or General Survey of the Antient and Modern State of That Island: With Reflections on Its Situation, Settlements, Inhabitants, Climate, Products, Commerce, Laws, and Government.* Vol. 3. London: T. Lowndes, 1774.

Lyall, Alfred C., comp. *Gazetteer for the Haidarábád Assigned Districts Commonly Called Berár.* Bombay: Bombay Education Society, 1870.

Mackintosh, Alexander. "An Account of the Tribe of Mhadeo Kolies" [Part I]. *Madras Journal* 5, no. 14 (January 1837): 71–112.

———. "An Account of the Tribe of Mhadeo Kolies" [Part II]. *Madras Journal* 5, no. 15 (April 1837): 238–79.

———. "A Sketch of the History of the Ramoosies." *Madras Journal* (April 1834).

Magez, Stefan, and Magdalena Radwanska, eds. *Trypanosomes and Trypanosomiasis.* Vienna: Springer, 2014.

Malcolm, John. "Essay on the Bhills." *Transactions of the Royal Asiatic Society* 1, no. 1 (1824): 65–91.

———. *A Memoir of Central India, Including Malwa and Adjoining Provinces.* Vol. 1. London: Parbury, Allen, 1832.

Malhotra, K. C., S. B. Khomne, and Madhav Gadgil. "Hunting Strategies among Three Non-pastoral Nomadic Groups of Maharasthra." *Man in India* 63, no. 1 (1983): 21–39.

Mande, Prabhakar. *Gāvagāḍyabāhera.* Aurangabad: Parimal Prakashan, 1983.

Mann, Harold H., in collaboration with D. L. Sahasrabuddhe, N. V. Kanitkar, and V. A. Tamhane. *Land and Labour in a Deccan Village.* University of Bombay Economic Series nos. I, II. London: Oxford University Press, 1917, 1921.

Manwaring, Alfred. *Marathi Proverbs.* New Delhi: Asian Educational Services, 1991. First published in 1899.

Marriott, McKim. "Caste Ranking and Community Structure in Five Regions of India and Pakistan." PhD diss., University of Chicago, 1955.

Marsh, George P. *The Earth as Modified by Human Action.* New York: Charles Scribner, 1874.

Marshall, Thomas. "A Statistical Account of the Pergunna of Jumboosur." In

Transactions of the Literary Society of Bombay, vol. 3, 349–410. London: Longman, Hurst, Rees, Orme, Brown, and Murray, 1823.

———. *Statistical Reports on the Pergunnahs of Padshapoor, Belgam, Kalaniddee and Chandgurh, Khanapoor, Bagulkot and Badamy, and Hoondgoond; in the Southern Mahratta Country*. Bombay: Published for the Government [of Bombay], 1822.

Martin, François. *Mémoires de François Martin, Fondateur de Pondichéry*. 3 vols. Edited by A. Martineau. Paris: Sociéte d'Éditions Géographiques, Maritimes et Coloniales, 1931–1934.

Mate, M. S. *A History of Water Management and Hydraulic Technology in India (1500 B.C. to 1800 A.D.)*. Delhi: B. R. Publishing Corporation, 1998.

McCann, James C. *Green Land, Brown Land, Black Land: An Environmental History of Africa 1800–1990*. Portsmouth, NH: Heinemann, 1999.

McCrindle, J. W., ed. and trans. *Ancient India as Described by Megasthenês and Arrian; Being a Translation of the Fragments of the Indika of Megasthenês Collected by Dr. Schwanbeck, and of the First Part of the Indika of Arrian*. Calcutta: Thacker, Spink, 1877.

McNeill, John R. *Mosquito Empires: Ecology and War in the Greater Caribbean, 1620–1914*. New York: Cambridge University Press, 2010.

McNeill, John R., and Peter Engelke. *The Great Acceleration: An Environmental History of the Anthropocene since 1945*. Cambridge, MA: Belknap Press, 2016.

Melville, Elinor G. K. *A Plague of Sheep: Environmental Consequences of the Conquest of Mexico*. Cambridge: Cambridge University Press, 1994.

Mitra, Sudipta. *History and Heritage of Indian Game Hunting*. Delhi: Rupa, 2010.

Mollison, James W. *A Text-Book on Indian Agriculture*. Vol. 3, *Field and Garden Crops of the Bombay Presidency*. Bombay: Times of India Press, 1901.

Moor, Edward. *A Narrative of the Operations of Captain Little's Detachment*. London: Author, 1794.

Moosvi, Shireen. *The Economy of the Mughal Empire, c. 1595: A Statistical Study*. Delhi: Oxford University Press, 1987.

Moreland, W. H. "The Pargana Headman (Chaudhrī) in the Mogul Empire." *Journal of the Royal Asiatic Society of Great Britain and Ireland*, no. 4 (1938): 511–21.

Morrison, Kathleen D. *Daroji Valley: Landscape History, Place, and the Making of a Dryland Reservoir System*. New Delhi: Manohar for the American Institute of Indian Studies, 2009.

———. *The Human Face of the Land: Why the Past Matters for India's Environmental Future*. Occasional Paper 27. New Delhi: Nehru Memorial Museum and Library, 2013.

———. "Pepper in the Hills: Upland-Lowland Exchange and the Intensification of the Spice Trade." In *Forager-Traders in South and Southeast Asia: Long-Term Histories*, edited by Kathleen D. Morrison and Laura L. Junker, 105–30. Cambridge: Cambridge University Press, 2002.

Morrison, Kathleen D., Seetha N. Reddy, and Arunima Kashyap. "Agrarian Transitions in Iron Age Southern India: Social and Environmental Implications." In *South Asian Archaeology and Art*, vol. 1, *Man and Environment in Prehistoric and Protohistoric South Asia*, edited by Vincent Lefèvre, Aurore Didier, and Benjamin Mutin, 185–95. Turnhout: Brepols, 2015.

Narain, Sunita. *Conflicts of Interest: My Journey through India's Green Movement*. Gurgaon, India: Penguin/Viking, 2017.

Nayeem, M. A. *Evolution of Postal Communications and Administration in the Deccan, from 1294 A.D.* Bombay: Jal Cooper, 1968.

Needham, Joseph, with the collaboration of Wang Ling. *Mathematics and the Sciences of the Heavens and Earth*. Vol. 3 of *Science and Civilisation in China*. Cambridge: Cambridge University Press, 1959.

Netton, Ian Richard, ed. *Golden Roads: Migration, Pilgrimage and Travel in Medieval and Modern Islam*. London: Routledge, 1995.

Olivelle, Patrick, trans. *King, Governance, and Law in Ancient India: Kautilya's Arthasastra: A New Annotated Translation*. New York: Oxford University Press, 2013.

"Open-Source Intelligence: Watching the Border." *The Economist*, February 19, 2022.

Orme, Robert. *A History of the Military Transactions of the British Nation in Indostan*. Vol. 1. 4th rev. ed. London: Printed for F. Wingrave, 1799.

Orta, Garcia da. *Coloquios dos Simples e Drogas da India*. New ed., edited by Conde de Ficalho. Lisbon: Imprensa Nacional, 1891.

Ostrom, Elinor. *Governing the Commons: The Evolution of Institutions for Collective Action*. Cambridge: Cambridge University Press, 1990.

Oturkar, R. V. *Peśvekālīn Sāmajik va Ārthik Patravyavahār*. Pune: BISM, 1950.

Pai, D. S., Latha Sridhar, Pulak Guhathakurta, and H. R. Hatwar. "District-Wide Drought Climatology of the Southwest Monsoon Season over India Based on Standardized Precipitation Index (SPI)." *Natural Hazards* 59 (2011): 1797–813.

Papers Relative to the Meywar Bheel Corps, under the Command of Major William Hunter. London: Acton Griffith, 1856.

Pathak, Shekhar. *Uttarākhaṇḍ main kulī begār prathā*. Delhi: Radhakrishna, 1987.

Peel, M. C., B. L. Finlayson, and T. A. McMahon. "Updated World Map of the Köppen-Geiger Climate Classification." *Hydrology and Earth System Sciences* 11, no. 5 (2007): 1633–44.

Pelsaert, Francisco. *Jahangir's India: The Remonstrantie of Francisco Pelsaert*. Translated by W. H. Moreland and P. Geyl. Delhi: Idarah-i Adabiyat-i Delli, 1972.

Pendse, N. V. *Pēṇḍse Kulavṛttānta*. Bombay: Author, 1938.
Pennant, Thomas. *The View of Hindoostan: Eastern Hindoostan*. Vol. 2. London: Henry Hughes, 1798.
Pinglay, Prachi, 2005. "Missing Tigers." *Frontline*, May 20, 2005. https://frontline.thehindu.com/other/article30204592.ece.
Pokharel, S. S., B. Singh, P. B. Seshagiri, and R. Sukumar. "Lower Levels of Glucocorticoids in Crop-Raiders: Diet Quality as a Potential 'Pacifier' against Stress in Free-Ranging Asian Elephants in a Human-Production Habitat." *Animal Conservation* 22, no. 2 (2019): 177–88.
Potdar, D. V., and G. N. Mujumdar, eds. *Śiva Caritra Sāhitya*. Vol. 2. Pune: BISM, 1930.
Pradhan, Queeny. *Empire in the Hills: Simla, Darjeeling, Ootacamund, and Mount Abu, 1820–1920*. Shimla and Delhi: Indian Institute of Advanced Study and Oxford University Press, 2017.
Prasad, Sushma, A. Anoop, N. Riedel, S. Sarkar, P. Menzel, N. Basavaiah, R. Krishnan et al. "Prolonged Monsoon Droughts and Links to Indo-Pacific Warm Pool: A Holocene Record from Lonar Lake, Central India." *Earth and Planetary Science Letters* 391 (2014): 171–82.
Prichard, Iltudus T. *The Administration of India from 1859 to 1868*. 2 vols. London: Macmillan, 1869.
Pritchard, Sara B. "The Trouble with Darkness: NASA's Suomi Satellite Images of Earth at Night." *Environmental History* 22, no. 2 (2017): 312–30.
Purandare, K. V., ed. *Purandare Daphtar*. Part 1, *1691–2 to 1773–4*. Pune: BISM, 1929.
———. *Śiva Caritra Sāhitya*. Vol. 1. Pune: BISM, 1926.
Pyne, Stephen J. *Fire: A Brief History*. Seattle: University of Washington Press, 2001.
Qaisar, Ahsan Jan. *The Indian Response to European Technology and Culture, A.D. 1498–1707*. Delhi: Oxford India Paperback, 1998.
Quarterly Journal of the Poona Sarvajanik Sabha. Pune: Dnyan Prakash Press, 1878–97, 1916–20.
Rackham, Oliver. *The History of the Countryside*. London: Weidenfeld and Nicholson, 2020.
Radding, Cynthia. *Landscapes of Power and Identity: Comparative Histories in the Sonoran Desert and the Forests of Amazonia from Colony to Republic*. Durham, NC: Duke University Press, 2005.
Radkau, Joachim. *Nature and Power: A Global History of the Environment*. Translated by Thomas Dunlap. Washington, DC: German Historical Institute; New York: Cambridge University Press, 2008.
Raikes, R. L. "The Mohenjo-daro Floods." *Antiquity* 39, no. 155 (1965): 196–203.

Rainger, Ronald. "Race, Politics, and Science: The Anthropological Society of London in the 1860s." *Victorian Studies* 22, no. 1 (1978): 51–70.

Rajan, K., and V. P. Yatheeskumar. "New Evidences on Scientific Dates for Brahmi Script as Revealed from Porunthal and Kodumanal Excavations." *Pragdhara*, nos. 21–22 (2013): 278–95.

Raman, T. R. Shankar. *The Wild Heart of India: Nature and Conservation in the City, the Country, and the Wild*. New Delhi: Oxford University Press, 2019.

Ramesh, Jairam. *Indira Gandhi: A Life in Nature*. New York: Simon and Schuster, 2017.

Ramsbotham, R. B. *Studies in the Land Revenue History of Bengal, 1769–1787*. London: Oxford University Press, 1926.

Rana, R. P. *Rebels to Rulers: The Rise of Jat Power in Medieval India, c. 1665–1735*. New Delhi: Manohar, 2006.

Rangarajan, Mahesh. *Fencing the Forest: Conservation and Ecological Change in India's Central Provinces, 1860–1914*. Delhi: Oxford University Press, 1996.

———. *India's Wildlife History: An Introduction*. New Delhi: Permanent Black, 2001.

Rao, Neena Ambre. *Forest Ecology in India: Colonial Maharashtra, 1850–1950*. Delhi: Foundation Books, 2008.

Raychaudhuri, Tapan, and Irfan Habib. *The Cambridge Economic History of India*. Vol. 1, *c. 1200–c. 1750*. New York: Cambridge University Press, 1982.

Read, Dwight, and Sander van der Leeuw. "The Extension of Social Relations in Time and Space during the Palaeolithic and Beyond." In *Settlement, Society and Cognition in Human Evolution: Landscapes in Mind*, edited by Fiona Coward, Robert Hosfield, Matt Pope, and Francis Wenban-Smith, 31–53. New York: Cambridge University Press, 2015.

Report of the Committee Appointed to Consider the Question of the Maintenance and Improvement of the Existing Cattle Breeds of the Bombay Presidency. N.p.: n.p., 1925(?).

Report on Crop Experiments in the Bombay Presidency. Annual publication of the Government of Bombay. Bombay: Central Government Press, various years.

Report on the Census of Oudh. Vol. 1, *General Report*. Lucknow, India: Oudh Government Press, 1869.

Richards, John F. *The Unending Frontier: An Environmental History of the Early Modern World*. Berkeley: University of California Press, 2003.

Richards, John F., and Elizabeth P. Flint. "A Century of Land-Use Change in South and Southeast Asia." In *Effects of Land-Use Change on Atmospheric CO_2 Concentrations*, edited by Virginia H. Dale. Ecological Studies, vol. 101. New York: Springer-Verlag, 1994. https://doi.org/10.1007/978-1-4613-8363-5_2.

Roe, Sir Thomas. *The Embassy of Sir Thomas Roe to the Court of the Great Mogul, 1615–1619*. 2 vols. Edited by William Foster. London: Hakluyt Society, 1899.

Rood, Tim. "Xenophon's Parasangs." *Journal of Hellenic Studies* 130 (2010): 51–66.

Roy, Tirthankar. *Monsoon Economies: India's History in a Changing Climate.* Cambridge, MA: MIT Press, 2022.

Ruddiman, William F. *Plows, Plagues, and Petroleum: How Humans Took Control of Climate.* Princeton, NJ: Princeton University Press, 2005.

Ruthnaswamy, Mariadas. *Some Influences That Made the British Administrative System in India.* London: Luzac, 1939.

Ruttan, Vernon W. "Induced Innovation, Evolutionary Theory and Path Dependence: Sources of Technical Change." *Economic Journal* 107, no. 444 (1997): 1520–29.

Ryan, P. A. "The Management of Burmese Teak Forests." *Commonwealth Forestry Review* 61, no. 2 (1982): 115–20.

Sarkar, Saswati, Sushma Prasad, Heinz Wilkes, Nils Riedel, Martina Stebich, Nathani Basavaiah, and Dirk Sachse. "Monsoon Source Shifts during the Drying Mid-Holocene: Biomarker Isotope Based Evidence from the Core 'Monsoon Zone' (CMZ) of India." *Quaternary Science Reviews* 123 (2015): 144–57.

Schama, Simon. *Landscape and Memory.* New York: Knopf, 1995.

Scoones, Ian. "New Ecology and the Social Sciences: What Prospects for a Fruitful Engagement?" *Annual Review of Anthropology* 28 (1999): 479–507.

Scott, F. H., comp. *Routes in the Peninsula of India: Comprising the Whole of the Madras Presidency and Portions of the Adjacent Territories of Bengal and Bombay.* Madras: Athenaeum Press for the Government of Madras, 1853.

Scott, James C. *Against the Grain: A Deep History of the Earliest States.* New Haven, CT: Yale University Press, 2017.

———. *The Art of Not Being Governed: An Anarchist History of Upland Southeast Asia.* New Haven, CT: Yale University Press, 2009.

———. *Seeing Like a State: How Certain Schemes to Improve the Human Condition Have Failed.* New Haven, CT: Yale University Press, 1998.

Seefeldt, Jonathan. "An Upwelling of Stone: The Precolonial Life of a Climate Infrastructure Project, Rajsamand, 1656–1818." PhD thesis, University of Texas at Austin, 2022.

Selections from the Records of the Government of Bombay, new series. Bombay: Government Central Press, various years.

Selections from the Records of the Government of Bombay, new series, no. 402, *Papers Relating to the Revision Survey Settlement of the Azra Taluka of the Ichalkaranji State.* Bombay: Government Central Press, 1900.

Selections from the Records of the Government of Bombay, new series, no. 531, *Papers Relating to the Second Revision Settlements of the Igatpuri, Dindori, Nasik, Niphad,*

Sinnar, Chandor, Yeola and Nandgaon Talukas of the Nasik District, with Reports on Inam Villages, 2 vols. Bombay: Government Central Press, 1916–20.

Selections from the Records of the Government of Bombay, new series, no. 539, *Papers Relating to the Second Revision Settlement of the Khed Taluka of the Poona District*. Bombay: Government Central Press, 1922.

Selections from the Records of the Government of Bombay, new series, no. 634, *Papers Relating to the Second Revision Settlement of the Man Taluka of the Satara District*. Bombay: Government Central Press, 1929.

Selections from the Satara Raja's and Peshwa Diaries. 8 parts. Compiled by G. C. Vad. Pune: Deccan Vernacular Education Society, 1902–1911.

Sengupta, Sandeep. "Defending 'Differentiation': India's Foreign Policy on Climate Change from Rio to Copenhagen." In *India's Foreign Policy: A Reader*, vol. 1, edited by Kanti Bajpai and Harsh V. Pant. New Delhi: Oxford University Press, 2013.

Sepkoski, David, and Marco Tamborini. "'An Image of Science': Cameralism, Statistics, and the Visual Language of Natural History in the Nineteenth Century." *Historical Studies in the Natural Sciences* 48, no. 1 (2018): 56–109.

Seppel, Marten. "Cameralist Population Policy and the Problem of Serfdom, 1680–1720." In *Cameralism in Practice: State Administration and Economy in Early Modern Europe*, edited by Marten Seppel and Keith Tribe, 91–110. Rochester, NY: Boydell and Brewer, 2017.

Shaha, G. B. "Khāndeś subhyācyā ujād mahālācī kamāvisī." *Saṁśodhaka* 49, no. 2 (1981): 31–36.

Shahabuddin, Ghazala, and Mahesh Rangarajan, eds. *Making Conservation Work: Securing Biodiversity in This New Century*. New Delhi: Permanent Black, 2007.

Sheikh, Samira. "A Gujarati Map and Pilot Book of the Indian Ocean, c.1750." *Imago Mundi* 61, no. 1 (2009): 67–83.

Shiba, Yoshinobu. "Environment versus Water Control: The Case of the Southern Hangzhou Bay Area from the Mid-Tang through the Qing." In *Sediments of Time: Environment and Society in Chinese History*, edited by Mark Elvin and Liu Ts'ui-jung, 135–64. Cambridge: Cambridge University Press, 1998.

Shuldham, E. W. *Table of Routes and Stages through the Several Districts under the Presidency of Bombay and the Adjoining Territories*. Calcutta: Printed at the Mission and School Press, 1826.

Simcox, A. H. A. *A Memoir of the Khandesh Bhil Corps, 1825–1891*. Bombay: Thacker, 1912.

Singh, K. S. *The Scheduled Castes*. Delhi: Oxford University Press, 1993.

Sinha, Surajit. "State Formation and Rajput Myth in Tribal Central India." In *The

State in India, 1000–1700, edited by Hermann Kulke, 304–42. Delhi: Oxford University Press, 1995.

Sinopoli, Carla M., Peter Johansen, and Kathleen D. Morrison. "Changing Cultural Landscapes of the Tungabhadra Valley, South India." In *Polities and Power: Archaeological Perspectives on the Landscapes of Early States*, edited by Steven E. Falconer and Charles L. Redman, 11–41. Tucson: University of Arizona Press, 2009.

Śiva Caritra Sāhitya. Edited compilations of sources, irregularly published, 1926 to present.

Sivaramakrishnan, K. *Modern Forests: Statemaking and Environmental Change in Colonial Eastern India*. New Delhi: Oxford University Press, 1999.

Skaria, Ajay. "Hybrid Histories: Forests, Frontiers and Oral Traditions in Dangs, Western India, 1800s–1920s." PhD thesis, University of Cambridge, 1992.

Sleeman, William H. *A Journey through the Kingdom of Oude, in 1849–1850*. 2 vols. London: Richard Bentley, 1858.

Smil, Vaclav. *Enriching the Earth: Fritz Haber, Carl Bosch, and the Transformation of World Food Production*. Cambridge, MA: MIT Press, 2001.

———. "Nitrogen in Crop Production: An Account of Global Flows." *Global Biogeochemical Cycles* 13, no. 2 (1999): 647–62.

Smith, Samuel. *The Cotton Trade of India, Being a Series of Letters Written from Bombay in the Spring of 1863*. London: Effingham Wilson, 1863.

Sörlin, Sverker. "The Environment as Seen through the Life of a Journal: Ambio 1972–2022." *Ambio* 50 (2021): 10–30.

Sörlin, Sverker, and Nina Wormbs. "Environing Technologies: A Theory of Making Environment." *History and Technology* 34, no. 2 (2018): 101–25.

Spate, O. H. K., and A. T. A. Learmonth. *India and Pakistan: A General and Regional Geography*. 3rd ed. London: Methuen, 1967.

The State of India's Environment, 1982—A Citizen's Report. Delhi: Centre for Science and Environment, 1982.

Stebbing, E. P. *The Forests of India*. 3 vols. London: Bodley Head, 1922–26.

Steingass, Francis Joseph. *A Comprehensive Persian-English Dictionary: Including the Arabic Words and Phrases to Be Met with in Persian Literature: Being Johnson and Richardson's Persian, Arabic, and English Dictionary*. New Delhi: Asian Educational Services, 1992.

Stevenson-Moore, C. J. *Final Report on the Survey and Settlement Operations in the Muzaffarpur District, 1892–1899*. Calcutta: Bengal Secretariat Press, 1900.

Stiglitz, Joseph E. "Information and the Change in the Paradigm in Economics." *American Economic Review* 92, no. 3 (2002): 460–501.

Stoneman, Richard. "How Many Miles to Babylon? Maps, Guides, Roads, and Rivers in the Expeditions of Xenophon and Alexander." *Greece & Rome* 62, no. 1 (2015): 60–74.

Sukumar, Raman. *The Asian Elephant: Ecology and Management*. Cambridge: Cambridge University Press, 1989.

———. *The Living Elephants: Evolutionary Ecology, Behavior, and Conservation*. New York: Oxford University Press, 2003.

Sykes, William H. "Land Tenures of Dukhun (Deccan)." *Journal of the Royal Asiatic Society of Great Britain and Ireland* 3, no. 2 (1836): 350–76.

———. "Special Report on the Statistics of the Four Collectorates of Dukhun, under the British Government." In *Report of the Seventh Meeting of the British Association for the Advancement of Science*, vol. 6, 217–313. London: John Murray, 1838.

Tanzi, Vito. "Uses and Abuses of Estimates of the Underground Economy." *Economic Journal* 109, no. 456 (1999): F338–F347.

Taylor, Eva Germaine Rimington. *The Haven-Finding Art: A History of Navigation from Odysseus to Captain Cook*. With a foreword by K. St. B. Collins. New York: American Elsevier, 1971.

Taylor, Peter. "Conceptualizing the Heterogeneity, Embeddedness, and Ongoing Restructuring That Make Ecological Complexity 'Unruly.'" In *Ecology Revisited: Reflecting on Concepts, Advancing Science*, edited by Astrid Schwarz and Kurt Jax, 87–96. Dordrecht: Springer, 2011.

Temple, Richard. *Men and Events of My Time in India*. London: John Murray, 1882.

Thomas, William L., Jr., ed. *Man's Role in Changing the Face of the Earth*. Chicago: University of Chicago Press, 1956.

Thomaz, Luís Felipe F. R. *De Ceuta a Timor*. Linda-a-Velha, Portugal: DIFEL, 1994.

Tone, William Henry. *A Letter to an Officer on the Madras Establishment. Being an Attempt to Illustrate Some Particular Institutions of the Maratta People*. London: Reprinted for J. Debrett, 1799.

Trautmann, Thomas R. *Elephants and Kings: An Environmental History*. Chicago: University of Chicago Press, 2015.

———. "Elephants and the Mauryas." In *India, History and Thought: Essays in Honor of A. L. Basham*, edited by S. N. Mukherjee, 254–81. Calcutta: Subarnarekha, 1982.

———. "Towards a Deep History of Mahouts." In *Conflict, Negotiation, and Coexistence: Rethinking Human-Elephant Relations in South Asia*, edited by Piers Locke and Jane Buckingham, 47–74. Delhi: Oxford University Press, 2016.

Tucker, Mary Evelyn, and Duncan Ryūken Williams, eds. *Buddhism and Ecology: The Interconnection of Dharma and Deeds*. Cambridge, MA: Harvard University Press, 1997.

Ullah, I. I. M., C. Change, and P. Tourtellote. "Water, Dust, and Agro-pastoralism: Modeling the Coevolution of Landscapes, Farming, and Human Society in Southeast Kazakhstan during the Mid- to Late Holocene." *Journal of Anthropological Archaeology* 55 (2019): 1–16.

United Nations. *United Nations Framework Convention on Climate Change.* 1992. https://unfccc.int/resource/docs/convkp/conveng.pdf.

Vad, G. C., comp., and P. V. Mawjee and D. B. Parasnis, eds. *Sanadāpatreñ.* Pune: Jagadhitechu Press, 1913.

Vora, Rajendra. *The World's First Anti-Dam Movement: The Mulshi Satyagraha, 1920–1924.* Ranikhet: Permanent Black, 2009.

Warde, Paul, Libby Robin, and Sverker Sörlin. *The Environment: A History of the Idea.* Baltimore, MD: Johns Hopkins University Press, 2018.

Watt, George F. *A Dictionary of the Economic Products of India.* 6 vols. Delhi: Cosmo Publications, 1972. First published 1889–96.

Webber, C. Elizabeth, Tuy Sereivathana, M. P. Maltby, and Phyllis C. Lee. "Elephant Crop-Raiding and Human-Elephant Conflict in Cambodia: Crop Selection and Seasonal Timings of Raids." *Oryx* 45, no. 2 (2011): 243–51.

Weil, Benjamin. "Conservation, Exploitation, and Cultural Change in the Indian Forest Service, 1875–1927." *Environmental History* 11, no. 2 (2006): 319–43.

Wellington, Arthur Wellesley. *Supplementary Despatches and Memoranda of Field Marshal Arthur, Duke of Wellington, K. G.* Edited by his son, the Duke of Wellington. Vol. 4, *India: 1797–1805.* London: John Murray, 1859.

Wingate, G. *Report by Captain Wingate, Revenue Survey Commissioner, on the Plan of Survey and Assessment Most Suitable to the Province of Khandesh.* Bombay: Bombay Education Society, 1852.

Wittfogel, Karl A. *Oriental Despotism: A Comparative Study of Total Power.* New Haven, CT: Yale University Press, 1964. First published 1957.

Zilli, I. A. "Two Administrative Documents of Akbar's Reign." *Proceedings of the Indian History Congress* 32 (1970): 367–73.

Index

acacia, 51–52, 136, 137, 154
afforestation, 157, 177, 179
Age of Regulation (*mandini*), 163–64, 172
agriculture: burning of stubble, 190, 211n5; China, 31, 47; clearing of forests for, 174–75; coastal, 93–101; Deccan, 125–26; and elephants, 48–49, 53; English, 126, 204n46; experimental, 184; fertilizing, 90, 95, 100, 126, 130–31; frontier zones, 30–31; Gandhi's views, 182; German, 38; implements for, 136, 137; plantation, 36, 38–39, 41, 95, 174; and rainfall, 48, 98–101, 102–3, 107, 120; shifting, 27, 41, 81, 91, 96, 146, 153–54, 165; South Asia, 47, 48, 53; and taxation, 123–24, 176; and village settlement, 111, 119. *See also* peasant farmers; rice cultivation; tillage
A'in-i Akbari (Administration of Akbar), 48, 57, 69–70, 76, 82
Akbar, 57, 71. See also *A'in-i Akbari*
Americas: crops, 126, 162; environment, 4, 24, 36, 37; mines, 56; native populations, 3–4, 8, 41; plantation slavery, 36, 38–39
animals: accompanying armies, 49–50, 54, 104, 156–57; consumption of, 102, 128, 132, 204n46; demands of, on environment, 13, 15, 132, 166; feeding of, 102–4, 106–7, 109, 157; human manipulation of, 20, 188; hunting of, 54, 57, 135; of itinerant communities, 15, 132, 133, 135; luxury trade in, 32; portraits of, 57; and raiding of peasant crops, 53, 143; symbiotic with elephant populations, 54; work, 102–4, 106–7, 109, 130, 148. *See also* camels; cattle; elephants; horses; oxen

Anthropocene, ix, 1, 3, 9, 190
archaeology and history, 10–11, 19–20, 21, 24, 29, 31; rice in, 91–92
areca (betel) nut, 87, 93, 95, 100, 128
armies: animals accompanying, 49–50, 54, 104, 156–57; effects on landscape, 15, 157, 166; field, 107, 156; Maratha, 102, 141, 151, 167; Mughal-period, 152, 156
Arthashastra, 47–48, 70; on landscapes and military affairs, 59–60, 89, 141; on taxation and economy, 54; on the village, 111, 116–18
Art of Not Being Governed (Scott), 158
Awadh (Oudh), 73, 168, 208n3

bamboo, 136, 157; thickets and defenses, 141, 142, 143, 144, 146, 150, 159
Banjaras, 147–49, 156
Bengal province, 64, 70, 77, 112; famine of 1943, 182; lordships, 73, rice cultivation, 92; teak plantations, 174
Bhil communities, 50, 113, 161–65, 166, 169, 171–72, 208n11
Bombay island, 87–88, 147, 201n51
Bombay Presidency, 84, 112, 118, 153; forestry, 128, 154, 177–78; rice cultivation, 99–100
boundary marking, 88, 116–18, 120–21, 146, 172, 185, 186
Bourdieu, Pierre, "habitus," 19, 20–21, 189
British Empire, 170*fig.*; army, 50, 152, 156, 184; bureaucracy, 73, 84, 175, 184; continuities and discontinuities from earlier regimes, 12, 15, 174; defeat of Marathas, 152–53, 163, 168, 170; forestry, 153–54, 173; and free-market

British Empire (*continued*)
theory, 173, 176; land surveys, 77, 96, 114, 117, 120–21, 122–25, 172, 179, 186; local administration, 75, 80–81, 84, 114, 164, 186; mapping and geographic knowledge, x, 15, 62, 66–69, 73, 77–78, 164, 169, 189, 199n102; military operations, 169–72; taxation, 77, 87–88, 96, 122–25, 169, 174, 176, 185; West Indies, 40–41. *See also* East India Company; Forest Department

British Parliament, 31, 35, 84, 126, 181, 186

Buddhism: previous births of Buddha, 20, 50; symbolic geography of, 24–25

camels, 61, 104, 107, 156, 157, 166

campgrounds: of itinerants, 111, 133, 149; military, 66, 67–68, 105; Mughal camps, 57–58, 61

carbon emissions, 1, 3, 42, 188; Mauna Loa carbon dioxide measurements, 4

cardamom, 93, 100

cartography. *See* geographic knowledge; mapping

caste, 205n74; horticulturalists, 100; occupational, 94, 95, 97, 119; and residence, 120; scribes, 71, 75, 82; watchmen, 80, 121. *See also* clerical class

cattle: dairy, 107; grazing grounds for, 52, 90, 103, 121, 132, 144, 165; herders, 93, 132, 133–34, 137, 146–49, 156. *See also* oxen

civil lines, 184

clerical class, 72, 73, 76, 82, 86

climate, 45–48; change, 1, 3–4, 5, 16, 42, 209n25; maps, 45*map*, 46*map*. *See also* rainfall

Coats, Thomas: on farmers and peasants, 103, 125–26, 128, 129, 132, 136; on migrant cattlemen, 134, 147; on village boundaries, 115, 119

coconuts, 83, 90, 94, 95, 97, 120

colonization: of Americas, 4, 8–9, 36, 38–39; and environment, xi, 8, 11, 15, 36–37, 40–41, 43. *See also* British Empire; Portuguese

communication networks, 59–61

contingency, 7, 16, 17

cosmology, ix, 4, 24, 37, 189; Greco-Roman, 195n56; sacred, 24–26, 42, 65; scientific, 42, 78

cotton, 126

"Criminal Tribes," 133, 134, 149

Dalit, 80, 120, 121

Deccan Plateau: cattle herders, 148, 149; early occupants, 146; farming, 98, 124, 125–26; forests, 169, 170; horses, 167–68; land surveys, 122; local chiefs, 151, 160; postal routes, 60; shrines, 26; villages, 113, 116

defensive use of landscape, 140–41; woodlands, 141–43, 146, 150, 151

Delhi: as British imperial capital, 185; smoke pollution, 190, 211n5; Sultanate of, 55, 56, 59, 71, 147

demarcation, 88, 116–18, 120–21, 172, 185, 186

desh, the, 89–90, 99, 102, 150

deshmukhs (regional lords), 74, 81–82, 115, 145, 200n6, 200n10

desiccationist theory, 37, 41, 173, 175, 176–77

displaced populations, 144–46, 147–49, 182

East India Company, 26, 77, 106; administration of Bombay island, 87–88; cavalry, 167–68; colonial demilitarization, 164, 169–72; and the cotton trade, 126. *See also* British Empire

ecological sciences, 7–8. *See also* political ecology

ecosystems: of the Americas, 36–37, 38; animals and, 4, 13, 15, 40, 51–52, 104, 166; and elite consumption, 11, 14, 125; historians' view of, 16, 23; human engineering of, 19–20; military effects on, 15, 166; and rice cultivation, 91–101; urban, 183; and war, ix, 188. *See also* environmental inequality; forests

236 | INDEX

elephants: African species, 32; "elephant forest," 48, 53–54; and environmental effects, 13, 15, 50–54, 104; habitat of, 49; and kingship, 50; military use of, 49–51, 156; nutritional needs and feeding of, 51–52, 53–54, 108, 157, 196n22; and peasant farmers, 48–49, 53; and political ecology, 78; in religion, 50; training of, 50–51, 53

elite consumption, 11; of animals, 102, 132; and effects on ecosystem, 14, 125; of ghee and spices, 93, 128; of humid zone plants, 100–101; of rice, 29, 91–93, 96, 99, 101, 131; and teak, 136

empire: age of, 40, 42, 190; and elephants, 13, 49–54; evasion of, 158–59; frontier zones, 30–31; and geographic knowledge, 16, 21, 47–48, 164; imperial gaze, x, 60, 70, 187, 189; improvisational working of, 186; Hellenic and Roman, 6, 31; Inner and East Asia, 30–31, 35, 49; irrigation projects, 27–30; maritime and transoceanic, 14, 16, 32–33, 36–37; models and structures, 6–7; and political authority, 59, 138, 163; and political ecology, ix, 23, 43, 159; Portuguese, 14, 32, 36, 87, 96; and race, 38–40, 43; standardization of measurement, 61–62; state-making, 44. *See also* British Empire; colonization; Maratha Empire; Mughal Empire; taxation

environing (Sörlin and Wormbs), 5

environmental history, ix, 6, 11–12, 16, 28, 49, 140

environmental inequality, 5–6, 9–10, 11, 16, 188–90. *See also* political ecology

epidemics, 36–37

equilibrium models, 7, 8

evaluative gaze, ix, x, 12, 22

extinction, 8, 32, 41

famine, 89, 90, 147, 162, 176, 182, 184

farmland, 119, 124–25, 131, 140; European field structures, 31; field assessment, 75, 87, 96. *See also* agriculture; land surveys; peasant farmers; rice cultivation; tillage

fertilizers, 130–31; oil cake, 100; synthetic, 42, 126–27. *See also* manure

fire, 2, 19, 27, 52, 99, 144–45, 154, 175, 206n46

firewood, 104, 109, 128, 136, 139, 154, 166, 180

fodder, 83, 93, 102–9, 137, 149, 156, 196n22; theft of, 132, 133

folk geography, 26, 89, 116–17, 122

foraging, 24, 92, 93, 95, 111, 128, 137, 161; by cattle, 56, 103, 106, 157; by elephants, 51, 53

forced labor, 92, 105, 166, 185, 209n45, 210n64

Forest Department: closure of woodland areas, 134, 169, 178–80, 180–81, 186; desiccationism, 175; forced labor practices of, 180, 209n45; government debate, 178–79, 211n66; grazing fees, 133, 178, 179; and peasant agriculture, 83, 95, 126; roots of, 173–74; scientific forestry, xi, 176–78; staffing, 176, 178; struggles against, 180–81

Forest Grievances Enquiry Committee, 180

forests: clearing of, for cultivation, 174–75; under colonial rule, 143, 166, 169–70, 172; as defensive woodlands, 141–43, 146, 150, 151; deforestation, 166, 175, 191n4; and elephants, 50, 52, 54; and fire, 154, 175, 206n46; as game reserves, 143; hill regions of, 127, 144, 165–66; military uses of, 141; as obstacle to visibility, 42; peasant use of, 91, 100; as refuge, 142–45, 161; regeneration, 157, 177, 179; resource demands on, 128, 136, 139–40; of the Sahel, 140; seasonal burning of, 205n6; and timber extraction, 136, 153–56, 166, 174; Vindhya region, 159; wild foods, 128–29. *See also* firewood; Forest Department; jungle; thorn forests

fortification, 139, 151–53, 154, 166, 205n1

free-market theory, 7, 173, 176, 183, 208n12

fuel, 109; dung for, 136. *See also* firewood

Gandhi, Mahatma: *Hind Swaraj*, 182; preface to Kumarappa's *Why the Village Movement*, 210n54
Ganges-Brahmaputra river system, 52
gardens, 86, 95, 96, 100, 123, 127, 184, 210n61
gentry landlords, 76, 83–84, 99. *See also* local lords
geographic knowledge: Arabic loanwords used for, 64–65; British Empire, x, 35, 62, 66–69, 73, 77–78, 164, 169, 189, 199n102; Chinese, 35; from communication networks, 60–61; early modern Europe, 34–35; folk and local, 26, 63, 89, 116–18, 122, 145, 151; as literary-descriptive, 70; maritime, 33, 34, 78; Mughal era, 47–48, 58–59, 78; routes, 61–62, 63, 66–69, 151; satellite and smartphone, 78; symbolic and pragmatic, ix, 13, 21, 24–26, 33, 42, 65–66, 70, 122. *See also* land surveys; mapping
global warming, 1, 3–4, 5, 16, 42, 209n25
globes, 70
Gole, Susan, *Indian Maps and Plans*, 26, 64, 117
Government of Bombay. *See* Bombay Presidency
GPS network, 5, 33, 45, 78, 191n13
grasslands, 31, 51–52, 134, 144, 165–66, 179, 205n6; competition for, 104–6, 108–9. *See also* cattle; fodder
grazing fees, 121, 133, 178–79
greenhouse gases, 4, 10
Grove, Richard, 40, 41, 173, 174

Habib, Irfan, 11, 58–59, 63–64
"habitus" (Bourdieu), 19, 20–21, 189
hedges, 31, 136; "bound hedge" as defensive feature, 142
hereditary landholders, 72–74; *khots*, 83–84, 99. *See also* local lords
hereditary officials, 84–86, 115–16, 118, 122, 145; accountants, 71, 73, 80, 84. *See also deshmukhs*

hill communities, 158, 162–63, 164–66, 171, 172, 181–82. *See also* Bhil communities
hillforts, 139, 151–56
Himalayan shrines, 25–26
Hind Swaraj (Gandhi), 182
Hindu sacred geography, 25, 26
historical analysis, 6–9, 10–11, 18–19, 23
history and responsibility, 9–10
Holocene period, 2, 3, 94, 95
horses: Dakhani horse complex, 167–68; demands on ecosystem, 4, 166; of itinerants, 31, 132, 133; of messengers, 60; Mughal and Maratha, 69, 90, 102, 104, 107, 141, 167–68; rations for, 102, 106, 121, 156–57, 166; war, 104, 140, 160
human development, 38–39, 42, 188; and niche construction, 19–20, 189
hunting, 51, 52, 54, 57, 105, 135, 136
HYDE (History Database of the Global Environment), 2–3, 191n4
Hyderabad, kingdom of, 70, 80, 81, 106

imperial gaze, x, 14, 48, 60, 70, 141, 187, 189
Indian Maps and Plans (Gole), 26, 64, 117
indigenous populations, 3–4, 8–9, 24, 36
Industrial Revolution, 3, 12, 169
inequality, x, 140, 183; history of, 2–4, 6, 10, 13, 21–23, 185, 188–90. *See also* environmental inequality
information as imperfect, 69
Intergovernmental Panel on Climate Change, 16, 209n25
Iron Age, 31, 91–92, 146
irrigation and drainage, xi, 26–30, 48, 92, 107, 165, 181–82. *See also* reservoirs and aqueducts; water management
Islam, 25, 26, 56, 71, 184; orientation toward Mecca, 26, 59, 63
itinerant communities, xi, 15, 115, 131; accompanying animals, 31, 132–35; Banjaras, 147–49,

156; campgrounds, 111, 120, 133, 149; as criminals, 132–33, 134; mendicants and performers, 135; studied by Atre, 131–34; studied by Mande, 134–36. *See also* pastoralists

jungle, 68, 104, 107–8, 120, 146, 160, 171, 174; wild roots, 129. *See also* forests; thorn forests

khots (gentry landlords), 83–84, 99
Klein Goldewijk, Kees, 3, 191n4
knowledge: differential access to, x, 13, 189; environmental, 5, 10, 12, 15–17, 188–90; historical, 18–19; local, 14, 61, 75, 77–78, 84, 85–88, 117, 121; and power, x, 16–17, 34, 36, 42–43, 47, 62, 75, 79, 81–82, 164, 185–86, 188; scientific, 1, 9; statistical, 78, 119, 179; and technology, 5–6. *See also* geographic knowledge
Kolaba district, 96
Kolaba Gazetteer, 91, 94, 97
Kolhapur, 104, 123, 127, 128, 151–53
Kolis, 152, 160–61, 168
Konkan, 89, 90–91, 94, 171, 180; agriculture, 94–95, 99–100, 125; taxation, 99–100, 125, 145
Köppen climate classifications, 45
kos: as variable measure, 62; *kos minars*, 61

land grants, 71, 72, 123
landmarks, 88, 116–18, 122–23
land management, xi, 38, 128
land measurement, 61–62, 123
land reclamation, 28, 35, 53, 95–97
land records, 44, 74, 76–78; as estimations for taxation, 54–55, 69–70, 71, 85–89; and field assessments, 75, 87, 96, 123–24; lists, 80–81, 84, 87. *See also* land surveys; village administration
land rights, x–xi, 147; hereditary landholders, 73–75
land surveys: British Empire, 15, 77, 96, 114, 117, 120–21, 122–25, 172, 179, 186; cadastral maps, 44–45; classes of land, 122–24; Down Survey of Ireland, 43; Goldsmid, Wingate, and Davidson, 120, 124; Pringle, 123–24; Sykes statistical survey, 122–23. *See also* land records
land use, x–xi, 5, 89, 104–5; classification, 2, 11, 115, 123–24, 169, 179
lentils, 92–93, 95, 100, 102, 127, 129, 156
lime mortar, 139
linear maps, 63–64
lions, 49, 53, 54
local autonomy, 70–76, 112, 114, 137, 158. *See also* Bhil communities
local lords, 72–76, 81–83, 85, 123, 151, 159–61; British measures against, 163–64. See also *deshmukhs*; hereditary officials

Madras, 177
Madras Army, 145, 148
Madras Presidency, Corps of Guides, 66
Maharashtra: geography, 45, 46, 65, 79, 89–91; nationalists, 182; nomadic communities, 134–36, 147; surveys, 118–22; villages, 102, 116–18, 137; western, 26, 55, 93–101. *See also* Bombay Presidency; Deccan Plateau; Konkan; Maratha Empire
maize, 158, 162, 164
malaria, 36, 151, 174, 185
manure, 94, 95, 130, 131, 201n51; from cattle of itinerants, 132, 134; and leaf mold, 100–101
mapping: aerial and satellite technology and, 1, 4–5, 69, 186–87; Arab, 58–59; British period, 15, 16, 62, 63, 66–69, 169, 199n102; Chinese, 35; climate, 45–46, 45*map*, 46*map*; colonial, of Asian geopolitical regions, 66, 67*fig.*; graticular frame in, 63, 198n75, 199n102; land, 44–45; maritime, 32–35, 78; mental, ix, 23, 24, 42, 117, 120; Mughal period, 58–59, 63, 72–73, 77–78; "portolan maps," 33; route, 58, 60, 63–69, 198n75; sacred and pragmatic, 24–26, 65. *See also* geographic knowledge; land surveys

INDEX | 239

Maratha army, 50, 141, 167; cavalry, 90, 102, 107–8, 141, 156, 167; defeat at Panipat, 60; war with Mughals, 82, 141, 151–53

Maratha Empire, xi, 106; and British defeat, 167–68; emergence of, x, 84–86, 89; lands, 89–91, 93–94, 152, 201n31; local administration of, 82, 84, 86, 108–9, 116, 117–18, 150, 160, 161, 163; mapping, 65–66; relations with Banjaras, 147, 149. *See also* Maratha army; Peshwa; Pune

Marathi language, 14, 82, 122, 155, 180

maritime maps, 32–35, 78

Marsh, George P., 6, 40, 43; desiccationist theory of, 37, 41

Maurya Empire, 11, 61, 71

Mawal region, 85–86, 89, 90

meadowlands. *See* grasslands

measurement, 12, 34, 61–62, 63, 77, 78, 96, 123, 186

meat consumption, 128, 132, 204n46

mehwas (recalcitrant) lands, 13, 142–43, 159, 161–63, 170

mental maps, ix, 23, 24, 42, 117, 120

mercenaries, 163, 170–71, 172

Mewar, 164–65; reservoir construction, 29–30

millet, 29, 101, 103, 127, 130; nagli, 91, 96, 101

modern statehood, 34, 44, 114

money economy, 54, 55, 56, 182

monsoons, 90, 93, 97, 100–101, 102, 115, 127, 154; and seasonal moisture, 45–47, 48, 89, 106–7, 115; and wetlands, 52, 91–92

Mughal Empire, 14, 189; accounting, 69–70, 72–73, 75–76, 77; British recognition of, 184–85; camps of, 57–58, 61; currency system, 56; land allotments, 72; and local elites, 72, 84, 85–86; mapping and geographic information of, 56–59, 63–64, 70, 72–73, 77–78; Maratha resistance to, 82, 141, 151–53; nomenclature, 64–65, 73, 74; village administration, 70–76, 84, 199n99

Mysore, 50, 101, 141; British attack on, 145, 156, 157

nagli (finger millet), 91, 96, 101

Nagpur kingdom, 81, 169

National Green Tribunal, 190, 211n5

nationalism, 180, 181–82, 209n45

New World crops, 32, 126, 158

niche construction, 19–20, 189

nitrogen cycle, 42, 188

nomadic pastoralism, 93, 131–32, 134; Northeast Asia, 31. *See also* itinerant communities

nomenclature, 64–65, 73, 74

oil, 28, 128

oilseeds, 100, 102, 107, 115, 129

oxen, 20, 134, 135, 166; fodder for, 104, 106, 130–31, 166; pack, 55–56, 101, 107, 115, 147–48; use by armies, 104, 156; use in farming, 83, 98, 99, 102, 107; worship of, 102

palm trees, 88, 94, 95, 96, 97, 127, 142. *See also* areca (betel) nut

"Paradise Lost" narrative, 37

parganas (village clusters), 71, 74, 114, 203n14; constituent units of, 118–20; record keepers and tax collection, 71, 76–77, 83–84; Saswad, 115–16

pastoralists: militarized, 147–49; of Northeast Asia, 31; of the Sahel, 140; seasonal burning, 205n6; seasonal migration, 93, 111, 133, 144, 146–47; villagers' complaints, 131–34. *See also* cattle; itinerant communities

peasant farmers: competition with military, 106–8; cropping decisions, 129–30; crops raided by animals, 143; Deccan, 125; diet of, 93, 101–2, 127–29; and geographic knowledge, 137, 145; hill regions of, 95, 165–66; housing of, 128, 155; and plot preparation methods, 126–27, 128, 130; purchase of

240 | INDEX

fodder, 103–4; refuge from raiders, 144–45; views of land and soil, 122–23, 124–25; and wood for implements, 136–37; work animals of, 98, 99, 102, 107. *See also* rice cultivation; tillage
peasant soldiers, 102, 168
Persian language, 64, 82, 184, 200n9
Peshwa, 60, 84, 99, 101, 104, 154; Bajirao, 105; cavalry, 105; lineage, 86–87; Madhavrao I, 80; overthrow of the, 167. *See also* Maratha Empire
pilgrimage centers, 25–26, 63, 133
plantation agriculture, 36, 38–39, 41, 95, 174
Plows, Plagues, and Petroleum (Ruddiman), 3–4, 8
political ecology, 12, 78, 188; emergence of the field of, 8; of empire, ix, 43, 159; Indian debates on, 10; of Western India, 79
population, 3, 47, 80, 191n4; increases in, 9, 26–28, 48–49
porters, 135, 156, 159
Portuguese: empire of, 14, 32, 36, 87, 96; introduction of maize, 162; navigation, 34; in South America, 8; traders, 60
postal routes, 59, 60
pragmatic geography, 21, 25, 32, 33, 36, 42, 78, 117
Pune, 99, 103, 106, 124, 131, 135, 196n22; and Maratha regime, 62, 86, 101, 109, 118, 163

racial theory, 38–40, 43, 195n67
railroads, 149, 166, 169, 174, 185
rainfall, 45–47, 46*map*, 68, 89–90, 209n25; and agriculture, 48, 98–101, 102–3, 107, 120; relationship to tree cover, 176. *See also* desiccationist theory; monsoons
regional lords. *See deshmukhs*; hereditary officials; local lords
remote sensing, xiii, 1, 5, 42
reservoirs and aqueducts, 29–30, 98, 99–100, 140, 165

Revenue Department, 174, 176, 177, 178, 211n66
rice consumption, 14, 29, 91–93, 96, 99, 101, 131
rice cultivation, 91–100; coastal, 93–94; farms and labor, 95, 98–100, 101–2; geology of, 95–96, 100; irrigation, 28, 29, 47, 92, 100, 165; on reclaimed land, 95–97; rice strains, 91–92, 95; taxation, 123, 125, 158
Rio Summit (1992), 6, 10
roads and highways, 55, 60, 61–62, 64, 148; route maps, 58, 60, 63–69
Roman Empire, 6, 31, 49
route maps, 58; British, 66–69; Mughal and Maratha, 60, 63–66
Ruddiman, William F., *Plows, Plagues, and Petroleum*, 3–4, 8

sacred geographies, 24–26, 33
Sahyadri mountains (Ghats), 46, 90–91, 94, 115, 144, 153, 172
Sariska Tiger Reserve, 187, 211n69
satellite technology, 1, 5, 42, 186–87, 189–90, 211n5; GPS network, 5, 33, 78, 191n13
scales of perception, 12–13
Schendel, Willem van, *Zomia*, 13, 146, 158
scientific forestry, xi, 38, 44, 173, 176–78
scientific racism, x, 38–40, 43, 195n67
Scott, James, 145; *Art of Not Being Governed*, 158; *Seeing Like a State*, 44, 114
scribes, 71, 75, 82
seasons, 51–52, 67–68, 89, 111, 138, 144, 162, 196n22. *See also* monsoons
Seeing Like a State (Scott), 44, 114
settlement patterns, xi, 14–15, 111–13. *See also* villages
shifting cultivation, 27, 41, 81, 91, 96, 146, 153–54, 165
ship-building, 95, 153, 154
shrines, 25–26, 193n17
smoke pollution, 190
social inequality. *See* inequality

INDEX | *241*

soil: "black," 120, 125, 134, 137, 176–77; classification, 122–23, 124–25; moisture content, 5, 47, 100, 102, 120, 124, 136; salinity, 27–28, 96
Sörlin, Sverker, 12, 191–92n14; *environing*, 5–6
Spanish empire, 8, 32, 36, 56
species extinction, 8, 32, 41
spices, 14, 93, 100, 128, 129
"stage books," 66–68. *See also* route maps
standardization, 61–62
subsistence strategies, 30, 101–2, 109, 111, 145–46, 158, 164
sugarcane, 125, 127, 164
summer resorts, 185
Survey of India, 77
swidden cultivation. *See* shifting cultivation
Sykes, W. H., 88, 90–91, 109; on British demolition of forts, 153; conversations with peasants, 122, 126; population calculations, 80–81, 115; on rural settlements, 150; soil survey, 122–23; on woodlands, 155–56, 173
symbolic geography, ix, 21, 24–26, 33, 65–66, 70, 122. *See also* cosmology

taxation: under the British, 77, 84, 87–88, 96, 122–25, 169, 174, 176, 185; cultivation and, 82–83, 96, 99–100, 125, 145, 173, 176; extortionate, 72, 84, 145; of fodder, 103; knowledge apparatus, 185–86; under the Mughals, 69, 71–77; under the Portuguese, 87; records and data, 11, 55, 69, 80, 83, 85, 87, 115; tax farming, 72, 80, 86, 123, 143, 200n10; tobacco, 200n10; village as unit of, 54–55, 64–65, 70, 84, 112, 114. *See also* British Empire; land records; Revenue Department; village administration
teak, 136, 153–55, 174, 206n46
thorn forests, 142, 146, 150, 159, 166, 168. *See also* jungle
tigers, 53, 54, 187, 211n69

tillage, 47, 94–95, 102, 107, 125, 126, 131; "overflow," 48
timber, 38, 137; extraction, 136, 149, 153–56, 166, 174; merchants, 181
Times of India, 178
trade: cattle, 134; export, 56; long-distance, 154; overland, 60–61, 107, 115–16, 164; timber, 179, 180; trading companies, 60; trading systems, 55–56
traditional medicine, 133, 135, 136, 164
Trautmann, Thomas, 49, 50, 52, 53; *Elephants and Kings*, 192n34; "Elephants and the Mauryas," 11
trees, 136–37, 154, 176–77, 179, 184; areca, 87, 95, 100; palm, 88, 94, 95, 96, 97, 127, 142. *See also* Forest Department; forests; timber
Trigonometric Survey, 199n102

uncultivated land, 82–83, 103, 104, 131, 179; terms for, 82, 200n9
ungulates, 52, 54. *See also* cattle
United Nations Conference on Environment and Development (Rio Summit, 1992), 6, 10
uprising of 1857–58, 168
urbanism, 27–28, 183–84

village administration: accountants and recorders, 71, 76–77, 80, 83–85, 112, 199n99; boundary marking, 116–18, 120–21; British, 113, 116; headmen, 86, 105, 108, 111, 112, 113, 115, 118, 132, 161; hereditary bureaucrats, 83–85, 86, 112, 115–16, 118, 122; landlords, 73, 75, 76, 83–84, 112–13; Mughal, 75–77; policing, 112; Portuguese, 87; tributary chiefs, 160, 161; using lists, 80–81, 84. *See also* land records; local autonomy; villages
villages: abandonment and repopulation, xi, 24, 80, 144–47, 150, 157, 168–69; as anachronism, 187; Atre's view of, 118–20; boundaries of,

242 | INDEX

116–18, 120–22; Brahman, 117; British view of, 116, 119; caste and, 120; clustering of, 64, 71, 83, 90, 111, 112, 113, 114, 115, 118, 160; cohesion of, 110, 112; defenses of, 113, 150–51; effective and administrative, 110; geographic knowledge of villagers, 26, 89, 116–18, 122, 145, 151; as human settlements, 14–15, 111–13, 120; independent, 160, 161; and itinerants, 15, 131–35, 137; and kingship, 14, 113–14; mental maps of, 120; self-sufficiency of, 182; as site and community, 118–22; as taxation unit, 54–55, 64–65, 70, 84, 112, 114; temples in, 120, 122; uplands of, 162–63; walled, 113, 119; wilderness, 193n45. *See also* local autonomy; peasant farmers; village administration

walled cities, 139, 165, 205n1. *See also* fortification
war and ecology, ix
watchmen, 80, 121, 135, 162, 181

water management: Chinese, 28, 35; embankments and reservoirs as, 96, 97, 99–100, 140, 165; mapping of water sources for, 66–68; water lifting, 29–30; in Wittfogel's political ecology, 28. *See also* irrigation and drainage
water supply, 89–90, 100, 140. *See also* rainfall
wells, 107, 113
Western India, 79; geology, 14, 95–96; inhabitants, xi, 161
West Indies, 41
wilderness: kinds and inhabitants of, 16; "elephant forest," 48, 53–54; "remote," 15, 193n45. *See also* forests; jungle; thorn forests
woodlands. *See* Forest Department; forests
world history, ix, 6, 31
world religions, 24–25
World Resources Institute, 10, 192n26
Wormbs, Nina, 12; *environing*, 5–6, 191–92n14

Zomia (Schendel), 13, 146, 158

Culture, Place, and Nature
Studies in Anthropology and Environment

Ecologies of Empire in South Asia, 1400–1900, by Sumit Guha

The Camphor Tree and the Elephant: Religion and Ecological Change in Maritime Southeast Asia, by Faizah Zakaria

Turning Land into Capital: Development and Dispossession in the Mekong Region, edited by Philip Hirsch, Kevin Woods, Natalia Scurrah, and Michael B. Dwyer

Spawning Modern Fish: Transnational Comparison in the Making of Japanese Salmon, by Heather Anne Swanson

Upland Geopolitics: Postwar Laos and the Global Land Rush, by Michael B. Dwyer

Misreading the Bengal Delta: Climate Change, Development, and Livelihoods in Coastal Bangladesh, by Camelia Dewan

Ordering the Myriad Things: From Traditional Knowledge to Scientific Botany in China, by Nicholas K. Menzies

Timber and Forestry in Qing China: Sustaining the Market, by Meng Zhang

Consuming Ivory: Mercantile Legacies of East Africa and New England, by Alexandra C. Kelly

Mapping Water in Dominica: Enslavement and Environment under Colonialism, by Mark W. Hauser

Mountains of Blame: Climate and Culpability in the Philippine Uplands, by Will Smith

Sacred Cows and Chicken Manchurian: The Everyday Politics of Eating Meat in India, by James Staples

Gardens of Gold: Place-Making in Papua New Guinea, by Jamon Alex Halvaksz

Shifting Livelihoods: Gold Mining and Subsistence in the Chocó, Colombia, by Daniel Tubb

Disturbed Forests, Fragmented Memories: Jarai and Other Lives in the Cambodian Highlands, by Jonathan Padwe

The Snow Leopard and the Goat: Politics of Conservation in the Western Himalayas, by Shafqat Hussain

Roses from Kenya: Labor, Environment, and the Global Trade in Cut Flowers, by Megan A. Styles

Working with the Ancestors: Mana *and Place in the Marquesas Islands,*
   by Emily C. Donaldson
Living with Oil and Coal: Resource Politics and Militarization in Northeast India,
   by Dolly Kikon
Caring for Glaciers: Land, Animals, and Humanity in the Himalayas, by Karine Gagné
Organic Sovereignties: Struggles over Farming in an Age of Free Trade,
   by Guntra A. Aistara
The Nature of Whiteness: Race, Animals, and Nation in Zimbabwe, by Yuka Suzuki
Forests Are Gold: Trees, People, and Environmental Rule in Vietnam,
   by Pamela D. McElwee
Conjuring Property: Speculation and Environmental Futures in the Brazilian Amazon,
   by Jeremy M. Campbell
Andean Waterways: Resource Politics in Highland Peru, by Mattias Borg Rasmussen
Puer Tea: Ancient Caravans and Urban Chic, by Jinghong Zhang
Enclosed: Conservation, Cattle, and Commerce among the Q'eqchi' Maya Lowlanders,
   by Liza Grandia
Forests of Identity: Society, Ethnicity, and Stereotypes in the Congo River Basin,
   by Stephanie Rupp
Tahiti Beyond the Postcard: Power, Place, and Everyday Life, by Miriam Kahn
Wild Sardinia: Indigeneity and the Global Dreamtimes of Environmentalism,
   by Tracey Heatherington
Nature Protests: The End of Ecology in Slovakia, by Edward Snajdr
*Forest Guardians, Forest Destroyers: The Politics of Environmental Knowledge in Northern
   Thailand,* by Tim Forsyth and Andrew Walker
Being and Place among the Tlingit, by Thomas F. Thornton
Tropics and the Traveling Gaze: India, Landscape, and Science, 1800–1856,
   by David Arnold
Ecological Nationalisms: Nature, Livelihood, and Identities in South Asia,
   edited by Gunnel Cederlöf and K. Sivaramakrishnan
From Enslavement to Environmentalism: Politics on a Southern African Frontier,
   by David McDermott Hughes
Border Landscapes: The Politics of Akha Land Use in China and Thailand,
   by Janet C. Sturgeon
Property and Politics in Sabah, Malaysia: Native Struggles over Land Rights,
   by Amity A. Doolittle
The Earth's Blanket: Traditional Teachings for Sustainable Living, by Nancy Turner
The Kuhls of Kangra: Community-Managed Irrigation in the Western Himalaya,
   by Mark Baker

Printed in the USA
CPSIA information can be obtained
at www.ICGtesting.com
JSHW021448030324
58207JS00004B/10